Russell Baer Photography

About the Author

Dr. Henry Cloud is a clinical psychologist with an extensive background in both the clinical and professional consulting world, and he has a well-established private practice in California. An international speaker, he is the author of the bestselling *Integrity, Boundaries, Nine Things You Simply Must Do, Changes That Heal,* and numerous other books. He has been a guest on numerous television and radio shows and written for many publications.

Also by Dr. Henry Cloud

Integrity

Boundaries

9 Things You Simply Must Do

The
One-Life
Solution

Reclaim Your Personal Life While Achieving Greater Professional Success

Dr. Henry Cloud

HARPER
BUSINESS

NEW YORK ● LONDON ● TORONTO ● SYDNEY

HARPER
BUSINESS

A hardcover copy of this book was published in 2008 by Collins Business.

THE ONE-LIFE SOLUTION. Copyright © 2008 by Dr. Henry Cloud. All rights reserved. Printed in the United States of America. No part of this book may be used or reproduced in any manner whatsoever without written permission except in the case of brief quotations embodied in critical articles and reviews. For information address HarperCollins Publishers, 10 East 53rd Street, New York, NY 10022.

HarperCollins books may be purchased for educational, business, or sales promotional use. For information please write: Special Markets Department, HarperCollins Publishers, 10 East 53rd Street, New York, NY 10022.

FIRST HARPER BUSINESS PAPERBACK PUBLISHED 2011.
Designed by Level C

The Library of Congress has catalogued the hardcover edition as follows:
Cloud, Henry.
   The one-life solution: reclaim your personal life while achieving greater professional success / Henry Cloud.—1st ed.
      p. cm.
   ISBN 978-0-06-146642-7
   1. Quality of work life—Psychological aspects. 2. Work—Psychological aspects. 3. Interpersonal relations. 4. Psychology, Industrial. I. Title.
   HF5548.8.C563 2008
   650.1—dc22 2008011285

ISBN 978-0-06-146643-4 (pbk.)

11 12 13 14 15   OV/BVG   10 9 8 7 6 5 4 3 2 1

To my parents,
Henry and Louise Cloud,
who both passed away during this book's writing.

Thank you for the integrated life you both led. You showed us that it is possible to make business, family, faith, service, and fun all come together. You leave your family, your friends, and your community much to be grateful for. We will miss you, and may we strive to give all of life its due, as you both did for more than ninety years.

Acknowledgments

I would like to thank several people for the role they played in the writing of this book:

Jan Miller and Shannon Marven, my literary agents, who make this whole process work. Jan, thanks for your big-picture counsel and for first taking me to Harper, where this content was really understood. And Shannon, for being nothing less than a rock star at guiding a book from the original idea to something that actually lands on a bookstore shelf.

Ethan Friedman and Steve Ross at HarperCollins. First of all, thank you both for joining me in the vision of this book and understanding the need for it. Ethan, your advice along the way has helped me shape it in the right direction to make it speak to both work and personal life. You were great at "keeping the main thing the main thing." And both of you were more than gracious in helping me negotiate the time line as I lost both of my parents in the process. Your care and the expressions of care from the Harper team were immensely helpful.

Sandy Vander Zicht at Zondervan for not only your editing of the book, but also your excitement about the content. Your enthusiasm for the ideas in the book was affirming as you validated the concepts throughout the process.

And a very special thanks to my family and friends who supported me throughout a difficult time in this particular writing season. The writing of a book is its own individual journey, and this one was and will be different than all the rest. In a very special way, you all showed me the reality of how life and work *must* work together, as we never know what either is going to bring. But when they do, we realize there is no other way, and strive even harder to make them serve each other well.

And, last, thanks to the leaders, companies, and organizations who give me the great privilege of being alongside you, in your war rooms, in your challenges, and in your victories. Thank you for opening up your teams and your inner worlds. I am always inspired by you, and I count it a gift to learn with you along the way.

Contents

Part One
FOUNDATIONS

one   Identifying the Problem—and the Solution   3

two   Your Vision and Your Boundaries   21

three   Structure and Boundaries   31

Part Two
REBUILDING BOUNDARIES

four   Reclaiming Your Power   53

five   The Audit   65

six   The Laws of Boundaries   85

seven   You and Your Words   107

eight   Make the "No-Choice" Choices First   133

nine   Follow the Misery and Make a Rule   145

Part Three
BOUNDARIES ON THE JOB

ten   Time, Space, and E-Mail   165

eleven   Getting Your Balance Sheet in Order   179

twelve   End Some Things Now   189

thirteen Communicating Your Boundaries   199

CONCLUSION: The Path Ahead   223

Appendix: Helpful Hints   227

The One-Life Solution

Part One

FOUNDATIONS

one

Identifying the Problem—and the Solution

MARIA, THE CEO WHO CAN'T PULL THE TRIGGER

Maria is the CEO of a tech company, and has a team reporting to her that has multiple functions, from finance to marketing and retail. She is ultimately responsible for both the performance of the business and for the culture within the organization. Profits have been good for several years, and because of that she has been able to hide a problem that troubles her in her more reflective moments.

Stan, one of her VPs, is a weak link in the team. She knows it, and so do others. A very nice guy, he is just not the kind of performer the team needs in that position. The momentum they have experienced keeps the overall picture looking good enough to hide what everyone at that level knows to be true. Stan is over his head and should be replaced. Other team members resent the fact that he is there for two reasons. First, they feel like their efforts are making him successful, and thus feel that the situation is not fair. But second, and more demoralizing, they know they could all be at a different level if Stan were replaced. They feel like they are being cheated of what they could all have if a real star were in his place.

So, they feel deflated about where they are, resentful of Stan, who is such a nice guy, and resentful of Maria, who will not do anything about him. When I asked Maria why she could not fix the situation, she said, "I just cannot pull the trigger with him. He is so nice. He is fifty-five years old, at the pinnacle of his career, and it would kill him. Where would he go? I don't know. I know I should do something, and I have to, but so far, I just have not been able to do it. I just keep putting off the inevitable."

DAVID, THE MANAGER WHO CAN'T STAND UP TO A BULLYING BOSS

David is a middle manager on an operations team. He is responsible for project management and keeping production schedules moving forward. As a result, he interfaces with many departments and several teams. He likes the complexity of his work, but at the same time he experiences a lot of stress, as much of what he is held responsible for is out of his control. He lacks real authority over some of the people with whom he finds himself interdependent.

His boss, Kenneth, does not understand this reality and is a bully. He goes off on David when schedules are not where they are supposed to be, berating him and not helping at all. After those interactions, no matter how motivated David was about the work itself, the company, or his own goals, he feels terrible about all of it, and sadly, mostly about himself. He gets sick over the fact that Kenneth has that much power over how he feels.

Unfortunately, not only does it affect him, but David takes it home as well. Too often when he gets home, he is not able to shake their last interaction, and Kenneth has now entered into David's home and his marriage. Too many nights when he gets home, he is not as available to his wife and kids as he would like to be as the crummy feelings about his work situation linger.

RYAN, THE MBA WHO CAN'T MANAGE HIS TIME

Simply put, Ryan is overwhelmed. He does not know how to stop the train—or even how to slow it down. The hours he is putting in never seem to be enough. The projects seem to grow in size and number, and the quantity of it all is beginning to get to him. But that is not the worst part. As an MBA fresh from graduate school, he is accustomed to massive quantities of work. Hard work tires him out, but this is different. This work is wearing him down.

Ryan feels as though he spends more and more time and energy on the things he cares less about, and less time on the things he loves. There are more meetings and appointments and deadlines—which drain his energy as soon as he sees them on his calendar—than there are activities that energize him. He is finding that most of his time is spent doing things that do little to engage his passion, talent, vision, or even best skills and abilities. This is not why he went to grad school.

Similarly, Ryan's personal life feels the same way. He and his wife often fall into bed and collapse. They remark about how it seems they never have time for each other, and are not spending time doing the things they love to do together with the people they really love being with the most. Their lives, just as his work, have become a treadmill. His work is part of the problem, too. He is often working on e-mail at night, taking calls at dinner, or checking his BlackBerry when they are out on a date or taking that walk they finally had time for. Ryan's wife frequently asks, "Do you have to do that now?" He feels like he has to, and then sometimes wonders why. His scariest thought is to project his current life ahead for twenty years. He envisions himself doing then what he is doing now— feeling like all he does is work and that it is somehow missing the mark.

SOPHIE, THE CREATIVE DIRECTOR WHO CAN'T FOCUS

Sophie has consistently had two parallel responses from her bosses and co-workers. They love her, and they are wowed at her creativity, vision, charming people skills, and her ability to get everyone on board with the newest idea she has spawned. And, at the same time, they get more than frustrated with how scattered she is, her lack of follow-through, and the chaos that surrounds almost everything she does.

For a long time, Sophie's creativity and all the good things were so exciting and energizing that they kept people on board and glad to be working with her. But lately, the enthusiasm for having to work around her lack of structure and order is growing thin. Her colleagues are getting tired of it, and the negatives have begun to wear them down to the point that they are no longer glad to be working with her. In fact, some gravitate toward projects in which they will not have to depend on her at all, and her boss is getting close to done.

SARAH, THE ASSISTANT WHO CAN'T CONFRONT HER BOSS

Sarah is fun, attractive, outgoing, and very serious about her job. She loves it, and she wants to please her boss. She has always done whatever he wanted her to do and more if she could—taking on more work, going the extra mile, whatever it took. And her boss always appreciated it.

Lately, however, his appreciation has taken on a different tone. It seems not to be as much about the work as it is about her. He comments less about the good job she did on this task or that, and more about her personally. At first, she thought they were just compliments, and they felt good. Sarah liked that her boss thought so well of her. But now it seems that his comments about her feel seductive, and he has begun to comment less about qualities that affect her work, and more about her appearance, personality, and desirability.

Sarah does not know exactly how to express it, but she now feels very uneasy around him. He has begun to stay around later and later, after everyone else is gone except the two of them. She is feeling increasingly uncomfortable. But she also feels that if she were to mention anything she would be out of line, since he hasn't done anything specific enough to which she can confidently point. She just knows in her stomach that his behavior is improper. As time goes on, going to work begins to make her feel sick. Yet, she feels as if she can't do anything about it, and so she doesn't.

KEVIN, THE SALESPERSON WHO CAN'T OVERCOME A PLATEAU

Kevin is really smart and likeable. Getting his position in sales was not a problem for him, nor was establishing a level of performance that earned him a secure place in the company. When he had been promoted to a regional level after handling a smaller territory, he thought he was on his way. But that has not happened.

Kevin has hit a ceiling. Finally, he has to call it what it is, as that is what his boss called it when he told him that Kevin was not going to get the next promotion. He had not wanted to admit that, but now that the words were out there, he knew they were true. He was not getting better. He had hit a plateau in his performance and seemed to be unable to break into the next level. Kevin knew it was possible, as others with whom he had started had made it. But, for some reason, his performance has progressed not upward, but in a flat line.

Having gone to all the seminars, and read all the sales books, Kevin was a little stuck as to what to do. He knew the techniques, the strategies, the tricks. But somehow they were not getting him to that next level. He thought he was smart enough—and talented enough—but whatever was wrong was also real. He had hit a wall.

THE CORE PROBLEM

It would be easy to look at these scenarios and put them into some clear kinds of categories of common business or training problems and prescribe the appropriate training: management skills for Maria, people skills for David, time management for Ryan, focus for Sophie, sexual harassment for Sarah, sales growth for Kevin. In fact, there is real value in doing so. Failing to fire the right person is a key management error and begs for leadership development and coaching. Bully bosses are a threat to any culture, and bullied people need help from HR, at least. When work increases, time-management skills and priority management are vital. Sexual harassment should never be tolerated. And salespeople, good ones, usually can be taught to sell more.

Often, when we see scenarios like these, we know something must be done. So we train people in the appropriate business practices, skills, and disciplines that apply to the individual problems that are quickly visible in all of these situations. These are important issues to tackle. Take a browse through the business book section in the airport and you will likely find good sources to address all of these situations with some helpful answers. But is that just treating the symptoms? Is that all there is? Is there something more, or something better you could do? More to the point, if you are one of these people or have one of these issues in your own life, is there something that you could do to be better and not ever be in that situation again?

As a business leader once said to me, "There is something missing from the way that we do training to fix problems. We give people a lot of content—the 'what to do' in specific problem areas—but for some reason that does not seem to be enough. A lot of times my people do not seem to be able to do what the training tells them to do. They don't seem to keep it going past the seminar and the initial enthusiasm of it all. I have seen it over and over again."

I agreed. While content training is important, there is an even bigger problem than a lack of knowing what to do. The bigger problem is this:

A person still has to go do it.

Whatever "it" is, whether in ethics, time management, or sales, the person is the ultimate piece of equipment, not just what he or she knows. There is a big difference between going to a seminar on anatomy and being able to do open heart surgery. One requires knowledge only, and the other experience, ability, and character. The page that says, "cut here" doesn't turn you into the person who can pick up the knife and slice someone open to heal them. The CEO knew the VP was underperforming, and yet could not pull the trigger. Something was missing *inside*.

So, if there is more to rectifying these situations than just the obvious ethics or management-training content, what is it? How would each individual turn into the person who can go do it, whatever it is in each of these contexts? Is there a magic bullet, a path?

Yes, there is.

THE ONE SOLUTION

What if I told you that there is one solution—one issue—that is the central issue in all six scenarios, as different as they all seem? What if I went beyond that and said not only is there one solution to the scenarios, but there is one solution that will affect not only their business problems but all of the other issues they have in life? And, what if there was one solution that made each of them the kind of person who was the same kind of person at work that they were at home, or with friends? In other words, what if they no longer felt like they had two lives, but one? Is there one answer that can integrate all of that?

What is that one answer—or issue—that drives all of these other problems?

That one answer is called "boundaries." In each one of the scenarios, the issue in common is that no matter what their positions—from CEO all the way to assistant—the people above had lost control of themselves in one way or another. They all lacked an internal core from which they were able to define themselves, and then express that "defined self" in a way that made life work. While there were six different situations mentioned, one issue underlies all those problems: lack of boundaries. The issue of boundaries is one of the biggest issues that all of us will face in business and in life.

> Boundaries provide the structure to your character that will make everything else work.

Here is the key. What the people in each scenario do not realize is that while they think they have certain situational problems, if we looked back over time and could see the video of their entire careers, or their entire lives for that matter, we would see that this is not the first time they felt that way. We would see that is not the first time that being controlled by external forces had affected their performance and well-being. And the common denominator in all of their past situational problems was *themselves.* They actually had done the same things in different situations over and over again. Once, when I pointed out to a fifty-year-old leader of ten thousand employees how this issue was affecting his performance, he said, "You have just described my entire career since college." It was only then that he was able to change the pattern that had held him back for three decades. He realized, at that moment, that he did not have a problem with one of his key reports. He realized that he had a problem with himself.

BOUNDARIES INSIDE AND OUTSIDE

Boundaries affect us on the inside—and the outside. They affect the ways we experience work and life, the ways we relate to others in work and life, and the degree to which we are successful in our pursuits. In other words, they affect the *emotional, relational,* and *performance* aspects of our work. To get a feel for how boundaries might be affecting you, review the descriptions in each category below with a pencil in hand. Place a check mark next to any statements that describe you.

The Emotional Side of Work

Whether or not we acknowledge it, how we feel has a great impact on how we work, and on the rest of life. How we feel goes to motivation, concentration, judgment, well-being, satisfaction, and overall functioning:

- You feel anxiety or even feelings of panic sometimes when workloads increase, when you cannot control an outcome, or when you have to face a difficult confrontation.

- You feel a loss of passion about what you are doing in most of your work.

- You experience burnout and a loss of energy for a lot of what you have to do.

- You feel a low-grade depression more than frequently.

- Your work has crowded out your recreational time, your exercise time, and your hobbies, and you are losing vitality and health as a result.

- Your boss or a co-worker has the ability to make you feel bad, depressed, anxious, inferior, or something else that is life draining or toxic.

- You feel resentful of the things you have to do, or of some controlling or manipulative people whom you feel "make you" do those things.

The Relational Side of Work

Every leader knows the power of relationships in performance, and people who work know the effects of their relationships at work on both their ability to do their jobs and to enjoy them.

- Your boss or a co-worker is making your life miserable, and you do not know how to deal with the relationship.

- Your work and your significant relationships—such as with your spouse, kids, or close friends—seem to be competing with each other for your attention, and you feel torn between the obligations of each.

- A co-worker is not pulling his or her weight, or you have become responsible for his lack of responsibility or performance in some way.

- You are resentful of another person's behavior or performance and feel powerless to do anything about it.

- You know that there is a difficult conversation that you need to have, even a confrontation, but you either avoid it out of fear of the outcome or do not know how to have it.

- You feel pressured to do more than you should, or to do things that you do not feel comfortable doing in your work, yet cannot find it in you to say no to those things.

- You feel overworked by someone, and yet do not address the issue with that person.

- You do not like something about how a person relates to you or to the team, but do not address it or know how.

- Someone you work with—either above you, a peer, a subordinate, or even a client or vendor—is able to get to you in some way, and you cannot shake it or deal with it.

- You are getting hurt at work, and yet are not doing anything about it and fear the outcome if you do.

- You are afraid to discipline, confront, or fire someone out of fear of hurting them or other outcomes.

- Someone is hurting you and you are thinking of leaving a good job or company to get away from them.

The Performance Side of Work

Performance and results are intricately tied to the structure of one's character and his or her ability to be autonomous, focused, initiating, goal oriented, and well defined. To get good results, one has to have an authentic and strong sense of personal power, and not feel powerless to impact the task or the outside world.

- Your workload is getting more and more out of control, and you feel like it is driving you, instead of the other way around.

- You are a leader, and you do not stay focused on the "real mission" or what really should get done or you let the organization lose its focus or "core."

- Your life feels chaotic and scattered such that you never get done what you truly want to get done.

- You procrastinate or are disorganized.

- You cannot close the deal.

- You cannot let go of things that are taking up your time and resources.

- The "wrong people" take too much of your time.

- You are so overloaded with e-mails that you know there is no way ever to get to them.

- You are a poor negotiator.

- You give too much away in deals.

- You agree to do things that take time away from what you really should be doing, yet you do not say no.

- You are often motivated out of fear, instead of out of purpose.

- You know that you could get better results, a better position, or more success, but you haven't.

- Your talents and brains and opportunities are not bringing you the success you know you are capable of attaining.

- You feel that you have somehow missed your calling.

- You have great intentions and plans but never bring them to fruition or completion, and they remain great intentions and plans.

- You are not focusing on what you have to do because you get pulled into what others should be doing.

- You have trouble delegating and letting go.

- You have lost your passion for work, or some other area of life.

- You let others get you off task often and on to their agenda.

- You are distractible and unfocused.

- You have not set goals, and even if you set them you ignore them.

Satisfaction in one's work, and often in one's life, is directly related to the emotional, relational, and performance aspects of work. In fact, people also change jobs for one of these three reasons: how it feels to be there, how the relationships are going, and how much success or fulfillment of their talents and passions they are achieving. No matter where you find yourself, however, staying where you are or moving on, you must be able to do the following three things in your work:

- Be emotionally healthy.

- Be relationally healthy.

- Be performance healthy.

If you can be the kind of person who can do those things, then either you will do very well where you are or you will find the right place where you will do well. As the old saying goes, "When the student is ready, a teacher will appear." We see the same thing in terms of work and relationships. You will attract into your life—and find—the situation that will fit the level of integration your character possesses. And the structure of your boundaries are an essential component to that actually happening. When you are ready, the right situation will appear—if you are not already in it. The challenge is for you to be the person who could make it work well for you no matter where you are. It is all about who you are, not where you are. The where will take care of itself if you are who you need to be. Reality always finds itself as water seeks its level.

Too often, just like in the world of relationships, we see people thinking that the answer is somehow "out there." If they just could find the right company, then they would be happy. If they just had a different boss, then they could really soar. If the market were just a little better, then they could be successful. You can probably imagine the people in the scenarios at the beginning of the chapter engaging in that kind of thinking: the CEO feeling that if he had just not inherited this employee the company would not be in this mess, the manager who thinks he would feel better at night if he had a different boss. While there is truth in the difficulty of those situations, the real and most powerful truth that you can do anything about is *yourself.* And that is what boundaries are all about. The truly happy, relationally fulfilled, and achieving people know that and are able to live that out. It is the goal of this book to help you become one of them.

YOU ARE DESIGNED FOR THIS

Just as children are designed to begin walking at a certain age, you are designed to become a structured and defined character with good boundaries. In order to develop these boundaries—and to become the person you want to be, or to develop in the areas in which you need work—you will need to grow in your ability to be in control of yourself. You must get to the things that are eroding your personal power, motivation, drive, autonomy, freedom, good aggression, and initiative. And to do that, you are going to need the internal structure that provides that kind of architecture for your character. If that sounds like a lot, it is not.

Developmental research shows us that you were designed to have a structured character that is free, motivated, powerful, autonomous, aggressive, and initiating. Everyone is designed to grow in this way, which is why it's not a lot to achieve. In other words, you were not designed to be a CEO and yet not be able to tell a nonperformer that he has to get with it or leave. You were not designed to be so overwhelmed that you could not find fulfillment in the work and home life that take every waking moment of your life and all of your energy—a total investment that is not giving the return it should. You were not designed to be so creative and yet so unable to deliver on what your creativity and talents bring that people no longer want to work with you. You were not meant to be sexually or otherwise harassed. You were not created to not be able to close the deal.

The obstacles that prevent a person from becoming a structured and defined character take root when the normal developmental path is interrupted, hindered, broken, or not properly resourced in some way. Some people get further along in that path of boundaries than others, but most of us have encountered situations that tell us we have room to grow and that, if we did, our performance and well-being would benefit. If you have not developed good boundaries, it is not because you are not able. It is because either the ingredients to develop in that way have not been present or there have been injuries, impediments, fears, and obstacles that have kept you from getting there. This book will help you get there by naming the reasons you have not learned to walk in this area, and telling you how to deal with them.

THE CHALLENGE OF INTEGRATION IN A "STRUCTURELESS" CULTURE

The title of this book is *The One-Life Solution*. I actually struggled with that, as it has a double meaning and therefore is difficult to communicate on a cover. But it reflects so well the felt need that most of us can identify with, no matter where we are in our careers. It came from the reality that today life has become so fragmented that people find it difficult to "bring it all together." The ways that work is performed today put more and more pressure on existing cracks we might have in the structure of our own makeup. For example, the traditional work structures that once helped you integrate and structure your life have all but disappeared.

Look at the simple question, "When do I work, and when do I not?" People used to have the structure of "work hours" that helped them know when work began and when it ended. They went to work at some appointed time and then left work and went home. Therefore, home to a great degree was protected from work. This work-free time zone served as a natural boundary to protect your psyche, your home life, your relationships, your recreation, your spiritual well-being, your health, and everything else that needs time and focus other than work.

But, in the last two decades, the line between being available and unavailable blurred. It began with paging. For the first time, your boss could always find you. Suddenly voice mail could be both left and checked after hours. Then, with ubiquitous and inexpensive cell phone coverage, bosses, co-workers, partners, customers, and others could instantly get around the no-longer-existent protective boundary of work hours. Simply having left work no longer meant that work had left you. It could now find you much more easily. Everyone became the doctor on call. But the difference was that even doctors are only on call a certain number of nights or weekends, and then they hand call over to their partners.

Then it got worse. Cell coverage continued to get better and cheaper, and then you really, really could not hide. After that came the ultimate work-hours buster: the Internet. With e-mail came two huge problems. First, anyone could send you work at any time and at any place. The volume that they could produce for you was no longer limited to how much they could create at the office during work hours. Now, they could create more, and they could send it to you anytime they wanted. The volume they could create and send went through the roof. They no longer had to walk down to your office during office hours or dial your extension. They merely had to hit Send.

Another problem was that not only could they create more and send it to you, but now you could actually look at it and work on it at home, past the safe zone of the office hours. You too were susceptible to the danger created by the erosion of the work-hours boundary. Not only were they not protecting you, but if you did not have the personal boundaries to keep you safe, you actually began to check that stuff after work—and work on it. At night. Sometimes late at night! So, work volume increased, as well as access to you. (I had a VP of a large company tell me that he could tell when things were not going well with a division or with one of his direct reports by the time stamps on his e-mails. He began to use those as a signal that the guy was out of control. In his words, "If he has to send that many e-mails that late at night, he is out of control. And I don't want anyone with that much responsibility who is that out of control. Besides, I don't want to create that kind of culture. I don't want people checking them either. It is sick.")

So, with all of that access, the time boundaries of work are virtually gone. And the reality-based quantitative boundaries of the amount of work that can be created are gone, while at the same time, no infrastructure increases are made to handle it. You are just the same person with the same job, only now there are no boundaries to the amount of work someone can create for you if they are manic enough to stay up that late. And there is no limit to how much you can take on without even knowing that your own "infrastructure" has been overtaxed. One sad result is that efficiency, always driven by limits, is no longer needed. Work expands to the time allotted, and now there is no allotment. It is infinite.

But it gets worse. If you noticed, it is not only the time boundary that got blown up, but also the "space boundary." Work has chased you home. If that were not enough, try to leave home, and it will still find you. Now you have a BlackBerry or some other PDA (personal digital assistant), and it will find you at your kid's soccer game, at a social gathering, at church, at coffee, on your walk or bike ride, or virtually anywhere you go. Work has no time limit and no space limit. Anytime, anywhere, you can be working—if you have no boundaries and structure of your own.

In addition to the space invasion that the Web has given us with PDAs, companies themselves have given us the ability to work anywhere as well. It is now considered good to "work at home today" to get away from "all those distractions at work." What a phrase! Now I don't have the boundaries I need at work to be able to work, so I have to go home to work. And the more mobile our society and businesses get, the worse this problem becomes.

The long and the short of it is that time and space—long-depended-upon boundaries on work—no longer exist. So, work has become an invader of the rest of life, in time, space, energy, and other ways. Family interaction decreases, and quality of interaction decreases. Other social ties suffer as well. Now people spend hours they used to spend on life together in front of some kind of screen instead—working.

And if we are not working, we are still in front of a screen. Technology has given us more and more ways to be in front of a screen, and thereby not engaged in the rest of the vital things of life. As the *Economist* reported on its Web site, "America takes the couch-potato crown, with households goggling at the box for an eye-straining average of 8 hours and 11 minutes every day" (*Economist*, October 20, 2007). Individuals in those households watch between four and five hours of television per day, and now there are more televisions in homes than there are people. Add to that the hours in front of a computer surfing the Net, or in front of a game screen playing video games, and we are spending less and less time doing the vital things of life, like connecting, exercising, parenting, relating, reading, developing our spiritual lives, and many other experiences that make us who we are. The digital world has invaded the boundaries of time and space in ways that we do not notice—if we don't notice. And remember, not only do you need all that time to watch all of that TV, you also have to do the e-mail that we mentioned above. No wonder other vital activities are suffering.

The result of this, and the disappearance of many other boundaries from our society—such as morals and values that used to contain a lot of destruction and help to integrate our characters—is that more and more we are living a "structureless" life. Or at least we are living a life in which our structure is always being eroded, the fruit of which is that we get more and more disintegrated as time goes on. We feel fragmented, out of control, and begin to lose ourselves over time. We lose our center, or feeling of being whole and integrated as more and more forces—and more and more people—pull at different parts of us. Before long, we no longer feel in control of our lives and yet do not know how to get them back, or design them proactively for the first time.

Therefore, the "one-life solution." The double meaning is that, first, there is one issue behind all of this, and one solution. The issue is that we have lost our boundaries in many ways. And the solution that will affect this in a very tangible way is to grow in developing those boundaries. As we do, whether you are a chairperson, a CEO, or anyone else, you will see an enormous effect in your performance, and quality of work life.

The other meaning is that we need to have only one life, instead of feeling fragmented between work and life. As work has invaded the rest of life, there is also a need to find what is referred to as "balance." People look to balance work and life, as if they sit on some sort of fulcrum or seesaw and the answer is to somehow get them to be equal. I guess that means adding or subtracting from one side or the other, which certainly has some merit. But I prefer a different idea. Instead of balance, let's talk about "integration of work and life"—but not in the way that means to take one to the other in more and more ways. The integration I prefer is not about the space and time boundaries of work and life themselves but the integration of the person who is doing both of those—you. As you integrate all of your different parts into one person—one core from which you do all that you do, including work, life, relationships, spirituality, health, and other parts—you will achieve balance as a by-product. Balance will be a fruit of your boundaries that will integrate your personality. Then you will not feel torn between many lives and be many different people, but one person, one life, with many different parts—none of them able to pull you apart from the others. That is the essence of one life, and the essence of balance. And it all will come from having better boundaries.

THE APPROACH

This is primarily a book about work. It is about your business, your performance, your career, you passion, and your sense of well-being at work. I hope it will help you to lead better, manage better, and do what you do better. So, our focus will be mostly in the context of work. But it is also a book about you and your overall well-being, and with the fragmentation of work and life we just looked at, we will also talk a lot about you and the way that your work affects your life and vice versa.

Our focus will be on constructing and developing better boundaries. We will do that first by talking about what boundaries are and what they do for your work and your life, and how they affect your power to do both of those well. That will lay a foundation for you to understand the concept in order to apply it better.

Next, we will move to specific boundary practices and structures as they are lived out in the context of the leadership, management, and work life. Some will be descriptive and some prescriptive. I will give you some tips on specific structures and practices that you can implement that will do two things. First, they will solve many problems in your leadership, management, and work. They will help your performance. Second, by doing them, they will also build better boundaries for you as a person. As you implement them, you will grow and change, as well as the people above, around, and below you in your organization.

Then, throughout all of it, we will be integrating life and work. Remember, this is about you as a person. It is not just about work problems and situations or personal problems and situations. This is about you, the person who has to live in both of those worlds. The intent is not necessarily to bring both of them together, but to bring *you* together to live in both worlds in an integrated way. As you integrate, you will be able to live more and more from a strong core, and create the life you were designed to live. The one life that only you can live, and live well.

two

Your Vision and
Your Boundaries

What are we trying to accomplish? In the words of Steven Covey, it's important to "begin with the end in mind." Let's be clear about that here. What is it we are trying to accomplish in *The One-Life Solution*? The simple answer is this:

Gain control.

We are not trying to gain control of other people or of all the circumstances or even all of the outcomes. Those things will take care of themselves as you gain control of the only thing you can ever control—yourself. As you do that, you will experience the things all of us desire in the integration of work and life.

The irony is that most people are so caught up in trying to control the things they cannot control—other people, circumstances, or outcomes—that in the process they lose control of themselves. And here is the real paradox. It is only when you do take control of yourself that you will begin to have significant influence on those other things: people, circumstances, and outcomes. People in control of themselves do the most to influence everyone and everything around them to good ends, results, and profits. But they start with themselves, and that is the essence of boundaries.

Before we get ahead of ourselves, let's get back to that desired outcome, the vision. What does that look like? What is it we are trying to accomplish by building good boundaries? How about this? What if . . .

Each day when you get up, you know that you will spend that day pouring yourself, fully engaged, into the things that matter to you. What if you know that you will do your work well, getting great results, enjoying the process and the relationships that come with them? As a result, you feel invigorated and alive when you think about what you are going to do that day. Throughout the day, although there will be challenges, difficulties, problems, and even problem people, you will feel competent and confident to deal with what comes your way. While you may get tired, even exhausted at times, you will not feel depleted, burned out, or dead inside.

When you put your head on the pillow that night, you know that you moved the ball down the field that day, in the right game, and in ways that matter to you. You are where you are supposed to be, doing what you were made to do, accomplishing all that you are capable of. You feel good through it all, knowing that your professional life works well with the other things that are important to you: your family, your friendships, your avocations, your values, your passions, your health, and your spirituality. The two lives, work and the personal things you value, are not in conflict with each other, nor do they even feel like two lives. Instead, you feel like one person authentically living out different parts of yourself in an integrated fashion, not allowing any one part to become the whole, or to get in the way of the other parts. That is what it looks like to be fully human—and fully alive.

Certainly, that sounds good. But, do you think it is really possible? Before you write it off as impossibly idealistic, think about it. It had better be possible. The alternative does not sound good at all:

You wake up dreading another day in which you will feel disengaged as you pour your time and energy into things that do not matter to you. You may or may not get results, and the process and most of the relationships will bring you down. You will feel demotivated and heavy when you think about what is ahead of you that day. The challenges, problems, and difficulties feel overwhelming, and you know they will somehow get the best of you, no matter what. You know you will feel drained, burned out, powerless, and passionless when you are done.

At night, you look back and realize you have missed another day of doing what you were made to do, and nothing you accomplished is really important to you. Through it all, you felt squeezed and conflicted about the choices you had to make between your work and your personal life.

You realize your work keeps you from having what you need and want in those personal areas that matter greatly to you. It seems like work, supposedly only a part of life, has infected the whole of life with its weightiness, and you are not sure what has happened or what to do about it. So, tomorrow does not look a lot different than today.

CAUSE OR RESULT?

These two scenarios are admittedly extreme. Life is not an either-or proposition in which everything is either wonderful or miserable. We don't get to choose between being the person in the first scenario who pretty much has a perfect life or the person in the second scenario whose life is a disaster. In different seasons of life, there are typically elements of both scenarios at work. I am not trying to paint the picture of a perfect, rosy life with no problems. We all have good times and bad times, and life is not about having either good or bad times. Those will always be with us. But there is another either-or choice we can make when it comes to how we will live the times that we do have, good or bad.

The first scenario describes a proactive life lived with purpose. While there may be hardship, losses, and even times of poor results in various areas, life lived this way has an intentional direction to it, even when bad things happen. This person feels empowered to live and exert positive energy to accomplish effects that are in line with who he is and what he wants. The second scenario describes a life that is dictated to, where the one living it has little choice and even less control over the circumstances of his existence. In short, he feels more like a result than a cause—a victim if you will. And that gets us to the essence of the vision for what we are trying to accomplish here:

You are a cause, not a result.

In other words, you will be empowered by your choices and your actions to bring about the results you want in your work and in your life, as opposed to your work and your life bringing about its results on you. When you think about the scenarios at the beginning of the last chapter, each one describes a person who envisions himself as the "result" of some force acting upon him or her:

- The CEO's inability to fire a nonperforming employee is a result of how she perceives the employee would feel if she fired him.

- The manager's emotional well-being is a result of a bullying boss.

- The MBA's feelings of being fragmented and having no life are a result of the work volume that comes his way.

- The creative director's disorganization and lack of follow-through is a result of too many ideas, directions, and creativity itself.

- The assistant's feelings of sickness, discomfort, and fear are a result of her boss's attempt at seduction.

- The salesperson's sales plateau is a result of not having high enough numbers and not closing enough deals.

If you were to talk to each person, they would describe feeling like they are stuck and powerless in the face of these forces or circumstances that are acting upon them. Our vision here is that after reading this book you will never feel that way. And even when you do encounter situations or people that test you, you will be able to be fully engaged and effective in dealing with them. In short, if you are a cause, not a result, you will be in control of yourself, which means you can experience the desired results in the areas we talked about in chapter 1:

- How you feel in your work and life

- How your relationships work

- How you perform and profit

- How you integrate it all with your transcendent or spiritual values

There will always be bullying bosses or toxic co-workers with their own agendas. Bad markets are a part of business, as well as pressures that come from all sides. If you are successful enough to be working and concerned about the topic of this book, that also means you certainly have more to do than you can find the time for.

You also have more things pulling for time in your personal life than you have time and energy for. Family, hobbies, friends, and more call for your energy and time. These are good problems to have, and they are constant for people with full lives. So, while pressures come and go, you are the one who remains through it all, dictating how you will engage and negotiate each challenge. You and your character are the constants in the equation. Let's look at how boundaries will accomplish this vision of getting you back in control.

WHAT IS A BOUNDARY?

Pure and simple, a boundary is a property line. It defines where you end and someone else begins, or where you end and something else begins. It is a structure that preserves order, a concept we will get back to a little later. For now, let's talk about it as a property line, and use a metaphor from the physical world.

In the physical world, property lines are relatively easy to see or to figure out. For example, a property line defines where your yard ends and your neighbor's begins. Often, there is a physical marker to show where that line is, such as a fence or a wall. Your house also has the structure of a physical boundary. It has walls that define it, and that is its structure and definition. You know what is inside the house and what is outside, and it is easy to determine precisely where the house is.

Boundaries, like fences, are easy to see and understand in the physical world of property. But what about in the personal and interpersonal world? How do they work there? Let's take a look at six key areas and consider some examples as they relate to work.

1. Ownership

Boundaries define ownership. We know that anything inside a boundary line is owned by the property owner, and anything outside the line is owned by someone else.

People with good boundaries feel as if their lives belong to them, and no one else. Their feelings, thoughts, choices, desires, opinions, behaviors, talents, and whatever else goes on in their lives exist on their property—their minds, hearts, and souls. They do not "*dis*own" these things by thinking they are someone else's problem. They do not blame others when they are not feeling good. They do not make choices and then act like the consequences of those choices are because of someone else.

These people "own" their lives, their opportunities, their successes, failures, fears, or whatever else exists on their side of the fence. If a boss or co-worker or the market leaves them feeling bad, they acknowledge that problem as their own. It belongs to them. It is their problem, no matter who might be on the other end of it, or the cause of it. If the distress is in their soul, they take ownership of that distress, even if they did not cause it.

> *Question: Which areas of your life—your time, energy, passion, and thoughts—do you own and to what extent? Do they really belong to you, or to someone else?*

2. Control

Once we know who owns something, we know who controls it. Owners get to do whatever they want to do with their own property (subject of course to the law). If we know that this is your property, we know that whatever happens on it is yours to control and no one else's. For example, no one can all of a sudden decide that your house should be painted purple and just overstep your fence—your boundary—and paint it. They need your permission to do that because you control the property. Likewise, you cannot go past your boundary and begin painting things that don't belong to you. You can control only your own property, not someone else's.

At work, people with boundaries realize they are in control of the things that are theirs alone to control—the things within their own hearts, minds, and souls. While they often cannot control the external realities within which they find themselves, they certainly can control their response to those realities. If they have a bullying boss who makes them feel bad, they realize that the boss does not have control of how they feel. Only they have control of how they feel. They also realize that they cannot control the boss's actions. So they begin to take control of only what they can control, which is themselves. They begin to see that they are not powerless victims of their boss. They can exert some control over themselves and do what is necessary to make themselves feel better, regardless of their boss's continuing behavior.

They also realize that external business forces are not under their control either, but their response to them is. A bad market, a difficult customer, or other external events are not under their control. But they realize they have control over their response to such challenges, and their focus and attention are always on what they can do, not on the negatives of the situation and the things they cannot control. "What can I do?" is their guiding mantra.

Question: How much control do you have over what happens inside your life? Your heart? Your mind? Your soul? Do you have sufficient control of your time? How you spend your energy? Your choices? Your emotional well-being?

3. Freedom

This self-control of your own property gives rise to the concept of freedom. It is totally your choice what to do with your property. Not only are you the one who controls it and has the power to do what you want, you also are free to make the choice about what that will be. No one can dictate that to you, only you can, within whatever limits that property has, such as homeowner's associations or the city's laws. Within those limits, you can do what you choose.

When it comes to work, a person in control realizes that no one is holding a gun to her head to remain a victim. She is free to make whatever choice she wants to make and, as a result, begins to make choices based on decisions that she owns and takes responsibility for, instead of being a passive victim and resenting her situation. When she realizes this, a whole world of choices opens up for her, and whether she chooses to change how she experiences her bully boss, or how she thinks about him or responds to him, or if she chooses to confront him or avoid him or even leave the company, she understands that she is totally free to make her choices. She can do whatever she pleases.

Question: How much do you feel free to do whatever you choose to do? Or do you feel like you have limited freedom because of outside forces?

4. Responsibility, Accountability, and Consequences

Once we know who owns the property and who is in control of it, we also know who is responsible for what goes on there. Ownership, control, and freedom all come with responsibility, accountability, and consequences. You can do what you want to do, but you also will reap the consequences of what you choose to do, good or bad. There are real consequences—good and bad—such as having a comfortable house if you take care of it or having the roof fall in if you ignore the termites. And there are interpersonal or legal consequences, such as getting evicted if you turn it into a fire hazard or getting sued by your neighbor if you endanger his property by the choices you make on your own. Either way, good or bad, you control it and you are responsible.

A person with boundaries knows that whatever the consequences of his choices are, those consequences are his responsibility, and he is not at odds with that reality. If he has chosen to be in his job, he takes responsibility for that. If he confronts the boss, he takes responsibility for the consequences. Or if he stays silent, he realizes that he has made that choice also, and takes responsibility for where it leaves him, whether the choice is good or bad, smart or dumb. He is not a victim. He is responsible and likes that fact. Whatever the consequences of his decisions and actions might be, he realizes that he is responsible for them.

Question: Do you take responsibility for the consequences of your choices? Your attitudes? Your beliefs? Your feelings? And, do you enforce consequences with others for their attitudes, beliefs, feelings, choices, or behaviors?

5. Limits

If you own your property and are free to control what goes on there, then you are also free to limit what goes on there. If people do trespass or do something on your property that you do not wish, then you can ask them to leave. If they won't, you can impose further limits, like calling the police. Ultimately, you can have them removed from your property, and you can hold them accountable for the damages they caused. But it is up to you to take control and to set the limits of what you will and will not allow.

If something is going on at work, maybe as a result of the choices of others, or if someone is acting irresponsibly, the person in control realizes that she can set some limits on how much she allows those actions or attitudes to affect her. She is not afraid to call a foul and say that there is a limit to what she will allow herself to be a part of, exposed to, or affected by. Limits also apply in saying no to herself in terms of what she allows herself to agree to, making sure that she does not agree to do things past her personal limits of time and energy, or against her values.

Question: Do you set limits with people or situations so that the effect they have on you has a clear end? Do you draw the line?

6. Protection

When you know where your boundaries and limits are, and you are in control of that property, then you can do something very important. You can keep the good things inside your property and the bad things out. Your boundaries protect the things that are valuable to you—your treasures—and you want them to stay inside, safe from the forces that might come to steal or destroy them. That is why you lock your door or close the gate in the fence around your house. Your boundaries protect the good things inside the lines. They also protect you from the bad things, like thieves and attackers, who are on the outside.

Those who are in control of themselves can stand up to persons or circumstances that threaten to hurt them or their organization. They have the boundaries to protect themselves, others, their organization, and its mission from forces and people who wish to cause it harm.

Question: Do you allow bad things to be dumped on your property or bad people to get inside the fence of your heart, mind, and soul? Or do you have a clear fence that says "keep out" to people or their behaviors that are not good for you? Can the wolves get in the yard or the toxic people dump whatever sludge they wish into your soul?

These are the functions boundaries perform: ownership, control, freedom, responsibility, limits, and protection. As you can see, these apply from the boardroom all the way to the front office person who answers the phone. Here is a quick example. If Maria, the gun-shy CEO from chapter 1, had these kinds of boundaries, she would have been in a very different place. She would have taken ownership of the queasy and fearful feelings that the prospect of firing the nonperformer left her with. She would have realized that her feelings are her problem, and how Stan might feel is his problem to own. She would have taken ownership of the consequences of his nonperformance. She also would have taken responsibility for the fact that as long as she made a choice to not act, she also made a choice to diminish the performance of the entire organization and to foster discontent in a lot of other people.

Boundaries are pretty simple when you think of them in physical terms like property, fences, walls, and gates. We can look at a person's yard or their house and see how much ownership, passion, care, and responsibility they put into their property. Just a quick drive-by tells us a lot about the person who owns it.

However, in the interpersonal world, there are no fences, walls, or gates. You cannot hide behind a physical fence to keep toxic co-workers, clients, or bosses from dumping their work or issues into the yard (so to speak) of your heart and soul.

Here is the reality. If you do not have good personal and interpersonal boundaries, that is exactly what happens. You begin to find your "yard" collecting the trash that goes on all around you, or just filling up with many more tasks to do than you desire. Your life gets junky and pretty soon you don't much like living there. Unfortunately, you can't sell or move to another property when the property itself is you. The only answer is to get some fences, take ownership, and reclaim control of your life.

In this book, we are going to explore what these "fences" might look like. To begin, let's talk a little psychology.

three

Structure and Boundaries

Fences are physical structures. You can bump into them. If you ignore them, especially the barbed wire types, you feel the consequences. So, what are the structures of the personal and interpersonal world? What are your fences made of? What happens if someone ignores them? Can they even see them? You probably know what it is like to be around someone with whom you get a clear feeling of where they end and begin, who they are and who they are not. You can bump up against them and feel as if you've actually run into someone. They are well defined. You can feel their fences.

Similarly, you know what it is like to be around the kind of person who feels "squishy" and not well defined. You wonder where they really are or what they stand for. Recently I was talking to a VP of a company who said this about his boss. "I just wish sometimes that he would stand up and just say, 'This is the way it is going to be and if you guys don't like it, that is tough.' He tries to get along too much with everyone and to make everyone happy. It leaves things too flimsy. I wish he would take charge, and not worry about how everyone else felt about it. Then things would be a lot better around here." What he was asking for from his boss is exactly what boundaries provide: the structure that creates security. Personally, inside ourselves, and for others' benefit as well, we need the security of clear boundaries.

THE IMPORTANCE OF STRUCTURE

What do you think of when you think of the word "structure"? For some people, it is their worst nightmare. "I do not want to be in an overly structured environment," they instantly think—and probably for good reason. Everyone has had some experience where rules, policies, and other structures virtually snuffed the life out of all those who were caged within its walls. If structures are too stifling, they can limit us to such a degree that we feel as if we cannot move. Ask any teenager with a rigid or controlling parent about the need for more space.

But, while problems with too much structure and not enough open space are one thing, a bigger problem is the lack of structure itself. We cannot live without it, any more that we can live without a roof over our heads. It provides the basis for us to know who we are, what we want, what we feel and think, and what our ability is to make choices and do something about those things. People use the phrase, "it is beginning to take shape" when speaking of a project, or a dream, to mean that it is beginning to have structure. You can actually see as the pieces are coming together and its form emerges.

A person is exactly like that, relationships are like that, and businesses are like that. Literally, the word "structure" comes from the Latin word for "to build." Think about the word "construction," where something is built. It is about the parts becoming organized into a cohesive whole. And when the whole is constructed, the parts hold together and work. But if the parts are spread out all over the place and there is no structure holding them together, or if they are too flimsy or movable, they do not work.

Your boundaries are the structure of your personality, and as you live them out, they organize the structure of your self, your relationships, your work, and your life. If they are secure, it all works. But, if they are too spread out, or too flimsy and movable, you will be, too. Let's look for a moment at the psychology of how all that happens, and how you came to have the structure you either have, or are lacking, today.

HOW STRUCTURE DEVELOPS

If you have children, or have ever been around them, you have seen a universal progression take place. They begin with almost no structure to their personalities whatsoever. While we might be able to see certain traits in infancy, like a bent toward aggressiveness or passivity or a tendency toward discomfort or contentment, they are pretty much undefined. We do not know what form they are going to take and how it is going to express itself later. If you look at the babies in a newborn nursery, you can see the future attorneys protesting and fighting or the passive ones who could turn into the future codependents. But you still don't know what they will actually be like.

As time goes on, they begin to take shape. They get more mobile, they develop language, and they begin to explore the outside world. They get in touch with their interests and desires. They move to express them and get them satisfied externally. But they are still chaotic and very easily upset. And what they want, they want—now.

Parents and caretakers surround them with the structure that they do not have for themselves. The ones who love them begin to set boundaries and limits around them, initially to protect them and manage them. Pretty soon, they learn the word "no." In fact, they not only learn to hear it, but they learn to say it, too. Toddlers are known to make a strong grimace, look at the powers that be, and say it with all their force. "No!" They are displaying their power and their will.

But, powerful as they may feel, they quickly find that there are limits to their budding sense of omnipotence. They run into boundaries and limits—fences—that are real. "No, you can't do that." "No, you can't keep playing. It is time for bed." "If you throw that, you are going in time-out." And this is a key in their developing the boundaries they are going to need for the rest of their lives. As structure is added to their experience, something is happening. They are internalizing that structure.

As the limits are imposed with them, an axiom of human development is occurring—a law, if you will:

What was once on the outside, becomes inside.

The limits that are imposed on them from the outside become part of their internal makeup. Those limits become the internal structure that makes them feel secure, allows them to feel safe, and also causes them to gain something referred to as "self-control." As limits and consequences are given to them for their actions, they learn that they can make choices that affect their well-being. "If you do A, then B will happen, and if you do C, then D will happen." The combination of getting rewards and getting in trouble gives them the structure and self-discipline that will later become the basis for the kind of self-control that will empower them to fulfill their destinies later in life—or not. They learn what the word "no" means, and are able to say no to themselves, to others, and to respect the "no" that others say to them. They have internalized that ability. Those who do not have these kinds of limits or discipline will flounder. (Have you ever seen an irretrievably spoiled child try to deal with the world on her own?)

Slowly, over many instances, the child's internal software is set to also do something else that will empower them for life. It will put into place a time-sequencing formula for outcomes and quality of life. When little Suzy learns that "if I do A, B happens," she is becoming more than an impulsive, do-what-feels-good-right-now kind of person. She is becoming a linear person who thinks in terms of cause and effect. She puts a time line to it, learning "if I do this now, there will be an effect later." She begins to link her choices with later results. First, her choices lead to results such as a time-out or an ice cream cone. Later, she understands that to study and do homework rewards her with acceptance to the college of her choice. Even later, she discovers that if she calls on enough key accounts she will be able to afford that house. Or as a leader, if she makes specific moves, the stock price will soar. The key here is that the software is being written that will get time on her side through the mechanism of choice. She will have a formula that will govern much of what she does.

"If I make this choice, good things will happen," becomes an organizing principle in her head, and it is one of the key components of boundaries and structure. The opposite will be true as well, and it will keep her from making other choices that will rob her of her desired goal. For instance, if she were in Maria's job, from the first chapter, she would know that not firing Stan guarantees a path to more misery for everyone, and thinking about the consequence of that for tomorrow and the day after would motivate her to pull the trigger. So if she had that kind of structure in her head, and did not have the fears and conflicts that would keep her from action, she would make the move that is necessary. That does not mean that she would be heartless, or not try to work with Stan to see if he could get to a higher level of performance, or that if she did fire him that she would have no empathy for his situation. But it does mean that she would be able to do what needed to be done.

As a result of being around boundaries, accountability, consequences, and rewards, children internalize a sense of structure that will serve them well. They learn to say yes to good things, no to bad things, and to gain the self-control they will need for a lifetime. All of that becomes an enduring structure in their hearts, minds, and even the neural hardware of their brains—for life. Their early experience of structure has become a literal part of who they are, part of their character.

WHAT STRUCTURE DOES FOR US

Structure performs six key functions: differentiation and separateness; containment; definition; limits; values; self-control, freedom, and autonomy. Let's take a closer look at each function.

1. Differentiation and Separateness

A key component of this developmental path of building character structure is something called "differentiation." It is the process whereby children find out who they are as distinct people, different from others. Remember the property line? It not only defines where your property begins and ends, it also defines where you end and someone else begins. It shows where the two properties are different and distinct. This side is yours, and this is not. That is the foundation of personal identity, to know that you are you and not someone else.

So, the child begins to exert that distinctiveness. He is given choices, and he chooses red as his favorite color or this activity as his favorite game as opposed to the other one. Even if Mom or Dad like a different color or choice for a toy, he will assert himself. So he begins to own his desires, thoughts, tastes, and uniqueness.

If all goes well, then later on, though he comes from a family line of bankers, he will feel the freedom and differentiation to become a musician instead, if that's his desire. He has learned that just because his brother is an athlete, he does not have to be one, and he pursues his own interest. He knows what he wants, feels, likes, and what he doesn't. He is different from his family, not in a weird way, but distinct as his own person. Even if he did like the same things as his brother or dad or mom, he would still be in touch with the fact that he liked them for himself and not because they wanted him to.

I remember an incredible experience in which I saw a parent exhibiting this kind of experience for his early teenage son. I have a friend who was a well-known football star, a real macho stud of a guy. We were planning to play golf one Saturday and he called to ask me if I minded that his young son join us, whom I had never met. I said, "Sure, no problem." In my mind's eye I pictured a younger version of this Goliath figure and wondered what position he played on his team and how many miles he could hit a golf ball.

When I got to the course, I was surprised. My friend's son was nothing like him. He was not studly, not muscled, not particularly manly. In fact, he was really on the other end of the continuum, somewhat artsy and much gentler and softer. I remember the striking contrast when we were introduced.

As we were walking toward the driving range, I asked a little about what how much golf he played or what other sports he was into. Before he could answer, Dad lit up like a Christmas tree. "Mark, tell him what is going on with your music! Henry, this is awesome!"

Mark started telling me about his musical pursuits, the orchestra he was a part of, opportunities that were opening up for him, and in the same breath, with a laugh from both of them, he said, "I'm not much of the sports guy. That's Dad's department." His father went on to brag to me about all that he was doing, and you could feel the enthusiasm and joy he felt in who his son was. I literally had to hold back my emotion at the sheer beauty of the moment. I saw a father with a son whose passions were so different from his own much-acclaimed athletic path, relishing his son's individuality, differences, and separateness from him, loving and supporting exactly who his son was. It was one of the most beautiful father-son moments I have ever witnessed. His son was fully differentiated, his own person, with secure boundaries of identity, a very structured view of who he was and what he liked, and the clear freedom to make choices to express that identity.

In differentiation, you can see how the concepts we discussed in chapter two—of ownership, freedom, choice, and responsibility—come to bear in business. If Mark becomes a leader or manager later in life, this differentiation will serve him well. He may have to take ownership for pushing his vision through when there are many voices telling him he should go a different way. But his clear sense that it is OK to have a separate and different path from other people's will empower him to stand up to the pressure. Remember the early computer entrepreneurs who were told that no one will ever want a personal computer? Fortunately, they were differentiated enough to think their own thoughts and say no to the pressure to think like everyone else.

If Mark found himself in Maria's situation from chapter 1, he would be able to stay separate and differentiated from Stan's protest and hurt over losing his job. No matter how Stan came back at him, his differentiated stance would allow him to maintain his position. If he were David, he would be able to stay separate from his bully boss's opinions of him as well, not joining those opinions and making them part of him. They would remain outside his fence.

If he later becomes a team leader who is setting the tone and the culture in a company, he will see differentiation as a positive thing for the team, and encourage the kind of team atmosphere in which people can have different ideas, put them out there, and feel free to express themselves. They would not have to think like him—or like everyone else. As a result, the team would be free to produce great things.

Recall postmortems in the *Wall Street Journal* or other business publications of CEOs or leaders who are fired, blow up organizations, or find a way to run things into the ground. You will often hear phrases like he "discouraged dissenting opinions," or "saw disagreement as a lack of loyalty," or "was threatened and hostile toward those who did not agree." Ultimately, a leader who cannot relish strong and differentiated team members loses the benefit of having them around in the first place, and instead develops a team that is merely an extension of himself and subject to all the diseases and foibles that exist in his own head.

Think about one more bent that Mark will have. He will act in accord with the findings of research on strengths, talents, giftedness, and performance success. He will pursue work that is congruent with his strengths and passion, and then he will spend his time focusing on those tasks instead of getting pulled into directions that were not him. His identity will always be an internal GPS guiding him toward the "me" he was designed to be, and not doing someone else's mission on earth. He will look at those other areas, and inside his brain will say the equivalent of "I am not a football player. I am _____." He will be separate enough to live out what he is actually good at and gifted at doing. Differentiation and separateness are huge.

Question: Where do you find it difficult to stand separate and differentiated from the pressures around you to be what they want you to be?

2. Containment

Another important function that the structure of boundaries provides is containment. Literally, it means to keep something that is destructive or harmful within limits or under control. Basically, it prevents expansion of something bad. Its business and life implications are enormous.

When a child is out of line or overwhelmed with negative emotion or even impulses and behavior, someone loving sets a limit with him or her. They intervene, and with gentleness and not reciprocal attack, they firmly and gently "contain" it to keep it from getting larger and expanding its reach. "I don't allow screaming like that. You are going to have to go sit in the other room until you can calm down and come talk to me quietly." The emotion and inappropriate expressions are limited. The same thing happens with the child's impulsive behavior as well. He is not allowed to have it spread. It is limited and contained.

Recently my five-year-old daughter was particularly upset about not getting to do something and was pretty whiny and becoming increasingly upset. When I told her the answer was still "no," she got more upset, and so I walked over to her, stooped down to her level, and said, "I want you to go sit in the other room until you can calm down, and when I hear you being quiet for two minutes, I will come talk to you, but not until you can be quiet." She was initially upset, but after a few minutes she quieted down and a few minutes later yelled out, "OK, Daddy. I can talk now." The structure and limits had helped her contain her emotions—and calm down. Through many experiences like that, children learn to contain themselves, and not lose it when they are distraught. Later in life, they can contain their own emotions in very escalating situations.

But, equally important, through containment they are also internalizing the ability to contain others as well. My daughter was around a friend's cat who was being a little crazy and she said, "Snowball, you are being too rowdy. You have to go sit in time-out!" She then went and put the cat in its bed and stood over it and made sure it stayed there until it got calmed down. She was internalizing the ability not only to contain herself but also to contain others.

This ability is so important later, especially as a leader. When there is chaos in the team or the organization or toxic attitudes or a crisis of some sort, the leader must step in and contain it. She must make sure that it does not spread, and instead give order to it all. Then, as she rights the ship, the people calm down. When a customer is "redlining" all over the place, and going to blow up the relationship, the person with the ability to contain does not react to the crisis, but proactively moves to contain and calm the customer's chaos, and moves the relationship along.

As I was working on this book, a series of fires were ravaging Southern California. A key theme in the news coverage of the disaster was how people in San Diego—the epicenter of the crisis—were so calm. Newscasters attributed this phenomenon to local leaders who created order that contained everyone's fear. They contrasted it with the lack of containment evidenced in the wake of the Hurricane Katrina disaster. The fires were raging, yet the structure provided by the leaders calmed everyone down in the midst of the crisis.

Are you that kind of boss? Account manager? Leader, parent, or spouse? Can you contain what should not be spreading and getting bigger? That is what good, structured boundaries do.

Many times in organizations, when there are changes or downturns, fear and uncertainty breed and performance declines because of the inability of the leader to offer the containment that is needed. He may be overwhelmed himself with the change and uncertainty—or merely lack the kind of internal structure that we have been talking about—rendering him unable to provide it for others. Either way, the inability of a leader to offer containment is a big problem.

One of the saddest situations I ever saw was a company whose incredibly talented management team was blown apart because of the CEO's inability to contain one VP's toxic interpersonal style. The VP was haughty, communicated a better-than-everyone air, and was very divisive. She put down people's ideas when they disagreed with her and assumed the worst of others instead of waiting to find out the truth of a person or situation. Slowly, over time, she eroded the unity that the team had once enjoyed, and significantly hurt a few individuals in particular.

When I was called in, it was because several people were about to leave, as she had created such a division that the board itself was divided in its commitment to the CEO. He had been there for five years and had up until that time enjoyed a good relationship with the board and the team. But the VP's politics and backbiting had managed to get the best of him.

A leader with good boundaries would have put up a fence to contain her destruction and not let it spread. My first task was to find him, the parts of him that should have been dealing with her in the ways that we saw above. Why didn't he say no? Where was his ability to differentiate from her, to stand separate and see what was going on and then take a stand and contain it? Where was his power? Somehow in the mix of it all, he had lost his mojo. When he finally found it, he stood up and began to lead again, first of all by communicating to the team that he saw the problem, had called in some help to address it, and that they were all going to lock themselves up in a room and not come out until they were a team again. By doing that, he said to them, "Enough! This is not going to destroy all that we have built and we are going to get back to being a team. I am going to stop the direction that we have been going." When he did that, he sent a strong signal that the chaos was over, and things began to turn around. Certainly there was more to this, as we will explore later in the book. But for now, understand that containment is a key component to successful anything.

> *Question: What is going on around you that is destructive that you should be containing and not allowing to spread further? When you've been faced with such problems in the past, how did you (or didn't you) work to contain the damage?*

3. Definition

Who are you? Have you ever thought about that? Many people, when asked that question, respond with the definition of a role. They might say "I am a VP"—or a project manager or a mother or in sales. But identity is not something that comes about from a role. Roles are structures that are created as contexts for you to live out an identity that is formed long before that role (parenthood, the VP position, etc.) ever happens. But your identity comes from being a well-defined person, before assuming a role. This enduring identity structure, which also changes over time, is composed of a lot of different parts of being a person, which all people inherently have. They are the treasures that lie within the fences of your boundaries, and at the same time actually form the boundaries themselves, as you take ownership of them and communicate them to the outside world.

You define yourself by first knowing—and owning—these elements of personhood:

- Your feelings

- Your attitudes

- Your behaviors

- Your choices

- Your limits

- Your thoughts

- Your talents

- Your desires or wants

- Your values

- Your loves

When you know what you feel, what you want, what your talents are, and what choices you are making at any given moment, you have a good sense of who you are. That is the first step, owning these part of you. But you do not really feel secure in that identity until you are able to go the second step and define yourself to the outside world as well—by communicating those elements of personhood.

Your fences are underground if no one else knows what you feel or think. They cannot be not forced to deal with you as you would like if your personhood is not being defined to the outside world. They certainly do not have to contend with you or adapt to you in any way, which is the essence of a real relationship.

In real relationships, we affect each other. The power of who you are affects another person. And they affect you. From infancy when the baby gets upset, communicates that to the mother, and she adapts the way she is holding him in order to make it work for him, all the way to adulthood when the spouse says, "Your work schedule is taking a toll on the family and you have to change it," we affect each other. We adapt to each other's feelings, limits, desires, and the rest of the list above. But, if you are not able to communicate these elements to those outside of yourself, you remain a nonentity, and certainly a "nonforce." The power of relationships is not experienced, and both you and others lose out.

Definition has three components:

- Knowing what you feel, think, desire, etc.

- Communicating those aspects of yourself to others

- Acting on them

When you do all three, you are fully alive and living as a defined person. If you are not, the world is waiting for you to show up.

> *Question: Do you allow yourself to truly be aware of your real feelings, thoughts, desires, etc.? When you are aware of them, how well do you communicate those to others? Once you know them, do you communicate them directly?*

4. Limits

Containment is an expression of a limit, but personal limits include more than the function of containment. They are the essence of the property line of you as a person. They define how far you are willing to go and where you draw the line.

Limits are developed first by having them imposed upon us. When parents and caretakers give us limits and consequences, we learn that we can go only so far. Then we internalize those limits and begin to obey them for ourselves. What is important is not the content of those limits but that the content changes over the years. (First it was "Don't go into the street." Certainly that limit changed with time. Later it became "Don't do off-balance-sheet deals.") The content may change but what is important is that you have a limit part of you, a line inside that says, "Don't go past this point." If you do step over that line, you will be someone who does not live within the very important limits that preserve life. You may use substances that destroy you, abuse your most significant relationships in some way, hurt those you work with, hurt yourself, or even break the law. Not good. The ability to obey internal limits is key to doing well.

Likewise, this personality structure gives you the ability to respect the limits of others. When someone says, "That is not allowed" or "I do not want you to do that," you listen and respect it. You might negotiate or try to persuade them to change that limit (sometimes a very good thing), but ultimately you will respect another person's "no." This ability is the essence of love, respect, and relationship—to allow another person to be who they are and not try to define them or control them. Co-workers and team members really appreciate that. If you have ever seen dysfunctional teams in a company, you can easily see at least one person's inability to respect the thoughts—or limits—of others.

Equally important is the ability to set limits with others—to say to them, "No, I will not do that" or "No, I will not allow that to happen to me." If you do not have a good sense of personal limits, then it is inevitable that your company, your customers, your friends, your in-box, your mission, the people you love, and the people you "shouldn't love" will all come to define you. And you will end up not being who you are but who they decide you are going to be. You will have lost control of yourself.

Your ability to set limits is paramount to good boundaries and to being a successful person. To be able to draw the line and say, "I will not go past here" is critical. It is what a lot of this book is about. If you think of the scenarios in the opening chapter, limits are what were missing in some form or fashion in each situation. If each person could have drawn some sort of line in the sand and said, "not past here," each outcome would have been different. In this book, we will look hard at your limits, how they are working, and how to make them better. But have you ever thought about what happens when you don't have limits, or they are broken?

- When a person pushes you too far, you go along with them and end up somewhere you don't want to be.

- When others' demands are more than you have time for, you do not set the limit and they control your time and life.

- When others' dysfunction or problems are causing you problems and more work, you do not stand up and say no to allowing them to affect you more.

- When there is a moral or ethical dilemma, and someone is pressuring you to do something that you do not feel comfortable with doing, you do it anyway and either feel bad about yourself or end up in trouble.

I can safely say that I have never seen a long-term successful person who did not have a good sense of personal limits. They are crucial. It has been said that your success is equal to your ability to confront. If you cannot confront a problem and set a limit on it, by definition it will overtake you. Limits save your life. The problem is that in our individual development, our limits get broken or conflicted or not built at all. So we find ourselves in adult life, where the stakes are much higher, sent to fight the wolves with no protection. And we get hurt, sometimes even destroyed.

In the next chapter, we will look at how your boundaries get broken and rendered impotent. Fear plays a big role, and we will see how. For now, just get the concept. Your limits help define who you are and compose the structure, shape, and outcome of your life. They are the reason a company has a mission statement, to define the identity and limits of what the company is and what it is not. "We do not do that" is one of most important things a company can say. It keeps its stakeholders focused on the things they should be doing. It is also one of the most important things an individual can say as well.

Question: Where are you being pushed past your limit and allowing something to occur that you do not want to occur, either by yourself or by others toward you? What limits of others are you not respecting that it would help if you would?

5. Values

Our values are another important aspect of our character's structure. What we value is ultimately what we enforce and stand for. To "value" means to hold something precious or of high worth. The things we value are the things worth fighting for. They are also the structures that organize our efforts into focused activity, with the aim of producing more of what we value.

If a family values education, for example, they will work to save for it, and then spend their money on educational activities, endeavors, and experiences. That is focused activity. They are saying yes to some things and no to others. That value is defining and organizing their resources into a focused direction. The values shape their identity in this regard.

If a company values excellence, for example, it focuses its resources, systems, and efforts to achieve it. It also enforces its values, and says no to behavior, attitudes, or work that falls short of or belies the value of being excellent. Nonexcellent performance gets rejected and sent back for improvement. Continued nonexcellent performance is not tolerated. It is contained, limited, and differentiated against. The values shape the identity of a company.

The same thing is true for your personal identity and character as well. Your values shape your behavior, focus, and direction. What you value, in a sense, you will ultimately become. It will be your true north, the compass setting that keeps you going in a certain direction. That is why instilling certain values in children is so important, as those values will guide them for life. They will seek expression and opportunities to live them out, guiding their behavior and choices.

Later, in chapter 5 where we discuss the "audit," we will talk more about your values and their role in the structure of your boundaries. But for now, just be mindful that you are living them out, one way or another. You are spending your time, energy, and resources on what is important to you. If you are not getting the results you desire, maybe some of the things you are valuing are not that helpful or even that transcendent. For example, maybe you value people liking you more than you value your own convictions, so you bend and become what they desire you to be in any moment. As a result, you are getting what your values are leading you to focus on: the immediate peaceful coexistence with several people at the expense of who you are as a person or the execution of your vision. Or maybe you value not making mistakes more than you value innovation (which includes the possibility of getting it wrong, and making mistakes before you get it right). Since wrong turns are a necessary part of the path of innovation, you don't get out of the safe zone and thus are true to your true value: no failure.

In any event, deciding what your values are is an important part of being an intact, differentiated, and secure person, as well as the ability to live those values out in difficult situations. The audit will help you identify your values, and the rest of the book will help you bring them about.

Question: What are the things that you value most in life? Would your actions get you convicted in court for caring about those things?

6. Self-Control, Freedom, and Autonomy

Dictionaries define "self-control" as the ability to exercise control over one's feelings, desires, behaviors, and impulses. Some add the idea of context, such as doing so in difficult situations. However you define it, self-control is the fruit of the kinds of structure we have been discussing. When it is all said and done, good boundaries put you in control of the only person you can control, and that is yourself. Ergo, self-control. You are free from others, and an independent, autonomous person.

Control over yourself is the essence of true power. The paradox is that in people's attempts to control others, which they can never do, they lose control of themselves, the only one they can control. In the next chapter, we shall look at how power works, and just as importantly, how it breaks down. But, ultimately, it comes from having control over you.

The point for now is the role that structure plays in self-control. If you don't have a No and a Go switch in your head, then you are not in control of yourself. If there are fears or conflicts that get in the way—or there never have been any of the above kinds of structures downloaded to begin with—then you will either lose self-control to forces from the outside or forces from the inside. But you will lose it, and suffer the consequences. You want to have a voice inside your head that steers you correctly and can at the right moment say, "Yes, do that," and at other times, "No! Do not go there."

People get into trouble when the yes-and-no voice points them in the wrong direction. They say yes to things that get them off course or into trouble because of pressures from the outside, or impulses and needs from the inside. And they say no to the very choices that they should be making for similar reasons, mostly based in fear or needs. What we don't often realize is that these abilities are also internalized from the outside, just like all the other structure we have discussed.

Many years ago I was visiting some friends and got to see an incredible example of this kind of budding structure in the mind of their three-year-old. We were all watching television one night, a DVD of the golden years of *Saturday Night Live*. Right about the time Weekend Update was beginning, Billy decided that he wanted attention and began to walk in front of the TV and block our view. His dad told him to move, and he did, but he came back and did it again. His dad told him again, and he moved, but the impulse for attention beckoned one more time. Billy started to walk in front of the TV again, and right as he was about to get into view-blocking range, his dad warned him. Billy stopped, hesitated, began to go forward anyway, and stopped again. You could see the war in his head. Then, with a big frown, he said, "I need to go sit in the Red Chair!" He promptly ran off and sat in the chair that they reserved for time-out discipline when he was in trouble. He knew that he needed to control himself, and he needed that external structure to do it.

The point is that the parents' discipline, from the outside, was getting internalized. They did not say, "Go sit in the chair," at least in that moment. Billy did. He said it to himself. He controlled the impulse that was going to get him into trouble, and he exercised his "no" muscle over himself. It was no surprise that years later we saw him awarded all sorts of scholarships, landing at Princeton, and on to a successful placement on Wall Street. He had internalized the ability to say no to himself—a key element of self-control.

Similarly, the ability to say yes and to use self-control to autonomously pull the trigger and go is just as important. I recall a CEO I worked with who was one of the most creative deal makers I have ever seen. He could look at a totally unworkable situation that many others had passed up and find a way to restructure it in ways that made "outside the box" not even come close to describing it. He would go for it and reach into markets and deals that others would be afraid of. He could pull the trigger.

But what stood out to me was that this ability to say, "Yes, go" was a real one, not an impulsive one. There are many business leaders who say yes to many things they should have passed up and later regret it. They are impulsive, out of control, enamored by the sizzle of the deals, and in denial about the downside realities that are staring others in the face. He was not like that. His yesses were real and not impulsive.

I saw the proof of this one day when we were reviewing the year's performance. The grand total of his overly aggressive activity that year? One deal. He had looked at many, many more, and passed on all of them. He said yes to just one. I thought about it later and it explained much about how he had built his multi-billion-dollar company. He had the essence of self-control, the ability to say yes residing in the same toolbox that could say no. One without the other is not self-control. A car needs an accelerator and a brake.

If someone jumps at everything that smells good, he is out of control, and if someone can't ever go for it when it truly is good, he is equally out of control. He is not free to be autonomous, take control of himself, and do what is right, smart, and congruent with all he desires. He loses control to his fears. True self-control means a balance of yes and no. That comes from the structures inside that are able to make those moves. And those structures came originally from the outside, people who said, "Don't do that or you go into the Red Chair," and people who said, "Go for it. Try to ride the bike without the training wheels. You can do it." Later, what was once outside, becomes inside—the voice that sometimes says yes, and sometimes no.

When you are three, it is time-out and bicycles. When you are an adult, the consequences and stakes are much bigger, but the structures are the same. You are in control.

When this is true, you are truly free, truly autonomous. What you do is up to you, and not some other force. And ultimately, freedom is soil upon which the one life that you desire is grown. Any other way, and you are either a slave or a child under the control of guardians. One life must be your life, and for it to be your life, you have to have control of you.

Question: Can you say yes and no when needed, or do forces from the inside or outside cause you to lose self-control? Is it harder for you to say yes, or is it harder to say no?

IF ALL GOES WELL

So, if all goes well in a person's development, the structures are in place that bring about the ability to do the following:

- Experience yourself as separate and differentiated from others.

- Contain destruction and keep it from spreading.

- Define yourself and know who you are.

- Set limits when needed.

- Possess and live out values.

- Have self-control and thereby be free and autonomous.

If you look at yourself and assess yourself in all of those areas, you will probably find two truths. First, you possess a lot of each or all of those qualities. Second, in certain situations, in certain contexts, or with certain people, any or all of these abilities can get threatened or become unavailable to you. You can sometimes let someone else make you an extension of themselves, and you no longer truly feel separate. Their force or their pain can get to you too much. Or you allow things that are hurtful or destructive to gain a greater foothold than they should. It is amazing how certain relationships can pull at you to make this happen.

Other times, you find that you somehow have lost a sense of who you really are and what is important to you, being defined by the company or relationships that are important to you—sometimes too important. Or your limits might waver, and you do not draw the line. You might not have taken the time or had the permission to figure out your own values and let them guide you. Instead, forces have caused you to lose the most precious thing you have—your freedom. If you are human, at least one of these and probably more than one can and have happened, given the perfect storm of the right person or the right time. Maybe it did not even take a storm, but just a drizzle. Either way, the truth is that you are human and your development, just like everyone else's, did not go perfectly. That is not only a given, it is also OK.

The good news is that because we know the kinds of structures that build these abilities—and also the ways that they get broken, eroded, or not even installed in the first place—we also know what to do about it. That is what the rest of this book is about and will help you to do. From here, we are going to talk about how these things get broken, and how they are fixed. And we are going to find out what kinds of boundaries help you get back in control and experience the kind of freedom that leads to having one life that works—both in business and in life. You will find that it is the same you bringing about results in both.

Part Two

REBUILDING BOUNDARIES

We have seen how boundaries are important, how they are developed, and taken a peek into how they affect business and life integration. The good news is that if you know how, you can grow in all of the functions of boundaries. In this section, we will begin that process, to regain control of yourself, your work, and your life.

four

Reclaiming Your Power

My client, Deb, was a particularly gifted businesswoman. She had it all: brains, charm, intuition, great people skills, a law degree, and an MBA from a prestigious business school—the whole mix. And she had been able to put it to good use in building her own customized marketing firm using venture capital. But there was one problem. Frequently, she found herself torn between the needs of her own business and the needs of another business, her father's. He was a physician who had gone into the hospital business and had done well building a chain of hospitals.

The problem would emerge when he wanted her to do what she did best, schmooze VIPs and the press at publicity gatherings in a new market. He would sometimes launch new medical centers with events, inviting city officials, investors, reporters, and others who were important to his business. And he loved for her to be the charming face of the event, hosting, emceeing, and just being the glue that held it all together. There was a time, when she was younger, that she did not mind doing this sort of thing for him. But now, at thirty-four, with two children and one on the way, a busy family life, and her own business, his requests were becoming more taxing with each passing season. She began to talk to me about it as she was preparing for the birth of her next child, when she knew her time was going to be even more taxed.

"So, what's the problem?" I asked. "Tell him you are going to have to bow out, that you just have too much going on right now to do any more of these for a while."

"I know I should," she said. "But I just can't. I have never been able to say no to him."

"Why? What happens when you do?" I asked.

"Well, it makes him mad, but he is not the loud-mad type. He is the quiet-mad type," she said.

"What is that?"

"You know, he just has the ability to go silent and say a few things to let you know that you are the scum of the earth for not helping him," she said. "I can't really explain it, but he just makes me feel so bad, so guilty. I always end up doing what he wants so he won't be upset. I can't stand it when he is disappointed in me, or mad at me."

We were working on this tendency to lose her boundaries in many situations when she finally had a wake-up call. Shortly after her baby was born, she got very ill with a flu. She was newly home from the hospital, sick, tired, and in need of rest—and he called. He told her that he needed her for a gathering that weekend with doctors and wanted her to come help—in a city halfway across the country. She told him that she was sick, with a new baby, and that she would not be able to come.

But, true to his colors, he pressed her. "I really need you," he said. "It is very important. We cannot let this event not be successful and without you, there is no one else that can do it. You have to come."

She continued trying to explain and told him that she was just too sick. There was just no way she could come, she told him. As she did, he interrupted her and said, "I'm FedExing you a ticket and will see you tomorrow." With that, he hung up.

The ticket came—and she went. Had she called me, I think I would have sent one of her teammates to kidnap her and talk her out of it. But she didn't, and she went. I found out about it later, and was astounded at what happened next, the truly incredible part. In her depleted state, she got on the plane and flew there. When she got off of the plane, she walked through security and there he was, standing there waiting, even after the last thing she had said to him was that she was not coming. She walked up to him, and he said,

"I knew you'd be here."

She told me that when he said that she almost felt like throwing up, sick to her stomach. The control he knew he had over her was staring her right in the face. She realized the degree to which he owned her life, and she did not. At that moment, she said, something snapped inside of her. It was finally clear to her that her father was ultimately in control of her life, and not her. It should have been apparent long before then, but what it took to break through to her was that he knew it. It showed her that all of her attempts to keep him happy, thinking that they had some true relational value, were really just the results of being manipulated by a truly controlling and selfish man. It was hardly worth giving her life for, she finally realized.

When she did, a pattern changed in the way that she did all of her business. She got mad, and then she got even. It was not in terms of getting revenge, but in terms of going through her entire life and figuring out how extensive the tendency for her to dance to the tune of others was affecting almost everything she did. Her employees, her customers, and her peers to some extent were more in charge of her than she was. All they had to do was pull the trigger that would make her swing into action, make her feel just a little bit bad. For her, feeling as if she were letting someone down was tantamount to an On switch, motivating her to do whatever it would take to avoid having someone be disappointed in her. And when we looked at it in some depth, it was extensive, even defining.

She would have said, and rightly so, that her highest business values were things like service, integrity, excellence, profits, good relationships, and the like. And she was right, except that any of those could be interrupted by her weak spot, the tendency to want the approval of people who were withholding it from her in some way that made her feel bad. When that happened, everything else dropped into second place. She lost her power, to use the popular phrase. Let's take a closer look at that now.

PERSONAL POWER AND POWER DRAINS

In some senses, I hate to even use the word "power." It seems hackneyed, like we are going back to the eighties. Power ties, power lunches, power suits. The last thing I want to sound like is one of those motivational speaker types telling you to find the power within. So accept my disclaimer. But pop psychology apologies notwithstanding, power is an important topic in work and in life. You can't live without it. You are designed to have it, as we have said, in the form of self-control. When you lose that and are controlled by others, you are rendered powerless.

And that is when the slippery slope that disintegrates life and causes you to lose your boundaries appears. What we know about the human experience of powerlessness is that it erodes functioning in all of the areas that are important to having one-life integration: your emotions, your relationships, and your performance. Decades of research have shown that the degree of powerlessness that people feel directly correlates with diminished functioning. And for powerlessness to occur, there must be a crack—a fault in the foundation.

If we take Deb as an example, we can see the crack in the armor that ends up in the disintegrated life. The crack was the weak spot she had for feeling guilty and over-responsible. Whether the pressure is from the fear of overidentifying with how bad someone is going to feel if she fires him, like Maria with Stan in chapter 1, or David's allowing his boss to make him feel so bad, or Ryan's inability to say no and therefore becoming too scattered, these situations can occur only if there is a soft spot in the character, a whole in the fence, a vulnerability through which people lose control of themselves. If the soft spot were not there, power losses could not happen:

Without a personal weak spot, power losses cannot happen.

Personal power, which is the beginning of the accumulation of any other kind of power, is about the things we discussed in the last chapter—separateness, containment, defining yourself, setting limits, living out values, having self-control and freedom—and it must be maintained, not subject to power losses. It is only through having these kinds of personal power that you will be able to build financial power, emotional power, relational power, political power, spiritual power, and the power to perform. You are powerful when you possess the ability to do the following:

- Experience yourself as separate and differentiated from others.

- Contain destruction and keep it from spreading.

- Define yourself and know who you are.

- Set limits when needed.

- Possess and live out values.

- Have self-control and thereby be free and autonomous.

Notice that power over other people is not on the list. You can only control yourself, and when you do that well, you will do well with others.

As you can probably tell, Deb's personal power was strong in so many ways. She was very successful, but when that little trigger inside was touched by her father or others, she would lose it. That was the personal weak spot that made it possible for her to lose her power. If someone made her feel bad, she could not stand separate from their wishes and stay differentiated with personal opinions and plans that were separate from theirs. If she could have, she would have felt like, "Gee Dad, that is tough. Sorry that you are going to have an opening in that city without an emcee." She would have stayed differentiated from his problem. But her weak spot kept her from being able to do that.

That does not mean that she would not care or feel for him. She could show empathy, but she could see that her life, her problems, her new baby, her illness, and all that she was responsible for were differentiated from his life, and ultimately she could allow him to have his problems without them becoming hers. That is not a lack of care. It is differentiation. A lack of care—or selfishness—is when someone lives a life of never offering to help anyone, totally self-absorbed. That is quite a different issue than not being free to determine when you are going to help and when you are not, and having that decision made for you, de facto, by someone who is making you feel guilty.

Similarly, if she'd successfully differentiated, she would be able to stay separate from his negative opinion of her when she did say no, and not join his invitation to feel like she was an ungrateful daughter or didn't love him. Even if he said those things, and even if at that time he believed that, she would be able to stay separate from his opinion and maintain her own. "I am so sorry you feel that way, Dad. It must be hard to think that your own daughter doesn't care for you. I do, but I understand that you don't see that right now, and that makes me sad, because I do love you." She would feel separate, perhaps sad for him, but not guilty, and certainly not recalculating her own direction based on how he feels. She would be too differentiated to do that—a separate person.

Further, you can just go down the list above and see how she would be vulnerable to losing all of those attributes at moments when her trigger was pulled. She would not be able to contain destruction that someone was causing if they could make her feel guilty for confronting them. She would lose touch with her own desires and goals as she put more and more energy into what other people wanted her to do. She would lose the ability to set limits, especially on her time and energy, like with her father. Her most important business and personal values would be endangered. Just look at the relational loss she had with her newborn to make a trip across the country on a whim so her father would not be upset. And, clearly, she was no longer autonomous, but an extension of him and his wishes.

How did this happen? It was from the hole in her fence, her need for her dad to approve of her and her inability to feel good about herself when he and others did not. That was her Achilles' heel. That was her power drain. So, that brings us to one of the most important questions that you will ever ask yourself:

> *Question: Where, with whom, and under what circumstances do you lose your power? What are the chinks in your armor? Where are the holes in your fences?*

To the degree that you can be honest about that question you will be able to get on the road to integrating your life and keeping your boundaries. But you have to be honest. If you are not, you are more vulnerable than you know. I remember a friend of mine, in his late sixties and having had a very successful career in business saying, "A person can lie to others and get away with it at times. But the moment he begins to lie to himself, he is in trouble. It is the beginning of the end." When you deceive yourself, you are in trouble and don't even know it.

IDENTIFY THE HOLES IN YOUR FENCES

So, let's get honest, at least with yourself. In this section, we'll look at a variety of unhealthy needs, fears, inabilities, and other conditions that tear holes in our boundaries. Each description includes assessment questions to help you identify the holes in your fences.

The Need for Security

When the immediate or intermediate future looks uncertain, do you begin to give away something of yourself to maintain security? If the job market looks scary, do you take some assignment that you would not readily agree to if you had the stomach to wait it out, thereby losing control of yourself and your direction? Or, because of fear, do you take on too much work, even with clients you do not want, because you are afraid that something may go bad? I am not talking about good diligence here. I am referring to a pattern of operating out of fear.

The Need for Approval

Like David, the manager with a bullying boss, do you have a need for others to like you and always approve of you? When they don't, do all of your systems begin to fire? Do you obsess about it after work, and worry about it at work? Are you overly vigilant in wondering what someone's opinion is of you, and if it ever seems to diminish, do you begin to dance and try to fix it until things are good again?

The Need to Be Perfect

If the possibility of something not looking good is anywhere on the screen, do you get motivated to action? While striving for excellence is a great trait, perfectionism is not. It gets you dancing around, spending time on things that are not worth spending time on, just because you cannot stand for them to be less than ideal. The need to get it right has turned into the need to have it perfect, and you spend hours and fret and stress over things that others are able to let go. As a result of your perfectionism, you are out of control.

The Need to Have Others See You As Ideal

This is the motivation to be seen in a certain light and expending lots of energy to manage your image in the eyes of others. I have seen people literally lose a month's energy and focus because they had a small interaction with someone they deemed important that left the impression they were not as good as they desired to be perceived. They were more motivated to work on fixing that impression than they were to address things that were truly important. Do you worry and obsess about how others are perceiving you? Do you fret and lose energy or time when you think you have left a less-than-ideal impression?

The Need to Overidentify with Other People's Problems, Pain, or Hurt

When other people are in pain, are you not able to stand it? Do you move in to rescue them from it? If you fear that confronting them might cause them pain, do you avoid the needed conversation to spare them the pain of going through it? Does their pain make it difficult for you discipline them or make decisions that negatively impact them? I am not talking about not feeling for people. I am talking about an overidentification with others' pain that stops you from doing what you need to do.

The Need to Rescue

This is the tendency to look at someone who is not getting it done, and be too much of a helper. Are you the kind of person who cannot stand to see someone get in over his head or have more to do than he seems to be able to manage? So you go into his yard and help him clean it up. Helping others and pitching in is a good quality, but this is different. It is the continuing pattern of getting drawn in to doing things for people that they should be doing for themselves. It is not the exception when help is needed, but a pattern of helping someone who always needs help, with things that are really not your job or responsibility.

The Fear of Being Alone or Isolated

Have you never gotten to that step of emotional independence in which being alone, at least for a while, feels good? So sometimes when it would be good for you to be alone, do you lose your direction and the objectives that are important to you just to be around people? You feel you have to go to lunch with that group or to that seminar, even when it would serve you better to stay in the office and complete something or work at home that day. You just need to be with people. You will feel too isolated if you aren't. Or, maybe just for the sake of being on a team, you give away too much of yourself. You lose important goals because of your excessive need to be with others, when it would serve you to be alone at times.

The Fear of Conflict and Need for Harmony

Do you get really uncomfortable when there is a conflict and people are not feeling harmonious? If there is disruption in the unity or togetherness for a time, is it difficult for you to allow that to be and just sit with it? Do you quickly seek them out to fix things or restore harmony, when often it would be better to let them fret or think about it?

The Fear of Disagreement or Differing Opinions

Do you feel that having different opinions is somehow a negative thing, no matter what side of the equation you are on? When you disagree with someone, do you feel like you have done something bad or hurt their feelings in some way, just by disagreeing with them? Or, when someone disagrees with you, do you take it as meaning something other than just a different opinion, such as an indication that you are wrong or inferior or stupid, or some other personal meaning other than simply different?

The Fear of Anger

Maybe you come from a background in which there was a lot of hurtful anger, or even abuse, and have suffered at the hands of angry people. So are you extra sensitive to it, such that whenever someone is angry or even might become angry you dance to their tune and lose yourself to make sure that they are OK? Or do you avoid conflict with them, avoid saying what you think to keep them from being angry?

The Fear of Feeling Inferior

Perhaps you have never really owned your own strengths, talents, and abilities, and you are still feeling sort of inferior to others. Do you feel a little like a kid and others are all adults? Do you feel that they are smarter, better, or above you in some way? If you do, do you give away your power to whatever they want or think, and not speak up when you really do have something to contribute? Do you just fold your cards instead and defer to the "real" experts?

The Fear of Someone's Position or Power

Sometimes we do not just give power to a person in our heads. They actually possess it in reality, like a boss. This person does have power over you in a certain sense, in that they are in control of your job. But, does the way you experience people having power over you exceed the amount of fear and respect that is normal? Does it take on the extra dimension of being able to define you, make you feel little, stupid, or powerless? As a result, do you notice that you are not yourself with someone who is over you?

The Inability to Say No

There is a power dynamic in all relationships. In the good ones, it is mutual. Each person shows up with who they are, their thoughts and opinions, wants, likes, and dislikes, and puts it out there for the other person to bump up against. That is a real relationship. But some cannot stand the force of another person's presence, another person's wants. They just by nature cave in. They blink first. How comfortable are you with standing up to another's request or wishes? Can you say no? Do you fold to other's thoughts, wants, likes, and dislikes just because to not blink is too uncomfortable? In negotiating, do you get too uncomfortable simply standing without giving in to the pressure?

The Inability to Hear "No" or Accept Limits

Sometimes it is not the tendency to back down that causes you to get out of control. It is the opposite. You fight and protest anytime someone says no to you or you encounter a limit or opposition. Is your problem with boundaries not that you give yours up, but that you encroach on the boundaries of others and are a control freak? Are you described by people as controlling or aggressive? Whenever you run into a boundary of anyone else and cannot be in control, do you protest and try to push them into giving in to you? Are you like a toddler having a temper tantrum and continually busting the boundaries of others? While this may have its rewards at times, it is costing you in some key relationships, and you can also see how out of control you actually are. All it takes is for someone to say no. (If you can't answer this one, ask someone who works with you.)

The Inability to Tolerate the Imperfection, Incompetence, Nonperformance, or Failure of Others

Do you lose yourself, your values, your emotional well-being, and stability when someone else is not doing their job? Are you the type who cannot stand nonperformance, and it makes you crazy? As a result, you lose control of yourself and act in ways that are not helpful, either to the person, or to your own goal of making it all work out well. Irresponsible people make you crazy, and as a result, you lose it and act in ways that do not help. Also, you might miss out on seeing the good parts of some people as well.

Idealization and Hero Worship

We all have people that we see as special or incredible in some way. That is a good thing. For example, if I played golf with Jack Nicklaus, my boyhood hero, I would feel like I were with a godlike figure. But sometimes when people idealize someone, for whatever reason, they cease to be a person around them. They fawn over them and give that person too much power over them, trying to please them or always get on their good side. Do you play up to the person you have put up on the pedestal, and give away much of your personhood just because you idealize them? Do you kind of lose your own brain and choices?

Lack of Internal Structure

It may not take a person or a situation to get you out of control. It may just take being awake. Are you an impulsive by nature, a perpetual ADD type, who just cannot sit within the bounds of any limit? If so, it is costing you. Your impulsivity—your inability to live within the limit of good structure—is taking its toll on you and/or some significant relationships to you, in and out of work. Sometimes people lose their power and effectiveness because they are out of control by nature. They are just impulsive and have never resolved that tendency.

Dependency

Are you dependent on others to help define who you are? Do you lack a sense of personhood, and look to others for validation, approval, significance, input, thoughts, security, etc.? Maybe something has happened in your development that has left you lacking that intact feeling of being an independent person in your own right, and as a result you are overly dependent on the judgment and input of others.

Vulnerability to Bad Conditions or Outcomes

Are you fine as long as things are going well, but, under stress, you become someone else? Do you lose yourself or withdraw and get overly stressed? You might get controlling or angry or argumentative. You might get scared and overreact in a myriad of situations, losing your best judgment and abilities. Either way, under stressful conditions, you lose ownership of your best self out of fear and anxiety. Maybe it is a loss of control or a fear of failure, but when things are not good, neither are you.

OK, if you did not identify with at least one of these needs, fears, inabilities, or conditions, then you live in a cave, and you need to get out more. In other words, we all have some sorts of situations and people that get to our underbelly and turn us into less than who we want to be. Becoming aware of your pattern, knowing when you lose it, is a key step in getting better.

It is essential to address those vulnerabilities in your personality. Without doing that, the problems will continue in every context in which you find yourself. You can go from job to job, thinking that the next one will be the one that will make it all work. But just like people who go from relationship to relationship without ever looking at what they contribute to the problem are destined to repeat it, you will too if you do not look at the underlying vulnerabilities to losing your boundaries. So identify the holes in your fences and own them. Watch for them and address them. Later in the book, we will address them as well, but for now, I just want you to see what is driving you to lose yourself.

Now that you know what boundaries are, why we need them, how structure is important to us, and the weaknesses that keep tripping you up, let's move toward the practical side of boundaries and building the structures that are going to make it all work.

five

The Audit

Everyone who manages anything knows the feeling at some time. You get the monthly, quarterly, or even yearly profit and loss, and gasp, "What? Where did all of that revenue go? We took in so much, it seems that there should be more left over at the end!" And if you have never been in the position of overseeing that kind of profit and loss, just think of your own personal checkbook. "What happened to all my money?" is a feeling that everyone has had at some time. So what do you do then? What happens next is where the real power is in the management of resources.

The smart people do a category-by-category audit and analysis and they find the gold. When your cost of goods is way out of line, you find out why and have a serious talk with suppliers. When your G and A is too big a slice of the pie, you look to find out why and cut the fat. All of this is designed to give you more of your resources to spend on the things that matter to you most, things like new business investment, new infrastructure that will fuel growth, more salespeople, research and development, paying employees better, or distribution of profit to shareholders.

> In the end, you want to maximize your resources to
> bring your real purposes to fruition.

The power of the audit is that it revealed where your resources were going, in ways that you were not aware of and did not want, empowering you to redirect them to where you really want them to go. Further, it brought insight into why that was happening. You found out there a was manager asleep at the wheel or some outdated system was costing you money and needed to be replaced. Resources do not just disappear for no reason. There is always a why and a how, good or bad.

Just as money is a precious resource to further the purposes of a business, and must be spent carefully and intentionally, so is another precious resource: time.

YOUR TIME IS YOUR LIFE

OK, now to the point about you.

> Your time is your life. Period.
> How you spend it ends up being what your life is.

No matter what you want to do, wish you had done, plan to do, or fantasize about while you are doing something else, the final reality of your life is how you spent your time. So, one of the greatest structures that you have to build the life you want to have is the direction of your time. But probably one of the reasons you are reading this book is that your time management is not working or is not being done at all. And there are reasons for that. Turning your time into a life that you want involves more than time management.

I remember an interesting conversation I had once when a Fortune 100 company called and asked me to do a workshop on time management. I asked the leader if they had ever had one of those before with this group, and she said, "Of course. Time management is a very important issue to us."

"What was the methodology that was taught?" I asked. I usually want to know what has been tried before, so as not to be repetitive or to get a better idea of what someone needs. She told me the system they had implemented, and it was one of those that was based around a set of tools, software, notebooks, etc. that promised to get everyone using their time better.

"So, did it work?" I asked.

"What do you mean?" she asked.

"Well, do you find that the people who went and now have all of those notebooks, software, and equipment are now managing their time well? Have the leaks been plugged?"

The phone went a little silent, and then we got into a very interesting conversation. The essence of it was something that she agreed with me on, but had never noticed. It seemed like two things were true, in both of our experiences. First, the people who were managing their time well before buying all the "tools" were still managing it well, and the ones who weren't were not helped that much by having a new system. Second, it seems that the more someone consistently buys the newest gadget on time management, that it almost diagnoses them as someone who cannot manage time. The takeaway? It ain't the tool. It's the carpenter. You can put the best golf club in a novice's hand, and it is not going to make him Tiger Woods. More to my point, time management has more to do with who we are as people—our boundaries—than it does with which system we use. And until we take a look at the ways that who we are is interfering with our use of time, we will still lose more and more time to the same patterns.

I told her that I would be glad to do the workshop, but only if I could do it in the way I believe that time management really works, and that would be to focus on the makeup of the people in order to find the leaks in their time. She immediately said, "That would be great. We need to plug the time stealers, like too many reports to fill out, that kind of thing, right? Not enough prioritizing correctly."

"No, not exactly," I said. "Prioritizing and lessening systemic time bandits is important, but that is not what I mean. What I mean has more to do with things like these:

- What happens when that talkative person, the one who never draws a breath, walks over and starts the engines? The talker goes on and on, and yet the captive listener cannot find the courage in herself to escape gracefully? Or doesn't know how? The interruption becomes twenty minutes that has blown a segment of time she thought she was going to use to get that report done—all because of a conversation she could not get out of.

- What if when someone sits at his desk for a while, he begins to feel a little lonely and wanders down to another office to have some contact with someone, maybe in the guise of asking an "important question" that really could have waited? And what if he finds it difficult to unplug and go back to work? Is he really just looking for contact?

- What happens if his own perfectionism makes him reread an e-mail or a report or a letter several times, and he is too anxious to just send it out and not worry about its being perfect?

- What about her own tendency to talk too much? What if when someone asks for the time, she tells him how to build a watch?

- What about his tendency to get distracted when working on something and as soon as he has another thought or an e-mail arrives, he leaves the task he was doing and is now off track?

- What about her inability to turn the ringer or her cell phone off and let it all go to voice mail for a couple of hours while she stays on task and finishes what she has to finish because she is afraid someone will be upset if she does not get right back to him, or that person is already bugged with her and she cannot stand to let it be for a while?

The manager paused for a moment and then said, "You know, I don't think we have ever talked about things like that. That would be really good." She didn't ask for the notebook. I think she was thinking about that talker who always wanders in to her office. We can all relate to that one.

The reality is that while time-management tools are helpful (we all need to write stuff down somewhere), there is still a person who has to use them. And in my experience, people do not take enough time to look at themselves and their use of time to find out what their patterns and issues are that are causing them to not use their time wisely. And that is the purpose of what I call the "audit."

It is designed to do for your time, and therefore your life, what a financial audit does for your financial performance. It tells you where it is all going, and thus explains the results that you are getting. Your time and your energy are the two biggest resources you have. With those working well, you can find any other resource you need. You can find more people, money, talent, and brains. But if you do not have time or energy to hunt, you can't. Or if your time and energy are being spent in ways that do not have anything to do with getting the results you need and desire, then you won't see the results happen.

Results are always dependent on how time and energy are spent.

But what I find is that often people do not know what they are actually spending their time on, nor why they are spending it in the ways that they are. They feel overworked, stressed out, spread too thin, and also dissatisfied with the results of all of that effort. Yet, they have never connected the dots to see that their results are a function of how they spend their time. They wrongly think that there is just too much to do. They miss the great truth that governs time. The truth is that there is zero to do. You are the one, unless you are in prison or elementary school or are dealing with an illness or other tragedy, who has chosen to go from zero to whatever you are choosing to do. How you are spending your time is exactly that—you spending your time. You are choosing to do with it whatever you are doing with it. What has to happen is that you have to take a look at what you are getting for your effort, and if you do not like it, then spend it differently. But you can't do that until you know exactly what is happening. The time and purpose audit will do that for you.

THREE AREAS OF AWARENESS

Conducting an audit will make you aware of three very important things: where you are spending your time, the (dis)connections between your values and how you spend your time, and the personal issues that contribute to the problem.

Awareness 1: You Know Where You Spend Your Time

The audit makes you aware of where your time is going, exactly where you are spending it. We are all subject to over- and underestimating the reality of how much time we are spending on various activities. So the first benefit of the audit is that the numbers don't lie. You may think that you spend only an hour or so answering nonimportant e-mail, getting sidetracked with meaningless Google searches or Web surfing, or getting drawn into solving an employee's problems that he should be solving for himself. But when you log it you find the same thing that people in Weight Watchers find. "There is no way I could be eating that many cookies!" But the numbers don't lie. Joe down the hall really is taking that much of your time. And you are not getting much fruit from your labor.

The truth is that we are very subjective about how we spend our time. I was in a meeting with a management team and the CEO and the VPs were in a little spat about who was pulling their weight and who was not. All the attention turned to one of the VPs, and the rest of them quizzed him on what he was contributing to the things that were their main objectives at the time, which required being physically present at the headquarters. He said, "What are you guys talking about? I have been here all of the last two weeks."

When he said that, they all went ballistic. "What are you talking about? You were here about a third of the time that we were!"

He resisted, and then they went to the audit. "OK, Monday. We were in a meeting all morning and you came in around lunch. Then, you left about three o'clock to go into the field. Tuesday, we were . . ." They chronicled the whole time, and the reality was that they were right. He had been there only a fraction of the time they had. But here is the point. He was not lying. He was just not used to being in the main office and to be there at all felt to him as if he were there *all* the time. It was very subjective. The audit helps us with our subjectivity about how much time we are spending doing what. Remember, your experience of time, which by nature is very subjective, and the reality of it are very different. Most Americans would not say that they actually watch between four and five hours of television a day, but that is what the research reveals. Think what would happen to health, obesity, and emotional well-being if they would capture just two of those hours per week in a brisk walk. The same thing will be true of your work when you really find where your time is going.

Awareness 2: You Discover the (Dis)connections Between Your Values and How You Spend Your Time

The audit makes you aware of the connections and disconnections between how you spend your time and your stated values, purpose, mission, gifts, and objectives. If you say that you have a high value for developing your leaders, and your audit reveals that you spent hardly any time focusing on making that happen, you have a disconnect between what matters to you and what you are doing. If you say that your main objective this year is to develop your strategic alliances, and yet your audit reveals that most of your time was spent getting drawn into managing details of projects, you have a disconnect. If your greatest gift is creating new opportunities and developing new arenas of business, and yet your audit reveals that existing, ongoing operations was where all of your time was spent, you suddenly realize why you are so de-energized as well as why your organization's growth is stagnant. There is usually going to be a direct relationship between how well something is going and the amount of focused time and energy it is getting. Since that focus is you, we are talking about your time. But without the audit, you will not really know what is happening. It will bring the necessary awareness.

Awareness 3: You Identify Personal Issues That Contribute to the Problem

This is one of the main ideas here. The audit will make you aware of your personal issues that are feeding the problem. Remember, it is rarely the tool. It is the person. You are not a victim. There are reasons you are making the choices that you are. There are power leaks, as we discussed in the last chapter. If you care about a certain area of your business or mission, and yet other things are eating all of your time, why is that?

You must get to the whys, the motivators of this misuse of time. Let's say you do your audit, and you find that you spent three hours last week talking to Joe about his problems in his department. Yet, Joe's problems are really Joe's problems, and he should be solving them. That is why you hired him. So, you have to ask yourself, "Why am I getting pulled into all of Joe's work or issues?" Look at the last chapter and reread the list of power drains and you will see how this works. Are you rescuing him? Are you afraid to say no to him? Do you feel guilty if you do not help him? Does your own work make you anxious, so you retreat into solving his problems to avoid the stress of what you have to do?

If we looked at Deb from the previous chapter, whose father had a tendency to dominate her time, we would find that there were several "missing weekends" from her main objectives and the things that she cares about. She was off track for herself and her family for a substantial amount of time, because she did the events for her father. But the audit shows that not only is she away a lot (the quantitative aspect of the equation), but it also shows that she is away with her father because she can't say no to him (the qualitative aspect). That diagnosis essentially gives her the key to her life. When she sees that the real issue with her time and being overstretched will not be solved by a notebook, but only by dealing with her personal issue that is feeding the problem, she is more than halfway there.

When you see the personal issue, you will ask yourself the key question, "Why am I spending time on that or on him or her or them? What about me makes me do that?"

We will talk about tools to keep these boundaries intact throughout the book, but first, let's talk about the essential measuring sticks for your time and energy.

AUDIT PART ONE: IDENTIFY WHAT YOU CARE ABOUT (YOUR VALUES, VISION, MISSION, AND GOALS)

Earlier we talked about what you value, what matters to you the most. Your values shape who you are and who you will become. In a sense, they are the DNA of the emerging you, your organization, your family, or whatever else you are involved in and influence. A company that values customer service, for example, spends time and energy finding out what contributes to that experience and focuses implementation toward making the customer's experience the best possible. Another company, whose greatest value is the short-term stock price, may make other decisions. You can look at a person's or an organization's behavior over time and see what they value as it comes to fruition. What you end up seeing in people's lives and organizations are ultimately what their values are. From there, a specific vision, mission, and goals all help provide the building blocks to seeing those values implemented into a focused expenditure of time and resources that accomplishes that vision.

In our discussion about structure and how our values are one of the most defining structures we have, we said that no matter what we might say our values are, our behavior sometimes reveals to us that there are other things we also value that are getting in the way of more important ones. We are in conflict. For example, you may value achievement and success. But you may value not making mistakes even more, so you avoid trying the things that you would have to do to be successful because you might also fail. As a result, your value of having no failure—your value of safety, of avoiding criticism—keeps you from getting the success that you also want. Your fears—your power drains—cause you to lose control of being able to move toward whatever will make you successful, losing what you value and not focusing on your goals.

I worked with a leader one time and we audited his time and matched the way he spent it with his priorities, beginning with his phone calls. I told him I wanted to look at all of his calls, who he made them to, when, and why. What he found was shocking to him, and changed the course of his work. He found that no matter what his stated agenda was for a day or for a week—the things he valued—when we looked at his calls, they often did not reflect those purposes. We found that he made numerous (often lengthy) calls to people who were not on his high-priority list. So obviously while he was spending time on them, he was not calling the ones he needed to call to reach his goals. Having seen that disconnect, we began to look at the reasons why.

"Why did you call this guy right then?" I would ask him. "Why did you meet with her at that time?" Over and over, I heard the same answer in different language. "There was an issue with . . ." or "I had gotten a call from so-and-so and he told me that she was . . ." Deciphered, all of these situations had one thing in common. On the other end of those calls and meetings was a particular kind of person, the kind who would get upset easily, get angry, be mad at him, and basically become a problem because they did not like something that he had done or a decision he had made. They were the kinds of people that we sometimes refer to as "entitled." They felt entitled to have things go their way, to not accept "no" like other people have to, and they felt like everyone else should make adjustments for them when they needed it. If the others did not comply, they would become "bad" in their eyes, including him. And he felt like he had to quickly call them and make it OK—to smooth it out and calm them down.

When we saw the pattern, he realized the key to his succeeding was twofold. Of course he would have to spend his time on the things that mattered. But, second, he was going to have to learn to recognize overly entitled people for who they are and become comfortable with letting them be upset and stew in their own juices without a call from him to make it all better. The audit revealed to him that there was one issue in his boundaries that was basically keeping him from having the accomplishments he desired to have: his inability to just let entitled people be upset. He did not know the truth of the Jewish proverb, which says, "A hot-tempered man must pay the penalty; if you rescue him, you will have to do it again" (n. Prov. 19:19 NIV). So, he just continued to rescue these people from their feelings when they would get angry, and not allow them to grow up. That was, in reality, where his time was going, and no new time-management notebook would have solved that problem.

When he saw that, it revealed a lot in terms of his whole motivational set. He could see that he was motivated to act much more by someone being upset with him than he was by the possibility of attaining a goal that would feel good to him. His entire motivation was negatively driven, out of fear. The fear of negative realities moved him into action much more than the possibility of positive possibilities. No wonder he was more of a problem solver than a leader who grew things. That is where all of his best energy was going, to solving other people's problems instead of gaining ground in the right direction.

He would say, rightly so, that what mattered most to him was reaching his goals and mission. But that is not what would get his attention first or consume the lion's share of his time. What mattered more seemed to be making sure that no one was upset with him. He could not let them sit with it while he dealt with the issues that were his priorities. So looking at how you actually spend your time will show you the things that, in reality, move you to action. Then you can see how in control you are, or out of control because of your power drains and the external forces that have gotten in charge of you.

The audit will show you how far off you are from investing time in what matters most to you, and why. But before we get to the mechanics of doing your own audit, look at your values, your vision, your mission, and your goals. When you know what those are, and you have them well-defined, then you can look at your time with them as a backdrop and see how you are doing.

Values

Listed below are a few examples of general values and character values to show you the kinds of things we are talking about:

General Values

Family
Close friends
Health
Recreation
Relaxation
Emotional growth and intelligence
Intellectual growth
Education
Career growth
Financial health
Spirituality
Giving
Service
Faith

Character Values

Honesty
Integrity
Love
Hope
Courage
Faithfulness
Freedom
Loyalty
Justice
Forgiveness
Excellence
Communication
Mercy
Tolerance
Trust
Wisdom
Patience

When you evaluate how you are spending your time, does it express your values? If, for example, health is important to you, where is it in your time allotment for maintaining your health? Is it on the schedule? How much time was actually spent on it?

Do you spend time on things that do not support your values? For example, let's say that patience is a character value of yours. But, if you looked at your time, you might see that you called a certain person multiple times in a day to find out if some outcome had occurred, just because you could not wait. And you lost all of that time. Or you could not wait until next week to meet with someone or to go look at a deal, even if there was no urgency. But your impulsivity made you want to go see it right now, as opposed to being patient. You just had to do it. As a result, other things that are important to you suffered. Or worse, you pursued something before it was time and lost money or blew the opportunity by trying to push it too early.

So take a look at your values first, to see if your time is spent in service of them.

Vision, Mission, and Goals

Next, look at your specific vision, mission, and goals. For some people, these terms are interchangeable, and for others they mean different things. This is not a book on strategic planning, so I will not debate the nuances of vision and mission, but what is important is that you are thinking in the general direction of defining what you are about, where you want to go, and how you are going to get there. These ingredients are always present in successful people's lives. There are few accidental successes, long-term. And they all must ultimately be connected to time. Let's take a moment to look at each one specifically.

Vision. Your vision is the picture of what you want something to look like in the future. Whether it is your company or your personal life, a vision is key to getting where you want to go. Without one, we flounder and become the result of whatever forces prevail upon us, or in other words, we become victims of circumstance. A vision captures your dreams and lifts your heart and passion to build something of great value. You would do well to have a vision for your career and areas of your personal life. Once you do, then how you spend your time should reflect investment in that vision, spending the resources of time and energy to make it come true. Take some specific time to write down your visions for what you want your personal and professional life to look like.

Mission. Your mission gets a little more specific as to why you exist and what you will do to bring your vision to reality. It is action oriented—what you are trying to accomplish. If you read Google's mission statement, you can see the match between it and how a lot of people have spent their time to make it a reality. "Organize the world's information and make it universally accessible and useful." They are certainly on track with that. And you can see how it provides a boundary to limit how resources are spent. If someone comes along and says, "Hey, let's take our big servers and use them to find the cure to cancer," while that might be a great plan for a bio-med company, it is outside of the boundaries of Google's mission. So, they say no and stay on course. As a result, you are now able to do a search and find the bio-med company who is closest to the cure.

So many times we see great leaders move into an organization for a turnaround or a new plan to make it grow, and the first thing they do is get rid of businesses and business units that are "off mission" for the organization. (More about "pruning" later in our chapter on ending some things.) The quotes always say something like, "We need to focus on our core business," i.e., "We need to stay on mission." When they do, the magic happens. So the more you know what you are about and what you are trying to do, the more you can focus your time and energy to that end.

Goals. The next things to consider are your specific goals to get you there. These tend to be measurable and have a time line attached to them. Goals give direction, deadlines, and organize effort in a focused direction. They force you to drill down and get it done. They provide more clear boundaries and structure for how time and energy are spent.

If my mission is to develop and communicate content that enhances people's lives, that only comes to life when I have a specific goal to write a book on the one-life solution by December 31. That goal is measurable, tangible, and brings the reality of time into the picture that forces specific action. Smaller goals are also necessary to know, for example, that I have to have X chapters written by the end of June in order to be on track for a December delivery date. So if I were to audit my time in any given week in May, and real writing time did not occur, there would be a disconnect and I would see that I have a problem.

In order to define yourself, choose your values, vision, mission, and goals carefully. They provide the anatomy for what your life becomes.

If you don't, other people, outside forces, chance, pressure, and happenstance will choose them for you. They provide the boundaries for you to measure decisions, activities, how you spend your energy, who you choose to be around, and a lot of other aspects of life. These boundaries judge your behavior, and say, "That does not fit here. Get that out of the yard, off the property of your life. It doesn't fit who you have decided you are going to be and what you have decided that you are going to build." You probably have heard someone say, "That [behavior, activity, relationship] is just not what I am about." That is what we are talking about.

AUDIT PART TWO: THE MECHANICS

I remember the first time I did this audit thing. I was working with one of my advisors talking about some long-term and medium-range objectives for my work. There were a few big initiatives that I knew had to be accomplished in the next six months at that time for some bigger things to happen. We were talking through it all and I was struggling with where I was going to find the time to get some of it moving forward. It seemed that there were a lot of projects I had going on that were keeping me from where I needed to go. So he suggested an audit. He told me to keep track of my time for a couple of months and then we would sit down, see what I was spending it on, and go from there.

So, being the good student, I did that. I kept a log of all of my activities, daily, for two months. I felt so good about it, and learned a lot from looking at it. It would say things like, "Friday morning, spent in the office catching up on administrative details after travel" or "Tuesday afternoon, conference calls and research." For a nondetailed person, I thought this was particularly anal. And I sent it to him.

When we got together, I was so proud of my accounting. But he wasn't. He showed up literally with a hour-by-hour journal, gave it to me, and told me to go do it again. He said that knowing that I was in the office making phone calls or doing admin told him very little that was useful. He wanted a log of every phone call and every kind of admin that I was doing. Only then would he get a clear picture of where my time was going. So, I went back to the drawing board.

What I learned from this was very valuable. I found out that I was spending a lot of time off objectives. But I did not know it until I really did the moment-by-moment analysis. If I saw, for instance, that I spent time in the office doing admin work or having conference calls, those could certainly be "on mission." My work requires that kind of activity. But, when I looked at each call, and that got me to look at each project or each relationship, the reality was that there was a lot of time that did not match my core objectives.

Then I got to the real issue. There were a lot of activities that had to go, but that I had significant resistance to letting go of. One was a graduate course that I taught. I loved it, loved the students, and it was very much in line with my general mission. But, for the time invested, there were some other activities that really contributed to advancing the ball down the field in a greater way than teaching was doing. It was clear, but not easy.

I resisted. I waited. I bargained, trying to figure out a way to make it all work. I even agreed to do another semester with a different structure to keep it going. When I did, though, I could feel the pressure that each class put on the time boundaries, and now that I was conscious of it, I had no excuse. The audit showed me the actual expenditure. The things that were suffering were a direct result of this choice and I knew it. I was responsible, and it had to go. I was sad, but I did it.

But without observing myself, I would not have known actually how much time the class was taking. I always saw it as the actual class time, but the closer look revealed to me how much drive time, prep time, etc. it was truly costing. And then more to the point, it forced me to look at the real reason I was resisting. It was my attachment to the program, the students, and the experience itself. There was also the feeling of not wanting to let the people down who wanted me to help build in to the department. They were good long-term friends and saying no was not something I wanted to do either. But looking at it all made me responsible for how I was not spending that time, what was not getting attention, and what was being lost as a result. And as I sat with that, I knew what I had to do.

So, the general mechanics look like this:

- **Identify your values, vision, mission, and goals.** Before you do anything, decide what it is you want to be, want to do, and want to realize. Decide what is important to you if you never have done that. Write them down in brief, memorable sentences. Your values, vision, mission, and goals provide the big boundaries for your life, which is your time and energy.

- **Find an accountability partner.** Covenant with someone to whom you are accountable, and ask him or her to join you in auditing your time with the purpose of finding out how directly your time connects with the things you have deemed important. Set up regular review times at intervals that you both will follow. Before beginning the audit, share your desired values, mission, focus, goals, purposes, objectives, and so on with your partner. This will set the target of where your time ought to be going. This is not a test that you are going to fail. Instead, it is your vision of where you want to get to as you go forward.

- **Do the audit.** Log your time in thirty-minute increments. This may sound tedious, but it is very important. It won't take you long, just keep a tally on your desk, or handy, and jot down your activities. Keep the log for a long enough period to capture the whole picture of your schedule. For those with fairly routine schedules, a few weeks may be enough. For those whose range of activities varies considerably from week to week, it may take a few months to get a complete picture. I had to do that because my work requires some travel, some studio time, some office time, and it takes more than a few weeks to get a full picture. This requires no thought, analysis, or tweaking. It is simple accounting and the smaller the increments the better.

- **Tally your time.** After auditing your time in thirty-minute segments—for weeks or months—look for the themes and categories of where your time is going.

    Write down what you discover using percentages. For example:

    - I spend 30 percent taking calls that do not relate to my stated objectives.

    - I spend 25 percent in meetings that do not further my real agenda.

    - I spend 40 percent on operations, and I need to be spending my time on vision and relationships.

- **Identify the disconnects and seek to understand them.** Compare your time percentages with your stated values, vision, mission, and goals, noting the discrepancies. Identify the disconnects. For example, if developing new business is your highest objective this year and you are spending all of your time on old business, that is a disconnect.

  Analyze the why and the how of time that is off target. Why are you taking those calls? Why are you going to those meetings? Why are you spending so much time talking to a colleague down the hall? How do all those meetings get on your calendar? How does that disruptive colleague gain access to you?

  Discuss the whys and hows of these behaviors with your accountability partner. What are the issues that you need to face that are in the way? What are the fears that are driving you to say yes, when you should say no? Who do you need to disappoint, confront, or delegate to? Where do you need to grow or add structure? What kind of help do you need to do that? (We will discuss more about that later.)

- **Develop some rules.** Come up with rules and steps and plans to deal with the discrepancies between your goals and the current activities that are consuming your time (more about rules in chapter 9). Do you need a rule of "no operational meetings on Tuesdays? Only new business that day." Perhaps a "no answering e-mail except for these two time slots each day" will help you manage your time. Maybe you need to make a new hire to take care of the things that are getting you off focus. Remember, you should be doing what only you can do as much as possible.

Keep this practice going until, like any other discipline, you do not need it anymore. When you are balancing the bike without training wheels, you don't need them. But reality is that this kind of thing, even though not needed daily at some point, is a good thing to do periodically. What we observe tends to improve.

ONE LIFE

To have a true one-life solution, this cannot be just a "work audit." While this is important in work, we are talking about your whole life. Do the same thing in your personal life as well. Take a real inventory of your time and energy.

If you have decided, for example, that your family or your close relationships are your number one priority, does your time investment reflect that? I was talking to someone the other day about raising kids and I told them what I think is an amazing story about time investment by a parent. Starting when I was about two-and-a-half years old, and continuing until I left home and went to college, my father would get me up at six o'clock on Sunday morning and take me to breakfast and out for the morning.

We would go pick up his best friend, and the three of us would go to a restaurant to eat. Then we would drop his friend off and he and I would drive around for another couple of hours doing various activities. Sometimes we would go look at building projects he had going. Sometimes we would go feed our horses or drive to look at a fishing hole. Other times we would go target shooting. On some days, we just drove around and talked, looking at sites. The activities varied, but the consistent investment of time did not. It was in those weekly uninterrupted hours of conversation that he instilled some of the most important values and lessons, especially on business. If someone were to ask him if building in to his son's life was a high value, and he said yes, and they asked him to prove it, he would have been able to do a log that proved it.

We all would do well to look at our personal lives and see if the time spent reflects the things that we value. If you are married, for example, is time invested in doing things together that build your relationship? Or, does your marriage just happen? Do you have a date night? What about set aside time for the kids? Regular structured time?

If you have a high value for a deep sense of community with a small circle of people, are you proactive to protect time with them? One of the most valuable practices I have ever had was a weekly dinner with a few close friends for years. Each week we got together and shared what was going on in life. It was a staple, something about which we did not have to call each week and see if we were on. It was in the schedule. That support structure was very important to me for many years.

A support group, a therapy group, or a prayer group are other ways that people do this same kind of structured investment that reflects their values. You can tell that it is important to them as a log of time would prove it. Health practices are similar. A regular workout is an investment in a value, vision, mission, and goal, and a log would show you how important being healthy is to you. Let your audit talk to you about who is really in charge of your life.

six

The Laws of Boundaries

OK, let's take a moment and review. So far, we have seen that what you find above the surface, the reality picture, always indicates that there is more of the iceberg below the water line than is visible. Whatever results you are getting in the emotional arena, the relational arena, and reaching your performance goals has a lot to do with what is going on inside your boundaries.

We have also seen that those boundaries are defined by structures that are built up in specific experiences in life, expressed in specific choices, and maintained by certain practices. Alas, the structures themselves are subject to having cracks in them, and can be shaky through what we called the power drains. Then, we saw that you could find how all of this is working through doing an audit of where your time and energy is going.

Now, it is time to make all of that even more practical. We are going to look at new experiences, choices, and practices that will help you develop the ability to do the following:

- Experience yourself as separate and differentiated from others.

- Contain destruction and keep it from spreading.

- Define yourself and know who you are.

- Set limits when needed.

- Possess and live out values.

- Have self-control and thereby be free and autonomous.

The next step is to understand the ten key laws that govern boundaries themselves. These laws constitute a set of principles that you can use to make decisions with people and situations, and also use to figure out why some situations are askew.

LAW 1: THE LAW OF SOWING AND REAPING

This is the principle that says the one who is doing a given behavior is the one who should be reaping the consequences of it, good or bad. It makes logical, common sense, but it is often violated everywhere from families to friendships to teams in major corporations. The result is dysfunction, demotivation, and poor results. One of the guiding thoughts to help you understand how it works is, who did this and who should pay or who did this and who should get paid? It is the law of natural consequences.

This is one of the laws that was being violated in Maria's situation in chapter 1. Stan was the nonperformer, but everyone else was paying for it. The consequences were not falling in his yard, if you will. They were draining over to everyone else's, in terms of the emotional fallout and the economic ones as well. If she would do the right thing, then the consequences would be falling where they should, and everyone would be better. Ultimately, that would include Stan, as the consequences finally touching him would get him to look at the patterns that were keeping him from performing at the level at which he should.

In many business situations where there is discord, this law is being violated. There is a person who is either not pulling his or her weight or is causing a lot of trouble, yet is not feeling any of the consequences for their behavior. And the sad thing is that others are, and that gets to the root of the problem.

In a cause-and-effect universe, there is no such thing as a choice, non-choice, expression of energy, mistake, etc. that is without a result. We know from quantum physics that even a butterfly flapping its wings on one side of the planet can eventually affect the weather on the other. So, the problem is that there is no such thing as a person being allowed to be dysfunctional or nonfunctional without someone paying for it. Someone is going to pay, either by having to work harder or in not getting the results that they should be sharing if the other person were doing what they should be doing, or in experiencing real pain. But, there is always a consequence to our behaviors. What this principle is about is making sure that the right person is getting the right consequence.

When that happens, there are at least four benefits. First, the problem gets solved—the primary hoped-for result—by being dumped into the lap of the only person who can do anything about it, the one with the problem. That is usually when change begins, as the consequences of the person's performance begin to affect them instead of others.

Second, faith is restored in the person who enforces the principle. The person who enforces the principle earns the trust and respect of others. An entire workplace's culture changes, and the boss becomes a leader again for getting this principle right side up.

Third, self-respect is restored. Abiding by the law of sowing and reaping sends a message to others that "I will not allow myself to be hurt by your behavior. Your behavior is your responsibility and you are the one who will suffer for it, not me."

Finally, the message goes out that standards are real, and they will be enforced. It improves performance and behavior when people know that there are real consequences to their actions. They begin to live up to the standard, because the standard is real. It has teeth.

LAW 2: THE LAW OF RESPONSIBILITY *FOR* AND *TO*

This principle says that you are responsible *for* yourself, and *to* others. It is realizing the boundaries of what you are to worry about and how. There is nothing wrong with helping another person. It is one of the foundations of relationship. But the lines must always be clear as to whether you are helping them to do what they should be doing, and thus empowering them, or if you are doing for them what they should be doing for themselves.

Stephanie is losing a lot of work time helping Diane. She was always covering for her, it seemed, when Diane was overstressed and overloaded. Diane had a lot of personal issues that were taking more and more of her work time, and as that was happening, she was coming in later, not getting pieces of projects done on time, etc. Stephanie was a big-hearted person and was glad to help her out, at least in the beginning.

Soon, however, it became clear that the reason Diane was overstressed and overloaded was not because a typhoon had hit her life, but because she was not managing her life well. She was not dealing with her problems and not managing her overload. As a result, Diane's problems were becoming Stephanie's problems. She was slowly taking responsibility for Diane. She had crossed a line. Her helping was not helping. She was dealing with things that Diane should have been dealing with, and in the process was doing her life for her.

A good friend would not do Diane's life for her, but be responsible to her and tell her that she was out of control and needed to do something about her personal life to get things back in order. Stephanie would be a better friend by telling Diane the truth, that she was worried about how she was doing and to get some help for whatever was at the root of all these issues, but to continue to cover for her was not going to help.

That is the essence of being responsible to someone, to not do for them what only they can do, and to love them by providing the help that would help them do it for themselves. Your job is to encourage, confront, empower, sometimes give resources, coach, cajole, support, or other things that help them fulfill their responsibility without doing it for them. That is the line.

Good bosses know this fine line. It is the essence of a job description. They do everything to be responsible to the employee to equip them with what they cannot do for themselves, require them to do what is theirs to do, and hold them accountable for doing it. That is being responsible to them and not for them. It is the axiom of giving a person the freedom and authority to do what you are going to hold them accountable to do.

Good co-workers know this, too. There is a line where your co-worker may be asking you to do things that are really his or hers to do. Figure out where that is, and begin to be responsible to that person like Stephanie had to do with Diane. Remember that saying, "That's not my department" or "That's not my job," may be a lame excuse in some situations, but it is a very good and appropriate answer in others. In a later chapter on communicating your boundaries, we will look at exactly how to say it. But you will ultimately learn to define and express the difference between what is your responsibility and something another will have to do for himself.

This is a huge issue also for managing up. I hired my first assistant when I began my consulting practice right out of grad school. She was a seasoned, retired executive assistant from a big corporate job, and was just looking for something interesting to do for twenty hours a week to get her out of the house and have fun. We really hit it off, and I was so glad to have her as part of my team.

Shortly after we began together, we met and I gave her a bunch of projects and work to do. She took it all and went back to her office. About an hour later she came in and said something I will always remember. It went something like this. "You have hired someone for twenty hours a week and given me forty hours' worth of work. Which twenty would you like for me to do?"

I did not know what to say. The reason was twofold. First, she was putting the problem right where it belonged: in my lap. She was not taking responsibility for my bad planning and saying yes to too many things, or being unwilling to hire someone full time. That was my problem, not hers, and she was giving it to me. She was being responsible to me and not for me. Second, she was not moving. She was steadfast. I could see it in her mature, deep blue eyes and "Now what are you doing to do?" smile. She was not distressed, stressed, or out of sorts. She was calm and clear. So, there was no drama to deal with like many less mature people would have created. The absence of drama made things very clear, which it always does, and it is one of the best by-products of a person being in control of themselves. It makes the problem the problem and they do not become the problem.

So, I had to take responsibility for myself and my planning—and prioritize. I had to make some hard decisions and get focused on what I needed to focus on. It truly was my problem, and she had helped me.

Perhaps you are thinking, "But you don't know my boss. She would say, 'Then you better find a way to do all of that in twenty hours or I will find someone who will.'" We will get to that threat in the chapter on getting your balance sheet together and on communicating your boundaries. But at the end of the day, you will have to figure out that if you are working for someone who is asking you to do the impossible, or do the job of three people, or work more than you have purposed to work, you have a problem. And you are going to have to solve that problem or go crazy. You do a good boss a good service when you make him or her aware of the problems that their overcommitment is bringing on the system. Remember the warnings to the captain of the *Titanic*? Those were a favor. If you are on a ship where dangers lie ahead, and the ones in charge do not heed them, then you may be on a sinking ship. That is no reason not to give the warnings, and if you find out you are on the kind of ship where leadership does not heed clear warnings, that is a clear sign to get your own lifeboat in order. I am sure that some people at Enron or other corporations that melted down in scandals could look back and see that the ones in charge were out of control, and they would have done themselves a service to have gotten out when the getting was good. Either way, be responsible for yourself and to others. In those situations, rejecting ineffective thinking like, "But you don't know my boss" or "What if they won't listen?" might have led to taking responsibility for their own lives—and maybe selling that stock while it still existed.

LAW 3: THE LAW OF POWER

We talked in chapter 4 about power drains and where they come from. If you look carefully, there is a common unifying principle in all of them. The principle is that all of the loss of power comes from you, not from other people. The reason for that is that power over yourself is all you ever had anyhow, so it is the only kind of power that you can ever gain or lose.

The law of power says exactly that. You have the power to control yourself and nothing else, including other people. When you understand that, you begin to truly get in control of yourself and your life while letting others be who they are. Then you're able to do the most powerful thing that you can do with them, which is to be a strong, positive force that influences them to be better.

In managing people, empowerment is a term we hear a lot about. But in so many interactions, the boundaries of empowerment are overstepped and people are actually disempowered. To empower people means exactly that, to not try to have power over them by nagging or controlling, but by giving them clear expectations, input, direction, resources, and finally the freedom to sink or swim depending on how they use their own power. Set the objectives, for example, the target numbers or goals. Resource them adequately, give proper oversight, and see if they can hit the number. If they miss it by too far or too consistently, they have shown that the job is not for them. Granting freedom, giving clear expectations, and providing accountability through clear consequences are principles that govern human performance from early childhood to the corner office. Set them free, and then act accordingly.

People also lose power over themselves when they give power to others to determine who they are, what they think, what they want, and especially how they feel. You have seen a situation where a team has a meeting and the boss basically spanks everyone there. Then, out in the hallway later, there are very different reactions. Some people are laughing at what an idiot the boss is, asking, "Have you ever seen anyone who is that big of a moron? How did he ever get his far? What a buffoon." A few more shrug and roll their eyes, go back to their offices, and get to work. They think, "What a jerk," and then are off to the important things they have to do. But there is another person who is now debilitated. She is now back at her own office, feeling like a loser, inadequate, that she will never amount to anything. Depression sets in, she loses motivation, and stares into space. Or she reaches into the drawer for a box of chocolates or suddenly feels the urge to smoke after going a year without a cigarette.

Why do people have such different reactions? The stimulus was the same, the jerky boss. But the ears that his words fell into were very different. And this particular woman, like David in chapter 1, who withered under the harsh treatment of his boss, finds herself particularly vulnerable to a certain kind of bullying jerk. That kind of person is always able to get to her. She loses her power to him, and all of a sudden someone else has the power to define her goodness, her potential, her abilities, and even her well-being. She has lost power over herself and how she feels.

We will discuss how she can deal with this in the chapter on getting your balance sheet together and communicating your boundaries, but for now, realize that many of the roots lie within the law of power. She has lost power over herself, and her boss has gotten power over how she feels. To get strong again, and to have the one life she desires, she is going to have to take the power back and realize that ultimately how she feels and what she thinks about herself are under her control and not that of the jerks of the world. You cannot have power over what another person thinks of you, over their choices, or their behaviors. But you can control your own emotional reactions, how they make you feel, your thoughts, your beliefs, and your actions. You can take that power back. In chapter 11, we will talk about how to do that.

The bottom line? Focus on what you can control—yourself. Then you will use the power that you have to behave in ways that influence others in mighty ways. And you will also gain other kinds of power that can have enormous effects for good: organizational power, relational power, financial power, political power, etc. But none of those will be granted to you if you are not taking the power to control the one person who can achieve all of those things—you.

LAW 4: THE LAW OF RESPECT

In my years working with people on boundaries, I've found that we love the message of boundaries. When we find out that it is OK to say no to abuse and control from others, and that you can still be a loving and kind person without giving in to whatever another person wants, that is a great, empowering message. It literally changes people's lives. When you tell an employee, "You don't have to put up with that" from a customer, they will love you. The power to say no is liberating. We will see how firing a customer is a needed example of the law of respect in our chapter on endings.

But what we don't like so much is the flip side. We like to say no, but we do not like to hear "no." From the time we are two years old, we will shout it out as our favorite word. There is so much power in it. But, when it is said to us, we just do not have a natural taste for it. That taste has to be acquired. This law is about developing that taste.

Think of the kinds of people that you dislike the most. Without a doubt, somewhere on the list is going to be what is referred to as a "control freak." The control freak is a person who does not respect the boundaries of others. They trespass over others' fences, not hearing the other person's "no," and then they take control of what is not theirs. In business, this can be totally demoralizing. If you have an area of responsibility that you have been given, and then your boss makes a decision that totally undermines you, you know the feeling. He has not respected the boundaries. You know also what it is like to be pushed and pushed by someone after you have said no to their request, and they just cannot let it go. That is annoying.

The law of respect says that if you are going to be in control of yourself and be an integrated person, that you not only command respect of yourself, but also that you are respectful of the boundaries of other people. This has implications.

First, organizationally, you must respect job descriptions and areas of responsibility. This does not mean that you cannot have influence in someone's yard, as that is part of what a good team player does. But influence and control are different matters. Respect the boundaries of other people's responsibility and you will get much greater cooperation and also influence. Trespass, and you will get stonewalled or retaliated against.

Second, when you get a boundary from someone, respect it. When they say no, respect that limit. That does not mean that you have to roll over and play dead, (especially if you are in sales). You must overcome objections. That is a big part of the job. But there is a huge difference between learning how to communicate with someone and overcome their objections through getting to a better answer—one they actually embrace—and getting the answer you want and that they are willing to comply with, but resenting you on the inside. That is not "buy-in." Buy-in is when someone has joined you in your position. I recently had a VP tell me that his leader wants consensus so much that he tries to control people into agreeing with him so that they all have buy-in. But they are just nodding without really being on the same page. They got bullied into buy-in.

True respect would entail really listening to their opinions (not just paying lip service and pretending to do so) and having a good dialogue whereby you get to the same place or you have buy-in without agreement. There is much more power in a leader respecting that someone has a different opinion, and at the same time saying that "I respect where you are coming from, but I have decided that we need to go this other way." Then, the buy-in comes from buying in to the fact that "you are our leader and we are on board, even when we disagree." While true consensus is best, of course, at times the essence of leadership, or even of being a person, lies in doing things and making decisions that others do not agree with, but it works best when done with respect.

Respect also means to respect people's ability to make stupid choices. Even with the addict, we have to do that. We ultimately have to say, "We want you to be sober. We will help you get there. But, if you choose to say no to our help and decide that you love your drugs more than us and being here, we will respect that and let you go." Freedom and responsibility also mean that at some point we let someone go. They make their choice and are going to have to suffer for it. We can try and try, but at some point, respect lets them go. And, paradoxically, many times that also serves to turn them around, but for the first time because they have made their own choice.

Respect has great implications for training and developing people. When you respect their boundaries, you give them an area of responsibility and set them free to screw it up. Of course, not enough to hang themselves, but enough to learn. You set them free, and oversee it so there is no disaster to the business, but so they are in over their heads just enough to have to learn. Let them learn from mistakes. That is when they will need and take your help. If you hover too much, they will spend more energy fighting for freedom than worrying about what they have to do. Need comes from freedom, not from control. You want them to need your input, not fight it.

Ultimately, respect is about being a good neighbor. Respect the boundaries of the fence, and don't jump into their yard without the right or without an invitation. And when they ask you to leave, get out.

LAW 5: THE LAW OF MOTIVATION

When was the last time you did something because you wanted to? Remember that feeling? There was energy, chemical reactions that went off in your head that you felt throughout your entire being. You did not have to make yourself do it. You just did. That is truly an awesome experience, one that people refer to in many areas of life.

When a marriage is strong, the couple says things like "I would rather be spending time with him or her than doing other things." When someone loves their work, they say things like "when you are doing what you love to do, every day at work seems like play." When someone is serving sacrificially in a task that seems so difficult, but for a cause or a reason that they love, even that is energizing.

The losses of energy come when there is the feeling of "having to do this"—not having a choice. It is coming out of a negative motivational set, and thereby is not fully engaging the person. In fact, it is worse than that. To do it means at the same time that a part of you is resisting it and working against it. That is what we see so often referred to as "sabotage," even of oneself. The real motivation won out in the end.

That is what the law of motivation is about. It is about getting to the essence of why you are doing what you are doing—and owning that essence. It is about realizing that no one is making you do whatever you are doing, but you are choosing it for some motivation of your own. Looking at that motivation is the key to figuring out if it is really worth doing, and if it is, then getting the motivation right so that you will have the energy and engagement to make it through.

There are generally two kinds of motivation: negative and positive.

Negative motivation. Negative motivation comes when we encounter pressure either from outside ourselves, or inside, that we do not want to say yes to but do not have the freedom to say no. For instance, let's say you have someone who is really pushy and does not take "no" for an answer, at least without a fight. So they push. And they push. Finally, you give in and agree to what they want. But, you are like the kid whose teacher made him sit down. Not wanting to, he says under his breath, "I am sitting down on the outside, but I'm still standing up on the inside." You have not truly given of yourself at all, you have given in. Inside you resent it, but it is because you do not want to go through the conflict that would be involved in saying no. So, you are doing it not out of any good purpose, but out of fear of some sort. You are afraid of their anger or of upsetting them or something, but the motivator is not positive. It is negative.

This kind of motivation can get compliance, but not energized, whole-hearted, sustainable effort. Leaders who motivate out of fear do not have loyal teams, and those cultures are rotten and ultimately implode. Same thing goes for parents who control kids through fear and guilt. Their kids may be "good," but ultimately they are going to either rebel or cave in on themselves in depression or worse.

The other kind of negative motivation comes not from outside pressure but internal pressure. It is life lived under the "shoulds." It is the people who have so many "ought to's" in their heads that they do a lot of things because they will feel bad or guilty if they don't do them. So, they are motivated out of internal guilt or fear. If they say no they will feel bad, so they go ahead and do it. Your co-worker wants you to go to lunch, and you really want to do something else, but you just can't say no because you will feel bad if you do. Or, worse, you will feel guilty if you don't do that extra work for them or stay late for some reason. None of that is going to bring more good into your feeling about them or the relationship, and it may ultimately drive you apart.

Positive motivation. Life, to be sustaining, must be lived on positive motivations. Now, do not go in the wrong direction here. I am not in any way saying that all of life should feel good, or suggesting that we revert to the motivations of the "me generation" when our society moved from the "if it feels good, do it!" of the sixties to the "if it doesn't feel good, I won't do it" of the seventies. That is the mentality of a loser. Anyone who ever accomplishes anything does many things that do not feel good. In fact, that is the big requirement of success of any kind, to do the things that don't feel good that others don't want to do. To win, you must do things that do not feel good, and past that, that you do not want to do. But that does not mean that the motivation for doing them is negative.

I saw an Olympic swimmer interviewed and she was asked if she liked all that practicing, swimming so many miles every day. She said, "No! It is cold at five thirty in the morning. My body aches, and I am so tired. Many times I hate it." But she was also smiling as she said it, because underneath it all there was a very positive, larger goal that she wanted: the gold medal. So, even though she did not want to get up at five thirty and freeze day after day, a negative feeling for sure, she did want what that was going to give her. That is positive motivation even when the particular task is negative. Winners do this each and every day. They delay gratification in the moment for something that will gratify them later. And that is sustainable for years and years, as any Olympian reveals.

Compare her with other athletes you might have known whose hearts were not in it, but were doing it for other reasons—negative motivations. They did it because their parents pushed them into it. Or they did it because they want to be accepted or could not say no to the pressure of peers who think it is so important. Think of people who are doing jobs for similar reasons, dancing to someone else's definition of their lives. That leads to burnout or acting out. Many midlife blow ups have come from a person's unconscious motivations finally saying that "I am not going to take this treadmill anymore. I do not remember choosing it. I hate it. And I am going to leave it." Usually the leaving of that sort is very,

very destructive for many people, including children.

What is important is that you are aware, in touch with, owning, and at one with the bigger motivations that are governing the smaller ones. For instance, you can do a job you don't really like out of positive motivation. You love your kids, for example, and want them to be able to stay in that neighborhood for another year until they get out of that grade. So, you continue to do the job that will provide for that. That is awesome and very positive.

You stay late at work to get it done, for the team, for the boss, for the company, and for yourself. It hurts, you are weary, and yet you do it for good reasons. That is positive. But to do that only because some jerk makes you feel guilty if you don't is not a good reason.

The law of motivation is one of the most powerful organizing and orienting principles in life. Its power is both for the big picture ("Why am I doing this career?") as well as the small ("Why am I going to lunch with this person?"). It will force you to get very honest with yourself and clear up a lot of your life by getting to the roots of why you are doing what you do. On the other side, you will find clarity, motivation, energy, and fulfillment when you stop doing anything out of fear or guilt and begin to do things out of higher purposes that have transcendent, lasting, and sustaining meaning—like love, your personal values, expression of talents, and the like.

It will ring true in all areas of your life. As a parent, why are you buying that new toy for your child? Because it will enhance her development or bring enjoyment or express your love? Or are you buying it because she will throw a tantrum if you don't or because you won't be keeping up with the Joneses? As a spouse, why are you doing what you are doing for your spouse? Is it truly helping him or her? In your extended family, why are you putting up with that nonsense? Because you always have and would feel guilty if you didn't? As a friend, do you really think that the friendship will suffer if you call and say that you are just too overcommitted and can't come to that party? If your friendship suffers because someone cannot respect your need to get some rest, maybe there is a bigger conversation that you need to have. Get clear and get free from negative motivations and you will resolve much that ails you.

LAW 6: THE LAW OF EVALUATION OF PAIN

I was talking to a leader who had a partner who was not performing. It was clear what needed to be done, but he was not doing it. I asked him when he was going to either take away some of the VP's responsibilities, get rid of him, or do something. It was getting past the point of obvious.

"I couldn't take away all of that from him," he said.

"Why not?" I asked.

"Because it would hurt him," he said. "He is a really good friend of mine and that would really hurt."

"Yes, I am sure it would," I said. "But what is wrong with that?"

"Are you serious?" he asked. "What is wrong with hurting someone? Isn't it obvious?"

"No, it isn't. I do not believe that hurting people is necessarily a bad thing. Life sometimes hurts. The truth sometimes hurts. But there is a difference in hurt and harm. I believe that harming people is not okay, and it should always be avoided. But hurt and harm are very different.

"If you take away some of his responsibilities, certainly it is going to hurt. But sometimes the truth of reality hurts. It just does. Do you feel great when you get painful feedback? Of course not. Sometimes it stings. But if you listen to it and use what it offers you, you are going to be better off for it. It helps you, not harms you, even if it hurts a little. Just like going to the dentist. Hurt can be helpful sometimes.

"But harm is a different story. Injuring someone is not good. That is not what we are talking about here. In this situation, you have to do what is best for the company and what is your responsibility and duty to do, and also do it in a way that may be helpful to him if he takes it to heart. How he takes it is up to him, not you. But to do it is not harmful, even if it is going to hurt a bit."

He got it, and that distinction helped him to talk to his friend and give him the bad news. He did it in a way that the friend could hear as constructive criticism and use in his life.

The law of evaluation of pain says that just because someone is screaming doesn't mean that something bad is happening. When a toddler gets put in time-out, the noise can be deafening. When you say no to a control freak, it is not pretty sometimes. When you set limits with an irresponsible person, sometimes he will protest. But just because he cries "hurt" doesn't mean that you are doing something harmful.

To evaluate the pain means that you are really looking at your actions and determining if they are harmful to someone, versus causing some discomfort that is just part of life. To abuse someone is not good, as it is harmful. Harm means that you inflict injury on to someone. You take something that is not broken and do damage to it. If I mug you, that is harmful. But, if I am a physical therapist and inflict pain on you by getting you to move a leg after surgery, that hurts, but it does not harm. It is discipline. To discipline, or to sometimes make necessary decisions that might be painful but are fair and just, is also a part of life. And for you to be effective, fair, just, respected, and fruitful, you must be able to do some things that sometimes people are not going to like. The law of evaluation will help you to put on the earplugs when some of the control freaks are screaming about your decision. They are acting like you are harming them, when in actuality you are not. They might be screaming, but the wise people will be cheering in another room, so take heart. (See the chapter on communicating your boundaries for how to deal with someone who resists correction or input.)

LAW 7: THE LAW OF PROACTIVITY

The online *Merriam-Webster's Collegiate Dictionary* defines proactive as "acting in anticipation of future problems, needs, or changes." The *New Oxford American Dictionary* puts it this way, "creating or controlling a situation by causing something to happen rather than responding to it after it has happened." The idea expressed in both is to be the cause instead of the result. I like to think about proactive as "to anticipate what is going to be needed and do it before it is needed."

Think of the functions we have said that boundaries perform, functions such as being a separate person, defining oneself, containing destruction, setting limits, living out values, and being free. When you think about it, there are two ways of doing all of those things. You can act, or react. Acting is better. One is a cause and the other is a result.

Ideally, adults are actors. Teenagers by nature are reactors; they react to the rules to define who they are. They rebel against what others try to tell them they ought to be. It is the time of life when they really need something to push against in order to find out who they are. Sometimes they do not even know what they want until someone tells them to do something and then suddenly they know. They want the opposite. They are not yet autonomous, defined, and independent. Instead they are oppositional.

The adult position is the one in which you become aware of something and act responsibly to do something about it. You are a cause, not a result. Certainly there are times in life when we do respond or react as things happen to us. But, there are many times when there is something that needs to be done, and yet there is no immediate force making us do it. In those times, mature people pick up the phone and get moving. That is ownership. It is the kind of flavor that companies try to instill in their cultures when they communicate that everyone should act like owners and not just employees.

A common example of someone behaving proactively is when there is a conflict. Sometimes people will say, "Well, if he has a problem with me, it is his responsibility to call me. He is the one who is offended, so he should make the call." A more mature response looks at the reality, sees that there is something wrong, and picks up the phone. "Do we have a problem? It seems that something is wrong." Certainly there are times when the other person is manipulative and you do not want to play into that by chasing them down all the time every time they pout. But, the point is that you move to resolve the problem. Even if someone is a pouter who is manipulating you, you could make the first call. "I notice that you are quiet and avoiding me, like yesterday in the hall. It seems that you do that when you are upset about something. I would like to get together and talk about what is wrong, certainly. But the bigger issue I would like to talk about is how we might handle conflict between us in a different way. That would be helpful to me."

To own your life means that you see what is needed and take action. That way, you are creating the life that you want. You are making your vision a reality, as opposed to taking whatever life brings you.

LAW 8: THE LAW OF ENVY

Ask any psychologist about the basest of all human motivation and emotion, and they will tell you it is envy. Envy is as bad as it gets, the motivator for untold destruction, to ourselves and to others. Narcissism is often fueled by it, as are quests for power, and the impulse to destroy the good of others.

All of us feel envy sometimes as part of the human condition, some more than others. Generally, the more we fill our lives and hearts with good things that are meaningful and are humble about how fortunate we are to have them, the more gratitude we feel and the less envy we experience. Nevertheless, all of us would do well to be aware of it when it creeps up in our hearts, minds, and souls.

Envy works this way. It defines what is good as what we do not have. In other words, if I do not possess something, it takes on a higher value than if I do. Likewise, once I attain it, it is no longer valuable to me, because I have it. It makes keeping up with the Joneses or climbing the corporate ladder or spending more and more on the next fashion fad or hot gadget a full-time job.

When envy dominates a person, he or she is looking over the fence at the yards of others. They think that another person's position or some other relationship or status or possession would make them happy. They think that the real things of value are the things that others have, not themselves. So, they never feel grateful or content. There is always a next thing that will make them happy, until they get it. But once they have the possession, the position, or the person, that used to be the object of their envy, they still aren't satisfied.

The law of envy says that instead of looking over the fence to find out what you want or what would make you happy, take ownership of your own yard and your real desires. There is nothing wrong with wanting things that you do not possess. That is desire. It is good. It drives you to achievement. You want a new house, so you figure out a way to make the money you would need to get it. It is great motivation, if the house is truly coming from your heart's desire. If it is, then when you get it you will be grateful and content. But if it comes from envy, then soon it will not be good enough.

The person who looks at his own life, takes a real assessment, and says, "I would like _____," whatever that is, and it truly fits who they are as a person and is a good thing for them is poised for the next step: to take responsibility for going and getting it. If it is the next step in your career, get the training you would need to fulfill your heart's desire and go for it. Desire means ownership and responsibility. Otherwise, it is just envy, wanting what you do not have and always not having enough. But true desire means you will do what it takes to get it—and love it once you do. It is the responsible stance in life.

So, instead of trying to find out what you desire in life by looking at what others have and thinking, "if I were only them" or "if I had what they have," look at your own heart and see what it is that you truly desire. What fits you? What will really make you happy that has nothing to do with ego or image or status? In business, we see this reality a lot when someone would truly rather be a VP or in sales or a manager, as that work fits them better. Yet, status needs drove them to seek being president or some other position. Once there, they find it does not fit.

If you are motivated by real desire instead of envy, you will have much greater self-control. The person motivated by what they do not possess is always out of control, by definition. They always need more and are crazy to get it. Do not lust after other people's position, status, possessions, talents, relationships, or whatever else. That is the road to discontent and out-of-control behavior. Instead, look at your real heart and soul, ask it what it truly desires, and take responsibility to get it. Then you will be fulfilled, and enjoy what you have.

LAW 9: THE LAW OF ACTIVITY

The law of activity is a cousin of the law of proactivity, but it is a little different. Proactivity is about addressing issues first instead of reacting to outside forces. Activity is about realizing that nothing happens if you do not do something. As Newton said in his first law, an object at rest will tend to stay at rest, unless acted upon by an external force. When we realize that we are responsible, i.e., must take ownership for our entire existence, then we also realize that the results we are getting are because of what we are doing, or not doing. And unless I do something different, nothing is going to be different. If I am experiencing some reality—and if I want to experience a different reality—I am going to have to do something to make things different. The universe is set up to reward activity.

So, if I do not like the sales numbers, what am I going to do about that? If I do not like the way my relationship with someone is going, what am I going to do about it? If it is going to be different, it is going to be because there was some activity that made it different. If there is no activity, then there will be no difference. Or maybe worse, if there is activity but it is not from me and what I desire the outcome to be, then it may be different but in a direction I do not like. So, I had better get active.

In my book *9 Things You Simply Must Do*, I talk about a concept called Do Something. The idea is that when we find something in our lives, our yard as we are referring to here, then it is our responsibility to do something about that reality. If we don't, it will not change, or it will change in a way that we do not desire. It is about getting moving.

People who possess good relationships, good careers, good financial results, and good health always do the things that result in those realities. Those things did not just drop out of the sky. Likewise, a (well-run) company that is not getting the results it desires does not wait around for the market to improve. It gets active. The bottom line is this. If there is something that lies within your boundaries—i.e., your life—and you do not like it, it is your responsibility to get active to do something about it. No one else. Yours. Get active, be a force, and remember Newton's first law translated into your life. This mess will tend to stay a mess unless I am a force that acts upon it.

LAW 10: THE LAW OF EXPOSURE

"I wish he would just come out and say what he wants us to do and then tell us to do it," said the upper-level manager about his leader. "You can tell when he doesn't like something. He stares at you with a heavy sigh, and gets this pensive look on his face. You know that he is not happy, but you really don't know why. And at other times he wants everyone to like the plan and be on board with it, even when we aren't. But if he would just tell us 'Tough. I don't care if you don't like it, I want it done,' it would be a lot better. Or, just tell me what he is mad about and what the rules are. I can't read his mind."

I think that the complained-about leader, like most indirect people, was probably trying to be nice, be the good guy. The problem was that in being nice, he was not being nice. People did not like it. They felt confused and did not know where they stood or what reality was. They did not know his expectations until they violated them, and then they had to guess when they had. In an attempt to avoid conflict he was creating a lot of conflict.

One person contrasted him to her previous boss. She said that she always knew where that boss stood. And, she said, it provided a certain sense of security and calm, even when you disagreed with him. "We did not have to wonder," she said. "We knew the parameters [what I call boundaries], so we knew where we could operate. It was clear. Here, you always have to wonder."

Group research reveals that groups that have the best outcomes are the ones in which the expectations are clearly known by the group. That is true also in individual relationships as well. When we know what is expected—and know when we violate it—we do better. We are just designed that way.

The law of exposure is about this principle. Everyone has boundaries. But not everyone's boundaries are known, or exposed where they can be seen. This law says that your fences should be visible, out in the open. They are seen in your words and in your actions. You tell others what you like, don't like, expect, desire, think, want, etc. And then, when there is a violation, you let them know, kindly and firmly. We will talk about how later, in chapter 13 on communicating your boundaries, but for now, just know that it is important to communicate them.

One of the other important benefits of the law of exposure is the absence of what is called "triangulation." Triangulation is where person A has a conflict with person B and yet talks to person C instead of B. So instead of direct conversation between the people who actually have the conflict, the conversation is happening between people who are not the real parties. So, two results occur, neither of them the desired one. First, the conflict remains. Second, there is now discord between C and B because A has turned one against the other. And in reality, they have no problem with each other.

When people expose their boundaries, they take the issue right to the person they have the conflict with. They leave others out unless they contribute something to the resolution, and they fix it with each other. That keeps the larger group immunized from conflict they do not have an interest in—and also solves the problem.

Then the big, obvious benefit is that problems are resolved instead of lingering. Avoidance fixes nothing, and it also changes the dynamic of a culture. The atmosphere created by having an elephant in the room is something known to everyone but loved by none. We do not like it when things are not well, but we like it less when they are not well and no one is talking about it.

Conflict is good. Good, strong organizations and good relationships are built on open dialogue and discussion, confrontation of ideas, and feisty debate. I do not mean debate that is demeaning or that tears people down, but disagreement that sharpens each side's thinking and from which the best ideas emerge. As we bump up against each other's thoughts, feelings, ideas, and experience, we all get better in the process. We influence each other, and our fuzzy thinking gets cleared up in the light where it is all exposed.

Direct, open, honest, firm, and kind boundaries that are communicated directly make every kind of relationship better. Unless you are a spy or a terrorist trying to sneak in under the radar, get it out in the open.

THE RESULTS OF LIVING BY THE LAWS

Think of the laws of physics. They order the way the physical universe operates. When we heed them, planes stay in the air. When we don't, we fall off of the roof. They don't play favorites, they just are. It is up to us to get on the right side of them.

The laws of boundaries are similar. They describe the ways that life is ordered. When we operate within them, we do well. When we try to break them, we suffer. The result of living these principles will be that your relationships will go better, you will feel better, and you will get better results. In addition, the big goal of having one life will be realized as you become one person, living out an integrated character in all of your life contexts: work, family, friendship, health, leisure. These laws will help pull it all together. They will accomplish the results of boundaries that we began with. They will help you to do the following:

- Experience your separateness.

- Contain destruction and keep it from spreading.

- Define yourself and know who you are and what you want.

- Set limits when needed.

- Possess and live out your values.

- Have self-control and be autonomous.

As you begin to live within healthy boundaries, you will experience more freedom and more effectiveness. Also, when you find yourself feeling fragmented or in the midst of a situation that is lacking clarity, refer to the laws to see which ones are getting violated. Then your path will become very clear and you will know what to do.

seven

You and Your Words

Have you ever heard yourself say, "Whatever possessed me to say yes to this in the first place? Why didn't I just say no?" Or, after negotiating a deal, have you ever thought, "Why didn't I ask for _____ ? I could kick myself!" If you have, that is pretty normal or at least common. However, if it happens often, it is also a problem. It reveals that sometimes you and your words are not on the same page.

> You desire one outcome, but your words
> take you to a different one.

As I said to a CEO recently who met with a key executive to terminate the relationship and then ended up extending the contract, "What happened? You went to break up and came back engaged!" In this chapter, we are going to take a look at some of the most important words in your vocabulary—and your relationship to them.

When I say you have a relationship to words, that may be an idea you have never thought about. But what we find is that in the depths of people's souls—where true behavior and its resulting success or chaos originates—there is a real relationship with certain words. The nature of that relationship dictates a lot of what happens in people's lives. If the relationship is good and they get along well with words, they use them to create and maintain a healthy structure and boundaries. But if they do not get along well with words, then structure and boundaries are compromised and their lives become fragmented as a result.

So, we are going to look at the words that have to do with why you find yourself in certain situations more than you might think. We are going to examine your relationship to some key words, including how you feel about them and how free you are to use them, or not. Before we dive into looking at specific words and phrases, it's important to understand how certain words become embedded, or internalized, in our lives.

INTERNALIZATIONS AND PATTERNS

One would think that when you say yes or no to something, your answer is based on the merits of what you want to choose. When you want to grant a request, buy a product, agree to a price, take an assignment, or go to lunch with someone, you say yes. If not, you say no. But in reality, that is not what always happens. Sometimes you may be on autopilot and have less choice in your response than you may think.

Think about people you know or even yourself. Have you noticed that there are people who routinely find themselves in some situation they do not want to be in? Inevitably, they land in some activity, relationship, scheduling conflict, or problem they did not want. The reason is not that they failed to just say no once or twice. They basically never say no. Their choices are rarely about what they want or don't want in a particular situation, but usually about their relationship with the word "no" itself. They are conflicted about the word at a very deep level. They reach down there in hopes of finding "no," but it eludes them.

Or, think of the person on your team you know you cannot send out to do that negotiation. When you need someone who can go into a meeting, ask for the moon, and expect to get it, this is the last person you'd call on. They just are the kind of people who never ask for what they want. For some reason, they can't pull the trigger. As a result, they rarely get out of life what they desire, and oftentimes they don't even get what they need. They get only what comes their way and nothing more. Then you know other people who go into a meeting, ask for the moon, and get it. You exclaim, "How did you get them to agree to that?" And they answer, "I just asked for it, and they said fine."

The difference is not that one person wants or needs the outcome any more or less than the other. In fact, often the person who needs something the most is the one who finds it most difficult to ask. The real difference is that some people have a longstanding relationship with certain words that renders saying them virtually impossible. The result of not saying those words when we need to, or saying them when we don't, is that our lives become fragmented and scattered—a far cry from the integrated one life we all want. Then we are truly out of control.

I know one CEO of a tech company who says "I will" almost as if it were part of his breathing. When something needs to be done, he is ever ready and just says, "Sure, I'll do that." He doesn't even think about it, until one of two things happens—either he finds himself way overcommitted and doesn't know how it happened or someone is frustrated at his lack of follow-through. He unconsciously avoids, procrastinates, and delays doing what he said "I will" to. He said "I will" when the truth is that he was not willing at all. But, he has been programmed to nod and say, "Sure, I will be glad to." He says "I will" on autopilot.

How does that happen? It happens when we learn to use these words in the context of significant relationships, and the outcomes of using them in those relationships become lasting structures in our heads. Those words are some of the most interpersonally loaded words that exist. They can bring you great satisfaction in a variety of relationships, or they can bring untold conflict and pain. If in your formative, significant relationships, using those words in a certain direction brought you pain, you developed a pattern of using those words in the other direction. Doing so either avoided conflict (or worse), or it got you other rewards. As a result, you developed a relationship with those words that became internalized.

Take the words "I think," for example. I was working with a team of VPs, helping them to develop a team dynamic that was safer and more creative and risk taking. One of the VPs, Dennis, was particularly gifted, but he seemed to keep his ideas to himself in meetings, especially when Steve, the president, was in the room. I knew a lot about the deals they were working on, and I was aware that there were a lot of times that Dennis knew more about them than the president. Yet he never spoke up to say what he thought.

I brought it up with the two of them together. I asked Dennis why there were times when he didn't say what he was thinking. I knew it was safe to do that with me in the room, as Steve had brought me in to develop that kind of team. If the president had a problem with others speaking their minds, he would be indicting himself, and I wanted that to happen with me there, not some other time when he would not be forced to see that he was the problem.

When I asked Dennis why he never spoke up, he froze and instantly, without realizing it, looked at Steve. "Why are you looking at him?" I asked.

"Well, uh, I don't know. I was just thinking," he said.

"Let me guess," I said, "The reason you don't say what you are thinking sometimes is that you are not sure how it is going to go down with Steve if you disagree with him. Is that right?" I asked.

"Well, maybe. I mean, he is the president of the company. It's his place to do what he wants," he said.

I turned to the president and asked, "Steve, is that what you pay him for? To just nod at whatever you think? Or do you want to know things that you might disagree with?"

"Of course I want to know," he said to Dennis. "Why do you think I brought you on? You have great experience in these areas that I know little about, and I need you to speak up. I am not going to shoot you."

From there we got into a great discussion and found out some important things. One was that Steve really did want to know when others disagreed, but he sometimes was unaware of how the ways he pushed back were intimidating to others. The proof of Steve's openness was evident in that there were others on the team who were not afraid to push back and speak their minds—and they still had their jobs. But if they did not have the internal freedom to do so and were afraid like Dennis was, they would never have done it. Steve had to recognize that while as a leader he desired honesty from his people, some of his behaviors made it difficult for them to be honest with him—the classic "say-do" gap.

We learned something else that was huge for Dennis and for the team. He realized that his fear of speaking his mind did not begin with Steve. Dennis had grown up with a military father who did not like dissenting voices in the house and ran the family like a combat platoon, handing out orders that were not to be questioned. Early on, Dennis learned to keep his thoughts to himself around authority figures. He developed a conflicted relationship with the words "I think." In the face of an authority figure, he kept those words to himself and just nodded. It was automatic response. He talked about this in one team meeting and it was big for him.

This is not to say that there are situations in which it would be wise to keep one's mouth shut. In fact, that is yet another reason why this issue is so important. In contrast to Dennis, there are others who were not compliant to an authoritarian parent, and instead felt like they had to speak up to them no matter what the consequences. They could not keep quiet, no matter how much trouble it got them into. In many ways, this could be considered an admirable response. But sometimes, in adulthood, it leaves these folks with a problem. Just as Dennis did not have a choice to say what he thought, they do not have a choice to not say what they think, even when silence would be the wisest choice. They are compelled to defy an authority figure, no matter what the consequences. This is just as much an autopilot behavior as the opposite problem, and both represent a loss of freedom.

But the issue here is not discernment or strategy. The issue is that relationships to certain words are often built in to us in the context of significant relationships, and we can find ourselves with a pattern of not saying what we want, what we think, or what we will or won't do. These responses often have nothing to do with the reality of the situation and everything to do with the patterns we have learned in the past. They become part of our character, our makeup.

In my book *Integrity: The Courage to Meet the Demands of Reality*, I talk about how our character leaves a consistent "wake" behind us. In this instance, the wake is one's patterned use or nonuse of these words. Look back and see for yourself. Chances are that you can identify many situations in which you would have been better off if you did not have that characteristic pattern of not saying no, or not saying what you really want, or not saying what you really think. Sometimes when someone sees this, their entire career begins to make sense. I had a leader say to me recently, "This explains my whole career path since business school." It was the wake he had left behind just as a boat leaves a wake. It was easy to see. The good news is that once he saw it, he could change it and leave a different kind of wake.

But there is another reason I mention the character wake here. In *Integrity*, I also talked about the etymology of the word "character." Too often we think of character too narrowly, as if it just means morals or ethics. But in reality it is about our entire makeup, how we are constructed. And the word itself gives us a beautiful picture of how we get to be that way, and why we can have characteristic ways of using or not using certain words. In Greek, for example, the word "character" comes from the word that means "experience." In English, it means "engraved mark." In other words, your past experience, especially in significant relationships, has engraved upon you a tendency to use or not use words in a predicable, characteristic way.

If you had bad experiences when you spoke your mind, you developed a pattern of keeping silent rather than speaking up. If dissenting opinions resulted in a slap to the face or a loss of affection, you kept silent. And you still do—without thinking. It is now automatic. But, if speaking up were rewarded, then you do it well now, too. It all depends on your past experience, until you have new experiences that change the pattern. We talked earlier about this dynamic in the section on how structure is built where we said, "What was one on the outside, becomes inside." It is now a part of you.

I once worked with a leader who found himself granting more and more policy exceptions than he felt comfortable with to one of his direct reports. This employee always seemed to have special circumstances or a reason he felt he needed to be given more flexibility than company policy allowed.

When I challenged the leader to look at it, he realized something. Although what he was doing did not make business sense, he was doing what he had gotten used to doing with a similar kind of person in his family—a brother who always seemed to need some kind of special treatment. This leader had the kind of sibling a lot of high achievers have, one who never really did pull his or her weight, was always sliding by, and yet the family for some reason never held that one accountable. His response to the special needs employee was an autopilot response based on his experiences with that kind of person in his family. Agreeing to requests for special treatment was automatic. So the thought of saying no never even occurred to him. He was just programmed that way.

Another executive I worked with had no difficulty asking for what she wanted for her company in negotiating contracts, making sales, and doing their business. For her, the words "I want," when speaking on behalf of the company, came freely and easily. But trying to utter those same words for herself was an entirely different matter. She was not nearly as free to say "I want" to her boss when negotiating her own contract, or to her team when expressing her preferences about which part of the project she wanted to do.

When I brought up the discrepancy to her, it blindsided her. She had never seen the difference in her abilities when she was asking for someone else versus asking for herself. When we explored the reasons for her behavior, we found a very different internalization in her own head surrounding the words "I want."

She had grown up in a family where serving and giving were very high values, which is obviously good. It trained her to stand up for people, to ask on behalf of others, and to use her power to get for others what they could not get for themselves. It had a moral high ground. But that same environment also taught her that wanting something for oneself is "selfish, prideful, and self-centered." She learned early that selfishness was one of the greatest of evils. But, as it was defined for her, it included not only the "I want it all for me" kind of selfishness we all deplore, but also the idea that wanting anything for yourself is bad. So, her relationship with the words "I want" was one that prompted an internal tongue lashing if she ever got close to uttering them. She felt guilty for wanting such a thing, and felt she should be thinking about others and not herself. Understandably, she developed a pattern of not asking for things for herself.

The takeaway here is twofold. First, you may have a pattern with certain words that you have never noticed, and that pattern is the reason you find yourself in unwanted situations. Second, that pattern was learned in experiences that have been engraved in you and have made their mark. They are now a part of the way you automatically operate. It is time to become aware of your autopilot behaviors and get your hands back on the wheel of your words and your choices. You would do well to see where you learned not to say what you want or think or will or won't do. There were probably good reasons you did that, but it is time to realize that those days are over and what might have served you well then is not helping you now.

THE WORD AUDIT

In chapter 5 we talked about the time audit. Now we're going to apply a similar practice to reviewing your relationship to words. See if you have a pattern and observe it. Remember, anything you observe begins to change just as a result of observing it. It is the first step toward having new experiences and developing new patterns.

The use of the words that we will explore next directly corresponds to the key components that your boundaries are designed to deliver for you. Recall that it includes the ability to do the following:

- Experience yourself as separate and differentiated from others.

- Contain destruction and keep it from spreading.

- Define yourself and know who you are.

- Set limits when needed.

- Possess and live out values.

- Have self-control and thereby be free and autonomous.

Consider the ways that the words listed below might affect your ability to experience the above outcomes:

- "I think . . ."

- "I won't . . ."

- "I want . . ."

- "I will . . ."

- "Yes."

- "No."

- "I don't know."

- "I was wrong."

- "When you . . ."

Let's look more closely at what each phrase might mean to you, to your work, and to your life.

"I Think . . ."

If you cannot say "I think," then you will not experience yourself as a separate person, fully differentiated from others. As a result, you will lose important aspects to your functioning, including the ability to self-direct, stand firm against difficult people, feel OK when others put you down, persuade and influence the direction of a conversation, deal, or team, and so on.

Telling others what you think defines who you are. It differentiates you from them, from their opinions, and from their beliefs. It forms community and true oneness and unity. Unity based only on compliance, rather than acceptance of differences, is not unity at all. Speaking your mind also develops your autonomy and helps you to access the good aggression available to you as you move forward and define who you are to the world.

Remember the salesperson from chapter 1, Kevin, who hit a revenue ceiling and could not get past it? It was fascinating to me. No matter what he tried to do to get past his plateau, he couldn't do it. Training, seminars, more contacts, whatever he tried—he was stuck.

After getting to know more about his life, I noticed that although he was very bright and could explain his thoughts and positions well in a discussion, there were times with significant others when he seemed to disappear. He turned nice, smiled and nodded at what the other person said, but didn't really give voice to his own thoughts. I saw this particularly with his wife, who might be mistakenly referred to often as a strong personality. In other words, she was pushy and somewhat dominating, which often is out of fear and weakness not strength. But others see it as strong and fold their cards. That is what Kevin did, and I could see he was becoming somewhat "led" in their conversations.

We began to work on his tendency to be led in a conversation and what that felt like so he could become aware of it when he was doing it. I gave him assignments that required him to speak his thoughts in many situations whether or not it mattered. The result was amazing.

After a period of time, his sales quadrupled. And, although that was a goal, I had intentionally not focused on customers but on other relationships. I did not want him to see speaking his mind as a sales technique, which it may or may not be. I wanted something different. I wanted his power to emerge.

Remember when we talked about power? Your power to think is part of it, and if Kevin could bring that power into the context of relationships in which he was afraid to do so, I knew he would begin to influence his customers in positive ways as well. He is the expert in his product. That is why customers came to him—to help them begin to think about what they needed to buy for their business. That is good power, for both parties. But his healthy aggression—which was needed to move people forward—was blocked, and he was getting only the sales that didn't require it. By changing his automatic pilot relationship to the words "I think," he freed up a lot of power, began to be present in those settings, and got customers to think differently and then to buy what he was selling. Customers wanted to be led, and he was not leading.

When you say what you think, you not only differentiate, you express the good amount of power you were designed to have. People do not feel dominated, but appreciative that you showed up. Everyone has something to offer, so get the words out and begin sharing what is in that head of yours.

"I Won't . . ."

If you find it difficult to say "I won't" or "no" then you are subject to being drawn into many destructive patterns, including everything from simply overextending yourself, to downright illegalities.

I recently got a call from a middle-level manager who had been asked by a sales manager to do something funny with some numbers, and she did not feel comfortable with it. But she said that the person was being promoted, and that his boss loved him. When she told the manager she felt uncomfortable with what he asked her to do, he told her that he was going places in the company and a little accounting change was not a big deal. He made it sound as if his bosses were really pleased with what was going on, which implied he was somehow above being questioned.

She felt caught. She did not want to do what the manager had asked her to do, but the ones above were so pleased with him she thought she might really be in trouble—either with him or someone above him if she caused a problem.

I had to jolt her back into reality because her "I won't do that" words were caught somewhere in her throat. This was a guy who was headed for a future harassment suit (there had already been two complaints), and other future indiscretions were certain as well. I told her he had a lot of legal exposure following him around as well as just good old ethics violations, and she had better find her words and say, "I won't do that." Otherwise, she could find herself someday pulled in with the rest of them when the auditors show up.

"What if I lose my job?" she said.

"If you do, good," I said, "You got out before the building burned down. But for now, just make sure you say, 'I won't.'" (We talk more about losing jobs later in the personal equity section.)

Ethics and legalities are only a part of the "won't" word. "Won't" is also huge in such areas as negotiations, working out alliances, and even in internal projects. Many people come to the table looking out for their own interests alone. They are there to get from you whatever they can. You must be able to draw the line and know what you won't do, in whatever arrangement you are making. If you have difficulty with that word, you will find yourself on the wrong end of a lot of agreements. There is a reason that controllers, or some risk management types answer the phone, "No. Who is this?" They have a limit-setting function. But what if they could not say those words?

In difficult situations, you have to know the bottom line of what you won't do. That is where you are going to stand. If you can't do that, your boundary lines will get moved past where you want them to be. If you can stand firm, others will have to come your way to make a deal, and that is the way any good deal works. Everyone gives up something, compromises. Give-and-take happens in a dialogue that works well for everyone. Any good relationship requires sacrifice for the greater good. So make sure you require that from the other side by knowing what you won't do.

"I Want . . ."

If saying the words "I want" is tough for you, then you are going to find yourself getting leftovers in many situations, and not getting the performance out of others that you need to move your projects forward. I once had an upcoming book release that was coordinated with several speaking events across the country. The publisher had just received an order from a national bookstore chain that seemed very low to me. With all the events

I had planned, I was concerned there would be much more demand for the book than the chain had committed to, which meant there could be a lot of people who wanted the book but would not be able to find it in their local bookstore. I felt there was a good chance the book's momentum would be derailed as a result.

I called the publisher and asked him to go back to the bookstore chain and ask them to order more copies. The publisher squirmed and said that they had a good relationship with the chain's buyers and did not want to offend them by pushing too hard. "Offend them? We are trying to help them," I thought. "Go ask for what we need."

The publisher would not do it, as the fear of being offensive was getting in the way. So, not out of any great skill on my part but strictly out of fear of the whole project not working, I flew to the bookstore chain's headquarters and met with the buyers. I told them that I would be doing a lot of events in their cities and I wanted people to be able to follow through while they were motivated to change, and they needed to be able to walk in and buy the book to do that. So, I said it plainly. "I really need you to do a lot more than you have committed to. Would you consider tripling your order?"

My publisher, who was present in the meeting, nearly fainted. But, the buyers looked at each other, nodded, and said, "Let's do it." It turned out well, and that chain performed better than all the others in sales. But it would not have happened if we had let the publisher's fear of offending them dictate the path. We had to go and ask them for what we wanted.

"I Will . . ."

To "will" means a lot of things. To be inclined toward, to determine, to assent, or to choose are usually mentioned. The meaning I like the best is "to desire, which adds a positive inclination to the mere choice to do something." I like to think the choices we make are actually the ones we want to make. Those tend to be the ones we are most likely to not only fulfill, but also to be fulfilled in carrying out. So, the question becomes, "How likely is it that when you say you will, you are truly in line with your desires?" The more what you say you will do is lined up with your desires, the closer you are to having one life, meaning the life you are living is also the life you desire.

Unfortunately, sometimes we lack alignment between what we desire and what we say we will do. We say we will when it is the last thing we want to do, but we say it anyway because we are on some form of autopilot. We are not truly giving of ourselves, but giving in. We cannot say no to the pressure (internal or external), so we say the words "I will" when we may or may not actually follow through—and if we do, we may resent it.

As mentioned before, this does not mean we only say we will do things we love doing. But even the things we do not want to do, to be authentic, should be connected to something we do want to do. The salesperson does not want to make one more call, but agrees to do it because she wants to make her numbers. She will do it, and while she does not desire to pick up the phone, she does desire (she has the will) to make the sales goal. So will and desire are still aligned.

The problem is that people sometimes say they will do things just to make someone happy or avoid conflict or because they are just used to agreeing to whatever anyone else wants. They learned it early in life to get a domineering parent off their backs, and then they developed a passive-aggressive personality to finally express their true desire. "I said I will do this for you, but watch me and you will see what I really want."

People whose will is not free from this kind of conflict are sometimes unable to go for a goal with vigor and persistence. They often fail to follow through on things or are not very good at pushing things along a path to completion. They have lost their will, and much of that has to do with the way they use the word. They use it automatically when they do not really mean it, and then they do not have the strength or power or impulsion of their will available to them in other ways to accomplish what they desire. They have lost touch with their drive, which in the final analysis has to do with will.

You know what this kind of drive looks like. These are people who when you ask something of them and they look you in the eye and say "I will" you know they mean it. There is not a shred of doubt that it will come to pass. They will. Period.

There are others you know who say they will, but you doubt it. They say they will but they won't. It makes you wonder why they said they would if there is no follow-through. There has to be a reason, and part of it is that the autopilot was probably on.

Your goal, to have one life, requires that the things you say you will do are the things you truly desire to do, even if you don't want to do them. Soldiers do not necessarily desire to go to war, but they say they will go because they do desire to serve the country. The will and the desire are truly together.

The expression of your values and how you live them out depends on your ability to will. If you have a value, yet cannot will it to occur, then the value is never expressed in real time. If you want to be a free and autonomous person and express your true desires and goals, yet have a conflicted will, that is never going to happen until your will is free.

Will can also be conflicted in the other direction. There are not only people who say they will when they do not want to, there are also people whose ability to will is conflicted out of fear. They do the opposite of overusing the word. They never commit to anything. They keep their options open and refuse to say "I will." The big joke about this always refers to commitment-phobic men with regard to marriage. They can't walk down the aisle and say "I will." But commitment phobia is not just a male disorder, nor is it limited to marriage. Both men and women can be afraid to say they will do something. Many people struggle under leaders who will not commit to a direction for the team or company. They stagnate. It could be out of fear of failure or other issues, but the result is the same. Their relationship to the word is stalled. But, and this is the point, this rarely tends to be an isolated incident. To the contrary, it is usually more of a pattern, and awareness of that pattern is what is needed.

"Yes" and "No"

Most of the uses of the words "yes" and "no" are pretty obvious, and they are also similar to the ways we use the words "will" and "won't." So I won't belabor them here to avoid redundancy. But they are the big direction setters in life. What we say yes to is where we are headed and what we say no to keeps us going in a particular direction. Yes joins us and no separates us. Therefore, they play huge roles in defining who you are and what you end up doing and not doing.

The word "no" is especially relevant to boundaries and structure. People's ability to say no is basically their ability to set limits, to define themselves, and also to establish their personal limits. Think of what your ability to say no does for you:

Shapes your focus
Determines the reality of your morality
Determines how you use your time
Determines how much people are able to control you
Determines what others can do to you
Determines what you allow others to do around you or in your organization
Determines what people can get from you
Determines what people can get you to do
Protects your energy
Protects your resources, including your financial resources
Protects you from self-destructive behavior
As a leader, determines you ability to keep people going in a direction
As a leader, determines your ability to stay on mission

In a sense, the word "no" is the boundary word. It is the first one we hear as children, beginning in the second year of life as we commence to do things that will harm us. Soon, we learn its meaning as our parents use it with us and as we want to use it ourselves. Mommy says stop doing something or come along, and the toddler looks up, takes a strong stance with a determined grimace, and says, "No!" He is exerting his will. It is very important. If all goes well, and when he uses the word "no" he does not get a thrashing or encumbered with guilt, it remains an important part of his vocabulary for life.

As a CEO, he can say no to a bad deal, off-the-mark requests from employees, customers, or other organizations. He can say no to team members who want to take the organization in a direction that is not on mission or would get them off focus. He can say no to uses of resources that are being spent in the wrong places and not utilized like they should be. The word "no" serves him well.

And, to have one life, he can also say no to the many different agendas that vie for his time. He will have enough time to lead the organization as well as know the names of his kids. And that is not only for CEOs. These functions are important for all of us, no matter what our positions. If you say yes too often because your "no muscle" is broken or weak, then you are going to be scattered. "No" defines the limits. And since both time and energy are finite resources, as we shall see later, "no" protects how they are spent.

Yet there are few words people have more conflict with than "no." It deprives others of what they want from us. While there is nothing wrong with that—in fact it is a good thing in good relationships—in some relationships it becomes a problem. There are people who interpret the word "no" as "What? You don't love me?" or "If you really cared, you would want to come with me" or "You would want to do that for me." Love, loyalty, devotion, and friendship get entangled with the word itself.

In business, the ability to say no is paramount to making the right deal, and to not giving away too much in projects and alliances. But, beyond that, it is in the day-to-day, moment-by-moment ebb and flow that our use of the word "no" leads us toward or away from success and fulfillment of goals. For example:

- You set aside the morning to get that project done, and then there is a knock at the door. Your co-worker asks, "Do you have time to look at this for me?" Can you say, "No, not now. I am tied up with this project today. How about tomorrow?" Or do you cave in and lose the morning for your own project?

- You know the objective you have set for your team and what you need to accomplish in the next week. To do that, you need Susan to do a certain task on a certain day. She comes in to your office and says she wants to take that day off to attend an event that is special to her, or that she needs to use the time to work on a different project. Can you say, "No, I need you to . . ."?

- You get a budget or an expense report from someone, and the funds are being spent in a way that you do not like; or you get a request for an expense that you know is important to the person who made the request, but you need the funds to go in a different direction. You know people are going to be upset, but can you say no?

- Your boss asks you to stay late and help with something. You have been looking forward to doing something that night right after work. Can you say, "No, I need to leave"?

- The team is discussing a strategic direction and people have strong feelings about which direction ought to be taken. Your boss wants a certain outcome, and is lobbying for it in a strong fashion in the meeting. He turns to you and asks if you agree with the plan he is proposing. You don't like it and don't want to do it. Can you say, "No, I don't agree"?

- Your client is pushing for more concessions than you want to agree to in order to do the deal. He is asking for discounts that reduce your margin to a point you don't feel good about, and he is also asking for more time than you want to give. Can you say no?

Your "no" keeps you in control, and it keeps you on track to having one life. When you lose it, you lose yourself. Certainly, there are situations, even some of the above, when ultimately you cannot say no and keep the job. There is such a thing as insubordination and refusal to carry out one's duties that will get a person fired. But most of the time in good and realistic scenarios that is not what happens. What happens if you say no is that you are going to get into a little bit of a conflict, upset someone perhaps, and life is going to go on. But, if your autopilot is set on "yes" and "no" does not come up on the options list, you will not be able to go that route. And you will be out of control. "No" preserves you.

"I Don't Know."

"I'm not sure what happens to me," the VP said. "Sometimes in big meetings with key investors, I almost can't think. I get anxious and just don't know what to say."

"What's going on when it happens?" I asked.

"Nothing," he said. "It just happens in meetings with powerful people."

"I bet that is not true," I said. "You have meetings with powerful people all the time. I bet there is a particular set of circumstances that brings this about."

"I have no idea, but I have got to get over this. I have to be able to think in those meetings," he said.

"OK, here is what I want you to do. I want you to start writing down exactly what is going on in the meeting when you begin to feel anxious.

I want to find out why this is happening and to do this, we have to know what is going on when you feel anxious," I told him.

So, he did. And what he found was that this feeling occurred when bankers or others used terms with which he was unfamiliar. He felt like he did not know what they were talking about, but also that he should have known. It made him feel stupid in front of the other people. When he figured out this pattern, we talked about it.

"So, what do you do when that happens?" I asked.

"I just get quiet and try to not let them figure out that I don't know what they are talking about," he said.

At that point, I had a thought. I knew the president of the company pretty well and also knew that if he were in the same situation, he would do something very different. So, I asked the VP to follow me down the hall to the president's office. We went in and I told the boss I had a question for him.

"When you are in a meeting with investors or bankers, do they ever use terms or talk about things that you are not familiar with?" I asked.

"Sure, happens all the time," he said. "A lot of times, I have no clue what they are talking about. I am not a banker and a lot of that sophisticated financial jargon is just not something I understand."

"So, what do you do?" I asked, fully knowing the answer.

"I interrupt them and tell them I am not familiar with what they are talking about and could they please explain it to me," he said. "Tends to make everyone feel better, especially me," he laughed. "Why do you ask?"

"Oh, we were just wondering," I said.

When we went back to the VP's office, he was stunned. He was stunned that his boss did not know some of the same things that he did not know. He thought anyone in that position would have known it all, just as he expected himself to know it all. It helped him overcome his grandiose and unrealistic expectations. But beyond that, he was stunned that his boss would just say it to them, just tell them he did not know what they were referring to with those terms. It blew him away.

This ability for people to say they sometimes do not know the answer is a powerful, self-defining act. It cuts down on the grandiose expectations people feel like they are under. Finally saying the words "I don't know" puts them comfortably in their own skin. It cuts down on the pressure to be more or different than they are and lets them be themselves. And that is a very powerful stance.

Whenever a person tries to fake it, or feels as if he has to, there is a crack in the foundation. And that crack will reveal itself in some say. To not fake it and be real requires taking a very strong stance that says, "I am secure enough in who I am to be who I am." And that security comes through. Often business situations are so full of egos and posturing that a real person stands out as a towering figure among the fakes.

The other powerful aspect of this stance is that when you admit you do not know something, you are on your way to finding out. You are learning, and as you learn you get stronger still. Humility is a very strong boundary, and pride a very flimsy one.

I can almost hear the pushback to what I'm saying. Perhaps you know that there are times when admitting you do not have an answer will cost you a deal or cause a difficult boss to hemorrhage all over you. If it appears you do not know something, the client loses confidence, many think. Bosses pay people to know things, and not knowing them could cost you your job or your political capital in the organization in which you are tying to ascend.

To these objections, there are obvious answers that involve circumstances, strategies, and particular personalities. But if you had those thoughts, it may mean that you have this problematic relationship with the words themselves. Obviously when you are at war, you do not want to reveal weaknesses that someone can take advantage of. In a hostile showdown, or an adversarial one, sometimes a guarded stance is wise. You don't need a PhD in psychology to know when someone is not safe or a situation is volatile. That is basic emotional intelligence. So, obviously there are times when "I will have to go find the answer to that" is going to get you shot, not increase your capital.

But that even proves my point. To sometimes not say "I don't know" presupposes that you have the ability to utter the words, yet wisdom and discernment prompt you to do something different in that circumstance. Wisdom presupposes that you actually have choices and options in your arsenal, and your experience and intuition tell you which one to use at that moment—"I don't know" or "I want to think about that one some more."

Admitting you don't know means you bring enough to the table and to the relationship that your value does not depend on creating a false perception about one point. If you know your stuff, if you have performed, and you are bringing talent, ideas, brains, experience, and other assets to the relationship, your boss or that client or potential JV partner already needs you. If your Mercedes performs for you, you do not have to act as if it makes lattes, too. Its value is proven.

Admitting what you do not know solidifies that what you do assert is actually true. It demonstrates that you are confident enough to show your underbelly, which also engenders trust and builds the alliance. All of this comes from strength, not weakness, and will be discussed further in the chapter on getting your balance sheet together. But suffice it to say for now that if you are good enough, what you don't know won't kill you. So, be competent and create real value, and then you can be yourself. If you asked Peyton Manning about a particular defense formation and he said he was not familiar with that one, would you really not want him on your team?

Realize that your discomfort in saying "I don't know" comes from some other kind of fear or expectation inside yourself. Maybe in your formative years there were interpersonal or other kinds of danger that required you to know everything—or at least appear that you did—or bad things would happen. But you no longer live there, and that kind of hypervigilance is costing you now.

And now, for all of you who have been squirming about this section, let me say one more thing. If there are things that you really should know and don't, which if you would admit would reveal that you have not done your homework, that is one of those times to keep your mouth shut, and sit there and look smart. Then leave the meeting, and go do your homework.

"I Was Wrong."

The lawyers say admit nothing, deny everything, and shift the blame to somebody else. And that is one reason Shakespeare was not always happy with them, I am sure. To avoid taking responsibility for one's side of something is one of the ultimate killers in any relationship, personal or professional. In fact, it makes real relationship impossible. When one person refuses to own something, true relatedness ends and managing one another begins. Your relationship has hit a wall.

If you are in court and the goal is to have a winner and a loser, then you can understand why "lawyering up" might be some people's strategy. But it should not be your strategy in life, either professionally or personally. The degree to which you are not able to admit when you are wrong determines the degree to which you have a crack in the foundation of your whole life.

Boundaries and the structure of the personality are based on secure lines of ownership of your own property. To be secure and to get good and strong, you have to own the things that are on your property. We looked at owning your thoughts, feelings, values, desires, and the like. To own your weaknesses and faults, although not as tasty at first, is just as important to becoming strong.

First, do the math. If you do have a fault or a weakness or make a mistake and you do not own it, you still have it. You will repeat it. It will occur again. You have seen this in people who cannot see their issues. They just stay stuck and those things never get better. Admitting quickly when you are wrong is energizing. It gives you a new path to go on and gives you solutions you actually have control of, like yourself. Not admitting something externalizes the problem. And if it is external to you, you cannot do anything about it. You have just become powerless. You are stuck at that point and become a victim. "It is not me" means also that you cannot do anything about it. You are stuck.

Second, you will get better when you own something and work on it, and by definition, you have gotten stronger and more competent by doing so. So, power, real power, the kind that you are designed to have (competence and self-control), goes up. You will have more security, more strength, more reality, and fewer future threats. When you fix the cavity, you can safely chew on that side.

Third, and this is huge, admitting your failures gives hope, trust, and good feelings to the other side. They appreciate you for it. When people do not own their mistakes, the other side of the relationship begins to lose hope. They unplug and adopt a negative posture because they know that whatever happens, whenever there is a problem, it will not be solved. Solutions come when responsible parties own their mistakes and fix them. And there is no hope for solutions with those who refuse to admit it when they are wrong. We will talk more about this in chapter 13, but for now, there is a question.

What is your relationship with the words "I was wrong"? If you cannot say them, then you will have the issues mentioned here and more. If you have difficulty with them, what is the structure of the problem inside your head? Where did it come from? Did you grow up with a lot of shame, feeling so bad that you avoid admitting when you are wrong? Did admitting failure mean you would be hurt in some way? I recently had an executive tell me about his background in an almost warlike neighborhood during his childhood. "You would never admit to anything or you would get killed," he said. "The same way in my house. My dad would have killed me. So, this stuff is all new to me. I am having to learn that it helps and does not get you murdered." But, his team members were glad that he was learning. It gave them hope.

Take a look and see if there is a pattern. And if there is, find out where it comes from.

"When You . . ."

And then there is the opposite side of admitting your own fault. That is when someone else, not you, is on the wrong side of behavior or of a mistake. This statement is about acknowledging that someone else is doing something you do not like, are uncomfortable with, or is flat-out wrong. This is not about when you are wrong. This is about confronting others when they are wrong or when you want them to own something. And it is one of the most important boundary structures there is, especially in containing destruction, remaining separate from other people's problems, and limiting someone else's toxic dynamics from taking over your yard. It is also one of the most, if not the most, difficult relationships with words that many people have.

I have called these words "when you . . ." But of course that is not the only phrase that is used when pointing out a fault or problem to another person. You might just as naturally say "I don't like it when you . . ." or some other way of saying what you mean. In the chapter on communicating your boundaries, we will take a look at some of the ways to talk to another person about problems. I use that phrase here to get you in touch with the main issue that tends to get stuck in a person's throat. "I am about to tell you something that I do not like about what you do, and I am going to hold you responsible for it." It is about the other person, and about how you feel or are inclined to think about his behavior. For example, "When you don't show up on time, I don't like it because it causes more work for me." The implication is that you are holding another person responsible for something, and for many people that is what is difficult.

If your experience in formative relationships, either in childhood or adulthood, was that you encountered a hurtful response when you expressed concerns about another person's behavior, then your relationship to the words "when you . . ." is going to be a fearful one. You will avoid saying them or be too long in saying them, sometimes after a lot of damage has taken place.

You may fear the other person's anger, their rejection, or just making them feel bad. While you see what needs to be said, you just can't bring yourself to say it. As a result, this lack of boundary is a gaping hole in the fence of your life and your work, and people will be able to bring things into your yard that are hurtful and destructive.

Is there a pattern with not being able to tell others when you think they have a problem, or there is something they are doing that you want them to stop doing? Do you allow problem people to continue to do hurtful or problematic things with no interference from you? Remember, in life, you will get what you tolerate. If you have a problematic relationship with words like "when you . . ." that would stop the hurtful or irresponsible behavior, that behavior is very likely to continue—in your yard.

FREE SPEECH IN THE FUTURE

Here are a few suggestions to help you reclaim your right to free speech:

- **Take this idea seriously.** Do not assume that you are immune from having a characteristic pattern of using or not using certain words.

- **Play the movie of your life, past and present.** Can you identify patterns that cause you to repeatedly say some words but also refrain from saying others, or from having hard conversations? What is consistently missing in your life that could be present if you could say the things you need to say to bring them about?

What are the fears, hurts, or relationships that brought those patterns about? Can you see that you are still relating to that person or those people from the past inside your head by allowing them to control your own use of words?

Talk these things through with someone—a coach, friend, or counselor. Get some insight, and get past this. You need free speech to be a part of your life. It affects everything you do, and it is a cornerstone of your personal power.

- **Seek out new experiences that develop new patterns.** Remember, your experience will become your character and your makeup. So you need some good experiences to replace the bad experiences. Attend some skills-building workshops, join a group, practice what you know you need to do with someone who holds you accountable. Remember, you will only grow and change as you have different experiences and different outcomes.

- **Write it down.** If needed, script your conversations and what you need to say in situations when it is difficult for you. Write it down beforehand and practice it with a friend. Role play the conversation. (See the chapter 13 for more about this.)

- **Make this a team exercise.** Talking about this issue of free speech is one of the best things a team can do together. Get this all out on the table and talk about how the team and the culture of the company work around these words. "What happens when you say what you think around here?" I will ask them. Or, what happens when you say no to each other? Who says an automatic yes to everything? When I asked that question of one team everyone turned to the CEO and laughed. "Never met a deal he couldn't say yes to" was what they all said. "And we are the ones who have to deal with the fallout. He just automatically says yes and then we get the trouble. He says yes to everything." It was insightful to him to see that he was an automatic yes person, and that his optimism was both his greatest strength and also a significant problem.

- **Get a coach or someone to help you.** Part of the process of change involves opening up our performance to a wise, experienced person who can observe us and speak to our patterns and practices.

Today, more than ever, executive and leadership coaching is readily available. Good coaches will understand this issue, even if they use different terms to describe it. Find one, invest the time and money in your growth, and reclaim your ability to speak the words you need to speak to get the results you need.

Your words are one of the most important boundary structures you have. Do everything possible to make the right ones available to you. Develop a good relationship with them.

eight

Make the "No-Choice" Choices First

If you are like most people, you either have a mortgage or pay rent. So, when the first of the month rolls around, you pay it. You don't think about whether or not you are going to do it, nor do you put it off and go spend that money on other things so it is not available. You do not have a choice, at least in the way you experience it. In reality you do have a choice, but not in your experience. You know that if you don't write that check, you are going to lose your home. Either foreclosure or eviction awaits you if you don't send it in, so you really don't think about it. You do it first, before you spend the money on anything else.

What I want you to see is the automatic nature of this particular choice. It is a choice, but you do not perceive it that way. You do not experience it as optional, something you will do if you have time or only if something better doesn't come along. There is little that can get in line before it, given the money is there.

Certainly there are a lot of other things vying for that money. There are wishes and desires, impulses, needs, and wants. They surround you. But they do not get in the way of the mortgage. The consequences are too high for that. So, you say no to the other things and send in the money. But, more important than just paying it, herein lies the key:

You never even perceive it as a choice.
Not paying is not an option.

That is the reason it gets paid. The consequences are so great that to not pay is not even an option. It is a choice to make something a "nonchoice."

The point of this chapter is to get you to look at certain other choices in life in the same way. They are not an option. But the paradox in all of this is that to do that itself is a choice. And that is why many, many people do not succeed. They never choose to make some choices a nonchoice. If you can do that, the things you care about will indeed go forward. If you don't, in the end you will lose them. It is not my role to tell you which choices in your life should be nonoptions. Your own value system will dictate that (even though I will make some suggestions). But I will tell you that to succeed in the areas you decide you care about, there are some choices that you will do well to see as not optional.

ROCKS AND PEBBLES: DISTINGUISHING THE VITAL FROM THE URGENT

There is an illustration you may already have heard by now about the professor who places a big jar, a few big rocks, and a box of pebbles on the table at the front of the class. The professor pours the pebbles into the jar first, and then he asks the students how many of the rocks they think will fit into the jar. They guess, and the professor is able to get some of the rocks in, but not all.

The professor then pours the pebbles out and puts the rocks in, and all of them fit. He pours the pebbles in, and many of them fill in the remaining space as well. In the end, there is much more room available in the jar than most students thought, but only because the big rocks were put in first. The big ones before the small ones.

The lesson is that your life is like that. All activities are not the same. Some are rocks and some are pebbles. The key is to know the difference and to put the rocks—the most important ones—in first. If the rocks get in first, not only will you fit more into the space, but you will make sure the important ones get their volume. Make sure that the big ones are getting the first space, and then you will have time for the little ones, but more importantly, you will have made sure that the big ones got in. When you pack your trunk for a road trip, put the suitcases in first. Then you can stuff other items in around the edges. If you can't, they were not as important anyway, or they would be in the suitcase to begin with.

In your life, there are some activities that are rocks. They are the big ones, and what I mean by that is that they are the ones that will define the outcomes of your vision, your mission, your values, and your life itself. They are the ones that are most important to you. If you put them in first, and give them the first of your time and energy, then you will live well and succeed. If you don't, you won't. And your dreams, goals, vision, and values will be foreclosed upon. You will be evicted from your own most treasured goals.

Simple enough. But, unlike the mortgage, the rest of the rocks of life propose a huge problem. The problem is that while the consequence of not paying the mortgage is right in front of you, all the time, the consequences of not performing the most important activities in life are not right in front of you. They do not come and bite you within thirty days. There is no notice that comes in the mail. The most important consequences in life rarely come immediately. They usually come much later and then, in full force.

Vital vs. Urgent

It is a truth of life that some of the most vital activities are not the most urgent activities. The word "vital" means that something is necessary to the maintenance of life. If you ignore vital activities, life is not maintained in some way. Death occurs. But, often, vital activities can be put aside, and you can do something nonvital instead, and feel no pain. At least for the time being. But if you continue to do that, something is dying.

For example, eating is vital. You must have food to maintain life. Ignore eating for long enough and you will begin to suffer at some point. But you can ignore eating (a vital activity) for something urgent and not feel the consequences right away. If you are late to the movies, you can skip dinner so you don't miss the opening of that film you have been dying to see. It's not a problem, as long as you eat sometime fairly soon before organ systems begin to fail. And you probably will eat soon, since your blood sugar will trigger notices, much like the mortgage company, to remind you at some point that you need food. But the point is that the urgent can replace the vital with no immediate consequence. Imagine, for example, that you can ignore talking to your kids any given day because you have work to do, and nothing bad will happen, that day. However, do it over time and you might find them on drugs. The urgent got in the way of the vital, and no one felt the pain—until later. But you will feel it.

Now to the point:

> There are activities that are vital to your business, your vision, your mission, your health, your goals, your soul, your relationships, your family, your future, and your life that you can ignore and not feel any immediate consequence.

The urgent can move them aside, and you will not have a blood sugar reminder. In fact, you may even feel more comfortable by ignoring the vital activities, not less. You might feel relieved not to have some of those difficult conversations, or do some things that are vital to your goals. As a result, ignoring them becomes reinforcing. You feel better in the short term when you do. But continue to do that and those things die.

Take a simple example. I have young children. I would die for them. They mean the world to me. I want them to develop well and be healthy and equipped for life. But for that to happen, they need a father who shows up—emotionally and relationally. Honestly, there are times when I return from a couple of days' travel or a very long day and just do not have it in me to engage with them at that moment. It is more comfortable to unplug. My need to withdraw feels urgent. And, if that were an option, a choice available to me, I could see myself doing it every time I felt like I wanted to withdraw into a hole where there is nothing pulling at me. Over time, I would become disconnected from them because the urgent got in the way of the vital.

There are certainly times when we all find ourselves dominated by the urgent to the loss of the vital. The pebbles take precedence in that moment. There is nothing wrong with that, either. That is life. Every now and then it is necessary. There are certainly times when the best laid plans do not get their planned moments. They get pushed aside. In your business, you could have a schedule full of important agendas that can get replaced by a crisis that is immediate. The fire must be put out. But, if that becomes a pattern, the important agendas get pushed aside in an ongoing way. Remember, the tendency in life is for the urgent and the comfortable always to vie for your best—and first—attention. They are in your face all the time, and it is easy for them to get the best of what you have. But, if you do that as a pattern, your important agendas will lose in the end.

Given that reality, add one more to it. And this may be one of the most important principles you will ever learn. What we usually depend on to stay on track is guaranteed to fail. What is that? It is human self-discipline—in the moment—to stick to what is vital instead of urgent. We think we will choose the most important activities and stay on track out of self-discipline in the moment, when the urgent is vying for our time. But the reality is that human nature cannot be depended upon, over time, to always make the right choice. And the less self-discipline we have in any one area, the more it will fail. We need help to be rescued from the temptation of the moment so we will not be pulled into the immediately reinforcing options that face us every day, and instead be pushed into doing what is not urgent, but vital.

> The answer to that is to make the decision to
> put the rocks in first.

Put the Rocks in First

Decide, proactively, to structure your life so that you never have to choose in the moment whether or not you are going to do the vital as if it were optional. You have already made the choice that they are nonchoices. And the way to do that is to structure them, just like paying a mortgage. Put them in your calendar and organize the rest of your activities around them, instead of hoping to get them in around the rest of your activities.

Take a financial example, and you will see how this kind of structure works. There are two kinds of people in the eyes of the IRS. There are those who pay their taxes and those who don't. Of those who do pay their taxes, although there are two ways they do it, there is only one real way: the way of the rocks first. Some of them are the ones whose taxes are withdrawn in a preset structure by their payroll system, called withholding. Every check is structured to take out the vital amount—rocks first. And, at the end of the year, vital taxes (at least vital to keeping you out of jail, maybe not vital in other ways) are already there in the jar—paid in full. It was never an option for them to spend the money, as it was never available to them.

The others are the self-employed whose taxes are not withheld by an outside payroll system, since they get no paycheck. But they have a similar structure whereby they never see that money as their own, and they pay it into a tax account to be sent in when the quarterly payment is due. They never see it as an option to spend that money. It is a nonchoice. It is not theirs to spend. It belongs to the IRS and so they do not look at it as if they can go out and do something else with it. It is put aside for the vital—rocks first.

Then, there is the other kind of person, the ones who do not pay. Typically, their taxes are not withheld, so they do have the option to spend it and not put it aside. They get the gross amount and can do whatever they want. And in the moment, not having the self-discipline to put it aside, they find something urgent to spend it on. Something they need or want to do, right then. Taxes won't be due for a long time, and there is plenty of time to gather the money to pay them, or so they reason. But "plenty of time" never comes because the same pattern of thinking governs all of those future moments as well. "Later" is the internal mantra for the vital, and "now" is the guiding focus for the urgent, always. And with people who live like that, the urgent always wins. Then, April 15 comes, and they do not have the funds. Why?

The reason is that they did not make the previous nonchoice choice. They did not choose to see that money as not being an option on the table to spend. In their minds, it was available, and if it is, as time goes on, the immediate and urgent desire will always take over at some point. That is human nature, the downward slide.

Your time and energy, as well as your money, are just like that. If you do not put the big rocks in first, in a structured way so they cannot be spent, then the goals and agendas you care about will always get pushed back by the urgent. If you see all of your time and energy as available to you to spend, and you are free to push the vital to the "later" category, you will never get to it. But, if the vital is structured, put into the schedule first, and not an option to spend, you will do it. That is the only way it will happen, day in and day out. Otherwise, those important, urgent needs will always push it back.

When my daughters were younger, I decided to take each of them to a weekly parent-toddler preschool. Each Wednesday, right in the middle of the morning, I committed to go. Being twenty months apart, they were enrolled in this for about a year and a half each, so right when the older one finished it was time for the younger one to begin. This represented about a three-year commitment. I entered into it not really understanding all that meant, just thinking about how cool this would be for them and for me. Then I learned something.

The way my week works, Wednesday morning was the first noncommitted time that I had available to do tasks. Mondays and Tuesdays were already committed, and those days were not available to just get work done. So, Wednesday was the first opportunity I had to do the urgent activities that are always pulling at me for time. By urgent I do not at all mean not important. The activities may have been very important to me and my mission, such as a pressing need to get a book proposal in to a publisher or involvement in an ongoing consulting project with an organization. These would be key activities to me. Each Wednesday, there was something pressing that would come up that had to get done. And that was true. Most of those tasks did have to get done or bad results would occur. So, whether or not they were important was not the question. They were. The question was when was I going to do them? With the urgency they all brought to the radar screen, I always felt like I had better do them right then, on Wednesday morning. These were important issues that needed my attention. They were much more urgent than going to preschool and singing "Five Little Monkeys Jumping on the Bed." There would be time for that next week, right?

After all, if I did not go that week, the girls would not notice. They had no understanding at toddler age what day it was. They would not miss it—that day. Life would go on, and I could get the proposal in, or whatever it was that was truly pressing for my time. But then I noticed something, and it was one of the most important realizations I could have had. From a business or mission perspective, there would never be a good time to go play finger painting games at preschool. There would never be a time when there was not something that was pressing for my attention at work. Never. There would always be a proposal or a conference call that needed to be scheduled. So, if that were the case, and there was always an available choice to do those things instead, then the way the math would work out is that they would get done and preschool could wait, as it was optional. I could put it off one more week and nothing bad would happen if I did—unlike the proposal—which would have immediate consequences for sure. The preschool wouldn't, so it could wait. But, when I saw myself reasoning that way, I got it:

> Being a father who showed up was a rock that
> had to go in the jar first. If I did not do that,
> there would always be something pressing that would
> get in the way on any given Wednesday.

So, I had to see that working on Wednesday morning from nine to eleven was not an option. It was not an available time for a meeting or anything else. It had to be blocked out, and just like tax money for the ones who actually pay, that time could never available to spend on anything else. It had to become, God forbid, a rule: no work on Wednesday between nine and eleven.

Once I made that decision, it was a different story. I did not agonize each Wednesday morning whether or not I could get away to go to preschool, whether or not I could afford the time and do that project later. I did not have to make that choice because it was no longer an option available to me. It was off the table. That time was not mine to spend because it was in the schedule, like my other nonavailable time. And that changed everything.

So, here is the takeaway. Figure out what the rocks are in your life, get your calendar, and put them in first—before all else. Pay your taxes, your dues, to your important missions in life, whatever those are, first, and you will succeed. Schedule them. Do not think that you will do them when you have time, because you never will. If you leave it up to the moment, and whether or not you can afford the time that day or feel like doing it, you never will. It just won't happen long-term. The most important things must be put in the schedule first, and not able to be moved unless there is something catastrophic or some higher reason. Certainly there were some Wednesdays I missed, like if I had to be out of town, but not like I would have if I had had the option each week to make a decision whether or not I had the time. If I had seen that time as spendable, I would have spent it.

The same truth holds in business. One pattern I see with some teams is that in the rapid pace they keep, the team cannot find time to get together. They blow and go all week, passing each other in the hallway, or for the more mobile ones, e-mailing and texting as a way of getting it all done. They know that they need to get together to pull all the pieces together and coordinate, yet the way they do that is thinking they will meet when everyone's schedule will work. While that may work for some meetings that need to happen as part of a project or a work flow, that does not work for a strategic team over time to keep themselves vital as a team, staying on track with the mission.

That requires that they see time together as a rock around which other activities must fit. I remember well having to learn that lesson the hard way when I began my first company. Dr. John Townsend and I founded a psychiatric hospital and treatment center company that grew to about forty markets in the western states, and we ran that organization for ten years. We launched it on a shoestring, and although it grew to a respectable size and enjoyed much success, in the beginning it was not easy. Having no money and virtually no infrastructure—like any entrepreneurial start-up—it was a whirlwind. We were basically passing on the freeways, catching up by cell phone, trying to make it all work without time to make it all work. Typical start-up fun.

Soon thereafter, we began to grow and brought on actual department heads—a COO, a marketing director, and others. We had a real team, yet we were not over the start-up hump quite yet, and still peddling hard to keep it all going. However, with a team, it was not like it was when we were doing most everything by ourselves. A team really required coordination. They needed time with us and time together for strategic and operational decisions. But we just did not have time for that. There was always a hospital to negotiate with to open up in a new city. There was always another doctor to meet with who could be the medical director of a new facility, or a media network available for new avenues of advertising to reach patients. And, if we did not have doctors or patients, we would not have much. Both of those needs were urgent. So, those needs always took precedence over getting together with the team.

Gradually, I could feel the reality that we would never get ahead of the curve. It seemed like we were putting out one fire after another. The team was getting frustrated at the lack of coordination. We would promise to get together, but then something important would come up. Then we would promise again, sometimes even desiring the meeting ourselves. "We should get together and talk about that." But getting together was not happening.

Finally, we bit the bullet. "OK, let's have a weekly two-hour breakfast meeting with the partners and the department heads. And let's put it in stone. No missing this meeting for anything other than a hospital burning down. And maybe not then. Call the fire department and go check on it after our meeting," was the way we set it up. It became a rock and it was in the schedule.

I learned my lesson. When we set the meeting in the schedule and saw it as immovable, something that could not be canceled, everything changed. The meetings that we always were going to have, yet weren't happening, began to actually happen. Coordination began to occur, and strategy was implemented. Time and money were saved. New ideas emerged, new product lines were created, and overall performance improved. We became profitable to a much greater degree in the season following the introduction of those meetings, and I would have to say that they were a big factor in creating that reality. In fact, it was in a strategy meeting that the idea of the book *Boundaries* first emerged, which took everything to a whole different level.

That may seem elementary, and to some it is, but to others whose business and schedule are not structured enough that regular face-to-face contact occurs in a written-in-stone way, it may be a revelation. Even for others to whom it is elementary, you would do well to take the principle and ask yourself where you need to apply it in addition to the built-in, face-to-face meetings you already have. Is there a direct report that you have with whom you repetitively trade the words, "When we have some time, we need to sit down and talk about that" and yet it never happens because you will not have the time? The time you have is the time that you structure as a rock. The urgent will have the rest. Whether business or personal, the rocks must be in the schedule or they will never happen.

TIME, ENERGY, MONEY

There are some finite aspects to life of which you only have so much to spend. Among these are time, energy, and money. The no-choice choice means that you decide what your rocks are in each of these areas first, and then you spend them in that way before anything else. Only you know what your rocks are, but just to help, here are some examples you may find helpful:

- **Structured rock family time.** It might include things like a weekly family meeting or certain meals that everyone knows everyone will be there. Research has shown that certain rocks, such as meals, family traditions, and the like, are linked to incredible benefits, such as how satisfied couples are in their marriage, the health of children and teen's identity formation, as well as how well kids do in school and the overall health of the family relationships.

- **Date night.** Making a consistent investment in time with a spouse, like a date night that is in the schedule—a rock that does not get moved—has a much higher probability of actually happening than defaulting to finding time to go out.

- **Scheduled, one-on-one parenting time.** An example would be a regular breakfast at a certain time each week in a restaurant with your teenager, alone and away from everyone else, or a regular activity of some sort.

- **Scheduled exercise time.** This means exercise time that is not a when-I-get-around-to-it event. People who exercise regularly do exactly that, regularly. It is in a routine, at a certain time or pattern as opposed to time that they have left over from other things. It is one of the rocks that is in the schedule. I have a friend who says that when the alarm clock goes off, she goes. She does not ask herself whether or not she wants to work out that day. If she did, she would never go. Not going isn't a choice she allows herself to make.

- **Automatic savings.** Follow the rule of paying yourself first. Make it easy by using direct deposit. If savings are first, and discretionary income after savings, you will save. If you spend before saving, spending will always win.

- **Planned vacations.** People who know when they are going to have a vacation actually take it, as opposed to just waiting around for when they have time. If your vacation time is set ahead, you will order and organize work around it. You will be more efficient.

- **Regular team time.** Teams who have structured times to get together will get together. Those who don't tend to pass in the night and always play catch-up.

- **Regular friend time.** There are friends who you might get to-gether with as time allows and works out in the ebb and flow of life. But there are others, the closest, who you might want to have "rock time" with, when both or all three of you have it in stone to get together regularly.

- **Scheduled recreational time.** Do you have a golf day? Or a bowl-ing night? Or a fishing day? Is there a regular time that everyone knows you are going to be doing something that recreates you?

- **Scheduled spiritual time.** Make a regular appointment that is a time devoted specifically to your spiritual life, and a time to be still.

- **Routine participation in a support group, accountability group, or regular appointments with a mentor, coach, or therapist.** You will be more grounded in life if you have a regular meeting of some sort that is devoted to supporting you than if you depend only on yourself.

- **Growth-oriented activities.** Some professions have continuing education requirements that must be fulfilled each licensure period. As a result, the professionals keep growing because these hours are not optional. Treat your own growth in the same way, requiring a certain number of hours to be in your calendar, and a certain amount of money budgeted to your own growth and development.

Even though this is just a suggested list, and on first glance it may seem like a lot, ask yourself, "Are there really any of these that I would want to look back at and realize never happened because I was too busy?" These all seem pretty vital, although not urgent.

In sum, do not depend on yourself to do the vital activities when you have time. The reality is that you won't have time if you wait until you do. Identify the things that are most important to you—your rocks—and give them a place in stone on your calendar. Then put the pebbles in. You will be glad you did.

nine

Follow the Misery and Make a Rule

Think about the process involved when something gets banned, when something is no longer allowed. Usually it comes about following some sort of bad occurrence, or a series of them. When people prove themselves to be unable to responsibly do something, that practice is no longer allowed. When too many drunken accidents occur on a college campus, a rule appears: no more alcohol on campus. When too many accidents happen on a certain patch of freeway, a rule against that level of speed is posted. If there are too many misuses of a certain freedom in a company, the brass reels in that misused privilege: no more corporate credit card. Rules are instituted to keep the order that people are not keeping themselves. They limit and they protect.

Sometimes, rules exist in the other direction. They are positive in nature, requiring the presence of some good behaviors. You must have a physical exam every year to get a special rate. A doctor must attend a certain amount of hours of continuing education to have a license. So, there are negative rules and positive ones—thou shalt nots and thou shalts.

Most times, the rules we encounter are imposed from outside ourselves. Our organizations have them, the government has them, schools have them, even private clubs, home-owner associations, and hobby groups have requirements. We run into rules as part of most external structures in our lives. In fact, they would not be structures or organizations without policies that hold them together and help define them. Those are their boundaries.

PERSONAL POLICIES

But what about you personally? What are your rules for yourself? I am not talking about the ones that your faith prescribes for you or that your moral code dictates. Again, those often arise from the outside or if even if they don't, they are probably somewhat universal in nature. Having a personal moral code against lying is pretty universal, so I would not call that a personal rule, just for you. What I am talking about are nonuniversal rules that are the policies of how to be you. They are rules that you make just for yourself.

These have to do with areas of your life in which you are morally, legally, and ethically free to engage, but that you have found are not the best practices for you. There is nothing wrong with them, per se, and no outside agency would have a problem with you if you broke the rules or engaged in the activities. No one would even mention it. But, your life would not go as well if you did. It is in these areas that wise people, although free to do otherwise, have self-rules that they have learned to live by. They are your own personal policies that protect good aspects of life for you and limit negative outcomes. They are the ways you either limit or exert your own personal freedom to make life better for you and to reach your own objectives, business or personal.

Often, they relate directly to the problem we discussed in chapter 1 regarding the disappearance of time and space boundaries for work. Whereas in earlier times, work ended at a certain hour and was done in a certain space, nowadays that is no longer true. With computers, PDAs, cell phones, and e-mail, you are free. You are no longer constrained by time or space. You can do work anytime and anywhere. But the downside is that while technology has given us all of this freedom from the boundaries of time and space in work, it has freed work to extend itself to all of our time and space.

> We are free, and now we are trapped in our freedom.

We cannot find a place to get free from all of this freedom. At times, we want to say, "Somebody lock me up, away from my freedom." As Jim Carey says, "Somebody stop me!" We need to be rescued from space-and-time work freedom—and from total accessibility. So, while it may be possible and moral for you to work anytime or anywhere you want, it may also not be good. That is where your personal policies or rules come in, to limit yourself from doing things that you are certainly free to do, but that may not be the best for you.

Other times, the need for personal rules is present in areas of freedom other than work. Not only are you free to work more than you should, you are also free to have conversations with toxic people, all you want. But just because you are free to do it doesn't mean you should. You are free to not have a regular bedtime and free to pull all-nighters several nights a week. But, freedom and wisdom are not always the same. You need some rules to protect you from all that you are legally and morally free to do.

So what you find is that in being your own local government, you might have to adhere to some local rules that in your experience are needed to avoid a lot of misery. Let me give you an example from my own life.

In writing books, there is no set job description. Those kinds of boundaries especially don't exist for me, as writing is not all I do. Unlike some authors who only write, like novelists, I do not take time off, or away, when it is time to write a book. I have ongoing activities that are usually in some way related to the ongoing process of change in people's or organizations' lives, and that requires that I be there. So, long stretches of time away from my other work is not practical. Therefore, I have to write in the midst of my other activities.

As a result, I have historically written at home, at night, on the weekends, and in many ways during my own personal time, and correspondingly, in my own space—home. I did not have writing hours. For the final few months, when a book deadline was approaching, two things happened. First, I did a lot of work late at night, at home, and on the weekends. This meant I was losing any time for myself. Since I had to get it done apart from work, it always crept into more and more of my time and space until there was none left for me. Second, and maybe worse, even when I was not working on it, I felt as if I should be. After all, I wasn't doing anything—just reading or watching a movie or thinking about going to the driving range or going for a walk or a bike ride. I have a computer at home. I could be writing and getting it done. And since I could, I felt as if I should.

Even when I was "off," I was "on." I felt like I was always at work even when I was not, because I could be doing it. It was there. So it was whispering in my ear all the time.

When my first daughter was getting a little older, I really began to feel it. She would want to play and I could feel the tug. I wanted to play with her, but hey, a book was due. I could—and should—be working on it.

Then I made a decision that changed everything. I needed a rule, or a few of them. I decided that I needed two things to rescue me from the freedom to work whenever I wanted to, as a writer. I needed the structure of a writing job. The kind of job that had two important structures to contain it: time and space. I needed protection from the ability of work to follow me home in a hovering kind of way, and to always be talking to me no matter what else I was doing. So, I made two rules: First, there would be no work at home. Second, regular hours must contain the writing task. I could no longer think that I could write whenever—at night or on the weekends. (Interestingly, I found that I needed to add another rule: no working on airplanes. I discovered that if I used that time to read a newspaper or watch a movie or read a magazine, the return I got was remarkable. But that is a different matter.) Regular work hours must contain the writing aspect of what I do.

I felt so empowered. I was going to get a life back—until I realized something. The space issue was going to be a problem. I could not write at our resource company office. That would not work at all. There would be too many interruptions, and it was too busy and noisy. I was going to have to have a special place to write in if I were not going to write at home. That meant something very painful for a cheapskate like me. I needed to rent a space. What? This is going to cost me not only time, but money? I don't know if I can deal with this, I felt. It is a lot easier to write books telling others that they need to make these kinds of painful changes than to do it myself. But I was determined. So I found a small space and bit the bullet. Space issue solved.

But there was still the time issue that remained that I had not anticipated. I had decided to write during regular hours, no writing after hours or on weekends anymore. I had regular hours and dedicated space. So, I began to do that. And then I discovered something. I could not be at that space and treat that time like the rest of the time at the office. I could not take conference calls, write e-mails, work on projects, and then write for a few hours. There were still interruptions. The space thing was better, but the time one was not solved.

Then, a miracle happened. I should have seen this, but a friend of mine talked me into a dedicated day for writing. She challenged me to block out a day and make a rule: nothing else on that day except writing. No projects or other work on that day of the week. All I can say is that it changed my life. Two simple rules to take away some freedom gave me more freedom than I could have ever had without them.

There would be no work after hours and no work at home. As a result of doing that, and a day for only writing, I found something else occurred. I lost a day of work, right? Since I had a dedicated writing day, I had lost a day that used to be available to me to do other things. But when I did, I found that I got a lot more efficient in my use of time on the other days because now, just like a budget, I had only so much to spend. I began to get things done in a whole new way. I was forced to focus on the things that were really important, because each time I had a "time choice," I knew that I did not have an unlimited bank account. If I spent my time on one thing, then I could not buy time anywhere else. It was gone. And now, with my new rules, I had to get it all done in regular time. My rules made me lean and mean. By having less time, I got more done.

That is the paradox of a rule—though it limits you in some ways, it simultaneously empowers you in others. The limit forces you to efficiency. It helps you make better use of what you have and gets you focused within a real space. Here is the principle:

Freedom that is unlimited causes a lack of focus.
Freedom within boundaries, within a structure, is real
freedom. You become all that you can be within that space.

I hope I will never go back to the old system. Interesting enough, in this particular book that you are reading, my publisher and I made a change in the structure of the book after I had begun, and with my final months of the year already booked with a lot of travel, etc., I had to break my rule for a couple of weeks. In other words, for a couple of weeks, I did some weekend writing and some at night at home. And I can promise you, from the pot calling the kettle black, it has reaffirmed to me in a million ways how true what I am sharing with you is. I was reminded

how much I love my personal policies and the freedom that a few structured, self-imposed rules have brought me.

There were two huge effects. First, I got my life back from the tech-
nological freedom of time and space. When I made a rule limiting the
unlimited time and space, I got more time, and I got my space back. I
picked up my nights and weekends, so I had time for myself again. And
my home was a work-free zone. When I went there, I could feel it all go
away. Work was not a fog that hung right above my head and below the
ceiling. It was no longer hovering. I was free.

RULES—THE CURE FOR MISERY

Now before you get defensive and push back at the idea of having rules in
your life, understand something. If you knew me well, you would know
that I am not a very "rulesy" person. I know those kinds of people and
they are usually not the ones I like to hang around. So, I am not coming
at this topic as a purveyor of rules for rules' sake. I am coming at it from
a different angle.

I think you only need rules when you find that something is continually happening that you do not want to happen, or something is not happening that you desire. And, some sort of misery is the result.

In the example about my writing life, it was a little of both. I was
having a lot of misery in that I felt like I had no free time, no getting
away from it all. And, I was losing other things that were not happening
in my life as a result of work taking all that time. I had operated under
the assumption that I could work here or there at home, get a little done
when I was able. But, after coming out of denial, I had to face the music
and admit that I was not able to do that well. I could not manage it. So,
I could not have that freedom anymore, thinking I might just do a little
here or there. I needed a rule to stop the misery and get the things that I
desired: no work at home and no extra hours.

Here is the point. I do not suggest that for everyone, but only for those
who can't seem to achieve some kind of desired result, like I couldn't.
That is when a rule is needed.

I was talking to a CEO recently about this topic and he said that it
took him thirty years to figure this out, but that it has changed his life
also. He and his wife have a little getaway cabin on a lake not far from
his home. They bought it to retreat from the hustle and bustle like many

couples do in various ways. They looked forward to owning it when they bought it, as they had very hectic lives. But he quickly realized something when he began going there. The space was not enough. He was free to take it all with him, at least in his head, when he was there.

He said that he would go there sometimes, have a plan to spend some time there, and then go back home because he would need to get some things done. But, when he looked at it that way, he would find himself at the cabin after spending the night, and early the next morning begin to feel the pressure, the gnawing inside, that he better get going and go "do all the things he had to do. Better get on the road and get to 'it,'" whatever "it" was, he said. He found that when he was there, he was actually not there. So, he made a rule: He would define the time specifically that he was going to be there as the no-work zone and make that a rule. "I will be at the cabin until noon, with no work, and then I will go back home and get some things done."

He said that a miracle occurred. Just because he had added the structure of a no-work zone until noon, he found that he could actually enjoy the time he was there. He was not fretting, thinking, "I need to get going, get on it." Instead, his mind had a time-off zone, and he finally allowed himself to be there. It would have not mattered, as he said, whether the time were noon, 11:00 AM, or 1:00 PM. That was not the issue as that could always change. What mattered was that he had a rule for when he would be there with no work, and in that time when there was no work allowed, he was able to enjoy it. He said that he now comes back refreshed and ready to go, and the cabin has been a lifesaver.

While you may not be in the position to have a space with your rule, like a weekend getaway, you can have the rule do the same thing for you in whatever space you use. You can do this in your office or at home or at a park. Just have a no-work rule for a space of time, if work is in your way. Set it in stone, and it will give you freedom as you already know that you can afford it when you set it aside. Here is the principle:

Find the misery, and set the rule.

Your rules can be related to work or other aspects of life, wherever the freedom to be miserable is taking over and needs to be limited. Here are some examples I have seen, in different contexts of life.

Toxic Relationships

There are some people who for whatever reason are able to make you miserable. We will look at various ways of handling that in chapter 13. But for now, realize that making a rule or two for yourself can keep you from a lot of misery.

I know one leader, Jay, whose CEO is a stress machine. He manages, by his mere presence and the heavy-handed negative loads he dumps on people, to make everyone's blood pressure go up. He gets agitated and infuses others with stress about business problems, off-loading all of his anxiety onto his direct reports. This tendency was becoming a problem for Jay in one recurring way. It seemed that often, right at the end of the day, his CEO would have one of his fits, and Jay would find himself getting overly stressed immediately before he left for home. Jay noticed that late in the day was the worst time for the CEO.

After these interactions, Jay would go home and find himself unable to relax, unable to connect with his wife and kids, and generally in a lousy mood. He was not taking his work home with him. He was taking his CEO home with him—in his head. So, until he could get this worked out, he made a rule: I will not allow myself to talk to the guy after 4:00 PM. Jay stayed in his office and worked, or set meetings with other people at that time. Of course, if there were some reason that Jay found that he had to see the CEO, he did. But as much as it was up to him, he realized that he needed to make this a rule. When he did, Jay said that everything changed. When he made it a rule that he would not interact with his boss right before he went home, he became a different person.

I have a business relationship with a person that is very, very difficult to talk to. This person can turn a simple conversation that should last two minutes into a fifteen-minute Supreme Court case. He just has a way of making it a lot harder than it needs to be. So, I have a rule: I never call this person if I have anything following the call that requires a clear head and concentration. I know that I am going to need a cold-water head dunk afterward, so, I just do not want to be in the position of talking to such a downer right before something important.

I know other people who have extended family members who are so toxic that they do not allow themselves to visit them alone. They make a rule: I will visit them only if I can take a friend with me. They find that to not be alone with that person is the only way that they can keep from being hurt by them.

I have instructed people who have mean and hurtful people in their lives to tell them, "I will be glad to talk to you about this. But I will only do it in a counselor's office." Just make a personal rule that you are not going to get into another hurtful conversation that you know is not going anywhere good. When they try to bait you, stick to your rule and do not have that conversation.

Several years ago, I was accosted by a drunk neighbor who did not like the way I had parked my car on the street. It became clear about a minute into the conversation that he was not going to be reasonable. I just interrupted and said, "I am sorry, but I have a rule. I don't talk to people who are intoxicated. Call me tomorrow and I will be glad to discuss this." And I walked off, with him screaming all the way. I never heard from him, as he probably did not even remember the incident, but what stood out to me was what happened with the friend who was with me.

She told me that that little rule changed her entire relationship with a difficult person in her life. She had never thought about it, but she could have rules that she lived by, and not talking to someone screaming at her could be one of those. It's a small thing, but for her it was a big one.

There may be people in your life with whom you are getting negative results, and with whom you need some rules. And remember, these are not rules for them, but for you. In the conversation with the drunk, notice that I did not say he was not allowed to talk to me that way. He could do whatever he wanted. Instead, I said that I did not allow myself to talk to someone who was TWI (talking while intoxicated). That is a big difference, and back to our original idea about self-control. The rule is for you, not the other person. Let him talk all he wants. I just won't be there listening.

In work settings, there may be some people that you need some personal rules with, even some they will never know about. It is your decision who you will allow yourself to talk to, who you will not allow yourself to talk to alone, when you will allow yourself to talk to some people, and when you won't, etc. Stay in charge of yourself, and when you do not absolutely have to interact with a certain person, don't let yourself get sucked into one of those conversations. If you do, then examine the power drain inside of you that drives that decision.

Look at the misery, and then make a personal rule that will keep it from happening.

Managing Energy for High Performance

Only you know where the misery or the lack of productivity is in your work, so only you can know where some rules are needed and what the rules should be. For some people, my rules of no work at home and no work after hours would create more stress than it would relieve. I realize that, and that is why I said they are personal. But the point here is that you need them if the normal ebb and flow of the way you are going about it now is not working. Remember, find the misery, and then make a personal rule that will keep it from happening.

Here is another example. As a speaker, sometimes I am asked to give a presentation that I have given before, and very little preparation is needed. If I am asked to talk about one of my books, for example, I pretty much know what I am going to say. But other times, the request is of an individual nature, as the organization has a particular need for a topic to be addressed. Many times companies have a theme to their meeting or convention or training, and much strategic planning goes into a given talk with their team and myself. It is then I need individual time to plan my part of it alone.

I noticed in the early years of doing this that I often did not understand how much prep time was needed until I was doing the actual prep. In other words, if I felt as if I knew the topic, and knew more or less how to speak to it, I thought I could plan the talk the day before I had to give it. But then something kept happening. Things would come up on that day, and my prep time would get pushed into the night or the next morning, many times on the road. I would be up late or up early, putting the final touches together. It always worked, but I hated the process. It seemed that I was always rushed at the end, and I was not enjoying one of the more enjoyable aspects of my work. I was not enjoying speaking. Misery.

But then I realized it was not the speaking I did not like but the stress surrounding it all. So, I made a rule with myself: If I were going to speak, I had to have my content organized a week or more before the event. That was the rule. So, I began to put an appointment in my calendar to plan the talk at a certain time, just like the event itself. Whereas I used to see only the event as the event, I realized that there were actually two events to every event. There were the speaking and the planning, and I had to treat the planning with the same rule as the event itself. I had to show up at a certain time. In the same way that I could not be late for the speech, I could not fail to show at the appointed preparation time either.

This simple rule restored the fun to the entire process. It is a whole different experience to not be rushed the day or night before, and to know way ahead of time what I am going to do and say. Nothing changed except that a little rule limited my freedom to make myself miserable.

I have found that energy management is similar, and in talking with many executives, they share that experience. In fact, I think that in performance coaching, energy management is as important as time management. It does no good to have time for something that you do not have your best energy to perform. And in the management of energy, rules are important.

To use my speaking life as an example again, I found that three things affected performance. First, meetings before a speaking event were an energy drain, and I learned to have a rule against them. Sometimes, especially when travel is involved, a big conference or convention is a place where not only the big event is occurring, but many people that you need to meet with are all gathered in one place, and it is a good time to get with them and save yourself another trip. So, often, if I were going to be speaking somewhere, I would get requests from someone to "get together before you speak." That is a great idea, and I would do it, until I found that after some of those meetings I did not have all of the creative energy available that I would need for the event. Even positive business interactions take energy, much less the problem-solving sessions. So, I found that I needed a rule: no meetings before giving a talk. That really helped.

Second, I found that a late arrival time the night before was an energy drain also. Weather delays, air traffic, and just getting in late and having no down time before an early event was not affording me my best available energy for the event. To go before an audience of thousands of people and not feel as if all the cylinders were firing was just not good, and sometimes even frightening. So, I made a rule: no late arrivals. I began to plan my travel in a way that got me in before dinner, and it made that part of my work totally different for me—and much better for the poor souls who had to listen to me.

Third, I have reactive hypoglycemia. That means that I can be subject to blood sugar lows if I do not have the right amount of protein in my system to ride out the glucose curve. I had one experience where in front of about seven thousand people I almost had to leave the stage. I found out afterward that they did not notice, but I was literally confused and about to faint. That was the extreme. There were other examples where it did not get that bad, but I had some energy lows with the low blood sugar. So, I created my third rule: Never give a talk without eating a high-protein meal beforehand.

Those three rules have changed that part of my life drastically. I allow myself no meetings, no late arrivals, and no skipping meals. If I keep those, the misery index is definitely lower.

Look at your own energy, along with your time, as your greatest resource. I find that many people allow the less important time eaters to use up the time when they're at their best, and then they give their leftover energy to some of the highest priorities. Ask yourself some questions to gauge your misery index, and then make some rules to address those issues. Here are a few examples to help get you started:

- **When do you need your best energy? For which activities?**
  You want to have the best of you available for the most important things. So, before you even think about managing your energy, look at your activities, work and personal, and ask yourself which are the most important and which are going to take the most energy.

- **When is your best energy available to you?** Is that when you schedule the most important activities? If you are best in the morning, try your best to give that time to the most important matters and activities. If you are so-so in the midafternoon, give that time to the less important meetings, or to tasks that do not require the most of you. Instead of scheduling things when there is an opening, weigh your openings and assign value to them. Just like hotels have high season and charge more for that time, you have a high season for your energy, and you should charge more for that time as well. Give it to the most expensive tasks. If I have to meet with someone and the issue is not that important, I always try to put it into a time slot that is not the best of my time. My assistant has heard more than once, "You gave that block of time to that meeting? Go get it back! I need that for better uses!" Give your best time to the best uses. Here's an example of an energy rule: Do not give mornings between 9:00 AM and noon to operational conference calls. Save that time for strategic alliances or client meetings, if that is the time you feel the more energized and creative.

- **What are your energy drains?** Are there certain tasks that take it all out of you? If so, and we all have them, quarantine their effects. Make sure that you do them at a time when whatever follows them is not an activity for which you need to be up. Do them at a time when you can afford to be miserable afterward. Here's an example of an energy drain rule: Do not do line-by-line expense budgeting before meeting with a new client. (I think it may be evident that microdetails are my particular energy nemesis. It may be the opposite for you.)

- **Who are your energy drains?** What people take it out of you? If possible you might want to make a rule against interacting with some of them, and give them to someone else. But if that is not possible, make another rule about when you will meet with them. For example, meet with Joe only if you have nothing important afterward—or a root canal scheduled.

- **What physical practices impact your energy?** I mentioned my blood sugar problems and travel/rest examples. What are those for you? Are you someone who needs a certain amount of sleep? Or a certain diet to have the energy you need? What about a certain amount of exercise? Do you know much about energy management physically? I find that many people do not, and they should. Your brain runs on two important fuels: oxygen and glucose. Do you get enough movement, which gets oxygen to the brain? Do you get the right food you need? (For a good book on this topic, see *The Corporate Athlete*, by Jack Groppel.) Figure out what rules you need to make for physical life to have the energy you need to make your life work. I have a friend who found that he was watching TV late every night and did not have the energy he needed for early morning meetings. Here's a good rule in this category: Do not watch any show that runs after 10:00 PM. Record it instead. Another friend found that local news was interrupting sleep, as it was all about murders and car accidents. Don't watch local news right before bedtime.

I mentioned earlier that if you have time and energy, you can pretty much find everything else you need. But if you do not isolate and quarantine the drains on both of these, you will not have it in you to go get what you need. You will feel one of the two most uttered sentences that prevent people from accomplishing what they need to accomplish. "I don't have time" and "I don't have it in me." In my experience, getting a handle on the misery that is creating both of those experiences and making a rule to prevent them is like finding a gold mine full of time and energy. And from there, the sky is the limit.

Wisdom and Random Rules

We saw earlier how in human development, structure is internalized from the outside and becomes internal. Teach a child that if he chooses A then B is coming, and he begins to think in a linear path. Therefore, he makes choices that are going to give him the B that he desires. In other words, before the misery comes, he learns to make a choice that is going to prevent it. That is the move to maturity.

Sometimes, we do not know the structure of life or certain situations or certain relationships until we are in them. So, we do not anticipate the ways that those jobs, projects, contexts, or relationships need to be structured. We don't know what causes misery until we are there.

But, once we are there, and the misery becomes a pattern, we need to realize that this is not a one-time occurrence. It is a pattern. And we need to take ownership of the reality that whatever internal structure we are depending on to not have this happen is not working. If it were, we would not be having the problem on an ongoing basis. That is the time to realize that "I do not remember that if I do A then I will hate my life because B will happen." Therefore, I need a rule to keep me from doing A so I will not get any more occurrences of B. Said another way: When "I better not do that or I am not going to like myself tomorrow" is not working, then we have to change to "I have a rule against doing that."

Wisdom is, among other things, knowing to not do what we already have experienced as not helpful. Wise people are not smarter than other people; they just have learned from experience or they listen to the experience of others and believe it. They do not talk themselves into "it won't be like that this time" or "it won't happen to me." They listen to experience, let it talk to them, and rise out of their denial that somehow "next time will be different." So, really, rules are about learning from your experience and not repeating the same misery for longer than it takes to learn what is creating it. To continue to do the same thing expecting different results is not wise. Listen and believe the results that you are getting, and make a rule to not do whatever is getting you the results that you do not want anymore.

An executive I know was having trouble in his marriage as his wife felt like he worked too much and was not at home enough. Upon further probing, I found also that he was not there when he was there. Thinking they might need to structure a regular night together to go out and just be together, I asked about what it was like when he did make time for the two of them to be alone. She immediately, reflexively responded, "It won't help."

"Why not?" I asked.

She took her hands and began to mimic using a BlackBerry, rapidly typing with her thumbs in mid air. "He will just be doing that the whole time we are at dinner," she said.

Wisdom would tell you that when you give time to your spouse and afterward she (or he) does not feel like the two of you were together because you spent the whole time e-mailing someone who wasn't there, going out again with BlackBerry as a threesome is not going to bring you different results. Maybe you are not mature enough to take it with you as a phone for emergencies only, and you need a rule: Leave it at home. Just leave it at home. No BlackBerry on date night. If he were to make that rule, I think his wife would be overjoyed.

I know another relationship where the wife said that their entire marriage and family was changed by one simple rule that her husband made for himself: no e-mail at home. He was aware of her feeling like he spent time on his computer that used to be time they were together, just hanging. Upon observing himself, he saw that a lot of that stemmed from getting sucked into doing work e-mail at home in the evening. But he did not see it as work. Because he would start out just surfing the Web or reading something online, he had not planned to end up working. But he did, and she would feel ignored—rightly so. So he made a rule, and he has stuck to it for several years. She says that the difference in their lives is amazing. Why? He saw the misery and ruled it out of existence.

Other couples I know put themselves on rules like their children have for television. As the average household watches more and more television every day and other vital activities such as talking get ignored, some are finding that they need to limit themselves and put themselves on a budget. Two shows a night or an hour a day or no television during dinner are all rules that I have heard espoused for those whose appetite for the vital activities of life do not rule their choices for use of time. They have to limit their cravings to use mind-numbing television in order for their more healthy desires to kick back in, like connecting with each other, taking a walk, reading a good book, practicing spiritual disciplines, working out, going to a class, or joining a support or prayer group. Just like kids who have to have snacks limited so that they will eat good food, adults sometimes need the same help to get to their higher and more vital selves.

Another executive I know has an incredible financial mind that instantly goes to work solving problems when given data. Add to that a little bit of an obsessive nature about his own finances, and if he gets to thinking about his or the family's financial picture, cash flow, savings, investments, or anything that produces mind activity or stress, his head is going to work on it. That is both a gift and a problem—especially if it occurs right before bedtime.

He noticed the misery. Often, as he and his wife have children, they would not get quiet time together until after the kids were in bed and that would be a good time to talk about a lot of things. Sometimes she would bring up an issue with financial implications, such as wanting to spend money on something, or becoming aware of a cost that she had incurred or was going to incur soon and would be a substantial chunk that would create some stress for him. When she did that, he found that he would lie awake, tossing and turning, unable to get to or stay asleep, as his mind could not stop working on the problem. Sometimes he would wake up in the middle of the night and hear and see his head working on spreadsheets in his sleep. Finally, he needed a rule: no financial discussions after 8:00 PM. If there is something to talk about, bring it up early or set a time to talk about it in the day, but not at night. If she did, he was guaranteed to be up all night, while she slept like a baby. With different personalities, they had different needs for rules. Once he did that, the misery was solved.

Someone else I know found herself slowly and steadily gaining weight. When she thought about it, nothing had changed in the big picture of food and exercise except one thing. Shopping at a new store had introduced her to a new kind of chips that were becoming a regular late night snack. Realizing this, this person decided that she was not going to eat as many of those awesome carbs as she had. She was going to cut back so this weight gain would stop.

Nice try. It did not work. If the temptation was there, it was going to happen. So, a new rule worked where willpower had failed: no chips in the house. She just had to face the fact that she did not have the structure in herself to not eat them, so the misery taught her that she needed an external rule to make sure that she was safe. If they were not there, she could not eat them. Sorry kids, if you can't control yourself, you can't be alone at home with the chips.

Addicts have known this trick for a long time. Where the self-control is not present, the misery will come unless you have some strict rules to protect yourself. The alcoholic who has not had a long time of proven recovery must make some rules to make sure the misery does not find him: no hanging around the old crowd; no going to bars; no going home alone after a trigger, go to a meeting; X number of meetings a week. Rules are not made to be broken—they are made to keep us from getting broken. The addict has learned that piece of wisdom. I just heard a woman say about an addictive romantic relationship that she had, that she did not break free until she made a rule: Don't take his call, and don't return it.

Figure out in the big areas of life, how you feel, how you relate, and how you perform—where the misery is coming from. Is there something that you do that renders you feeling awful more times than you can write off as random? Is there a person or a relationship pattern that continues to get you? Is there a practice that is interfering with your desired results? Find the misery, and rule it out. The dictionary says the word "rule" means to have things like dominion, control, and authority over an area. Self-control in your life means that you rule. So, make some.

Part Three

BOUNDARIES ON THE JOB

ten

Time, Space, and E-Mail

I was recently in Manhattan and was awestruck by the sheer volume of skyscrapers, those incredible monuments to ingenuity, reaching up to the sky for as far as I could see. I just found it to be incomprehensible how much time and brainpower had gone into the creation of such a skyline. It really is mind-boggling to take it all in at once.

Then, I started to look more closely at just one of them, an older building, probably dating from shortly after World War II. I thought about the reality that at one time that amazing structure did not exist except in an architect's head, and then on a piece of paper. From there, countless communications, phone calls, documents, blueprints, meetings, steam shovel loads, drillings, foreman's commands, crane lifts, hirings, firings, hammer blows, and the like brought that initial vision into reality. The amount of activity by human capital that went into its completion is incalculable.

Then it dawned on me. When all of that was accomplished, there were no computers. They did all of that without one PC. They got all of that done without sending one e-mail or even one word-processing document.

Then I thought of all the great books in the world written before the 1980s, and the same thought hit me. The authors wrote all of those books without one computer, one e-mail, or one Internet search. And it brought up a question. Is all of this technology really helping us?

Of course it is. I would hate to go back to typewriters, much less no e-mail. But I do think about it, and you probably have also. It seems that those folks, while having no e-mail, sure did get a lot of work done. And there are a lot of times, I have found, that because of e-mail, we don't get a lot of work done. And that is the subject of this chapter.

E-MAIL GAINS AND LOSSES

I am not here to decry e-mail or conclude that it is worthless. Not having access to e-mail today is nearly equivalent to dropping out of the world of commerce. E-mail communication is the way business is done nowadays.

I realize the benefits of e-mail all the time. In writing books, for example, I used to have to type a chapter or a manuscript, print it out, FedEx it to my editor, and wait days until changes were mailed or FedExed back to me, look them over, and then repeat the process. Editing a book and making changes took a long time and a lot of excess work compared with the process now. Today I shoot off a manuscript, it gets butchered by the editor, and he e-mails it back to me with visible tracked changes in a Word document; I look it over, make a few more changes, hit Send, and we are finished. This happens sometimes within hours, whereas the old process could take days, sometimes weeks. Nowadays, every business beyond selling hot dogs on a cart is like that. We save so much time with e-mail.

But, while we are saving so much time, we have lost some time as well. The employees in your organization and many outside it have direct access to you if they have your e-mail address, and it is a lot easier for them to shoot you an e-mail than it used to be to call or write. It takes little time or effort. Also, it is very easy to just "cc" you on whatever they are sending to everyone else within six degrees of separation of their project. So, now you are included on communications that, before, you would have never known about, nor needed to know. Both access and volume have increased, and those two factors alone can way outweigh the time savings that e-mail provides. If you are a leader, for example, who used to communicate with only a handful of direct reports, you might now have literally dozens or hundreds of people who communicate with you without going through any walls, doors, channels, or other protective boundaries of your time. They used to have to make an appointment or get through an assistant on the phone. Now, they just shoot you an e-mail.

What may be the worst part of it all is the implied assumption that because someone sent it to you, you should respond. So, by definition, you have lost control of who you need to talk with or not, and if and when you choose to talk with them. They now have more implied control of that, through e-mail, than you—if you use e-mail like a lot of people do.

Let's say you have an important meeting for one of your most important projects. But, instead of closing the door to the conference room and putting the "meeting in progress" sign on the door, you leave it open and throughout the meeting a dozen people walk in, walk up to you, and begin a conversation. You stop interacting with the people around the table and change the agenda to whatever the new one who walked in wants to talk about. When that conversation is over, you begin to turn back to your meeting and pick up where you left off. Right as you restart the conversation, a new person walks through the door and starts a new conversation with you, putting the meeting on hold again. You do this a few more times, all the while not really moving the agenda of the meeting along at all. Then, the time is up, and everyone has to go. Try pouring the foundation of a skyscraper that way. "Oops, gotta stop. Joe wants to ask me something."

Now that is a ridiculous example. No one would run a meeting in that fashion, especially for anything important, because you would lose control of what is important to you, and the interrupters would set the agenda for what gets your attention. But that is exactly what has happened with e-mail each and every day when people are at work. They sit down at their desk with an important agenda, task, or project to focus on and finish. (If not, why are they there?) So, they begin to work on that project, and then, after moments of focusing on what they really need to focus on, a little sound goes off or a small box appears on their screen, alerting them that an e-mail has arrived.

They then turn their attention from what they were working on, presumably what they have deemed important, and they read the e-mail. Then, they either answer it or go back to what they were doing. If they answer it, it could take a moment or two, or it could take them onto a whole different path of work and focus. That e-mail, just by showing up, has changed the agenda. It is like a person walking into a meeting and changing the whole focus.

Sometimes people interrupt what they are doing to respond to e-mail because they are afraid to not answer right then and there, thinking, "This person is waiting on a response. I have to get back to them."

(Remember the power drains?) Other times, they just get distracted into that task because of their own garden-variety ADD. And for still others, the e-mail distraction is a way of avoiding the task they were working on—a task that was producing anxiety for them, that was difficult, or that was simply boring. But regardless of why they got distracted, they did. Just by a simple message showing up, their entire agenda has changed, at least for the moment.

If they did not reply but just read it and returned to what they were doing, it still took a few minutes to read it, and they lost concentration and focus on what they were doing. At the very least, it was a distraction. Multiply this example by literally a hundred times for some people, and you have lost a lot of focus, attention, and I would submit, completed work and agendas.

Now, even worse than these examples are the people whose very agenda is set by their in-box. In other words, they show up at work without a clear agenda of what their goals and objectives are for that day. Instead, they immediately open their e-mail program and go to work. Whatever is in there is their work. They scan it, answer some, and skip others, with little or no plan based on anything objective or purposeful. Some answer or work on the ones that are simple or that make them feel good, and they avoid the others that are more difficult or produce anxiety. Other people focus on and go to work on the ones that tap into their own power drains, as we discussed earlier. They have psychological and relational cracks in their foundations, and holes in their fences.

In all of these cases, the point is that e-mail is in control of the person's agenda, instead of his or her own purposes driving it.

Whatever is in the in-box is what gets the attention. There is little difference in this person's goal setting and the person working the counter at McDonald's. Both serve whoever walks up to the counter.

Going back to our meeting analogy, there is no way you would run a meeting that way. You would put a boundary around that meeting, a sign on the door, that says, "no interruptions, meeting in progress." But think for a moment about your workday. Are you really in control of what you have decided is important to you, or are you allowing others to decide what you will focus on? When you get an e-mail, do you move on to that person's agenda for you, or stay on your own? That is the big question here. Who decides how you spend your time and focus?

Obviously, you cannot ignore e-mail. As I said, that would be like ignoring work itself. Instead, you would do well to think about how you are working with it. Here are the two questions I think we have to ask:

- Who is in charge of your agenda, or what you work on? You or your in-box?

- Who is in charge of your time, or when you do what? You or your e-mail?

CREATE TIME AND SPACE BY CREATING YOUR OWN AGENDA

Remember the problem. More people have access to you, and they have access to you whenever they want, just by hitting Send. They can get to you, and they can get to you now. That is not a bad thing in and of itself, as long as you can close the door and focus on your "meeting," at the times you need to. The only problem with e-mail is that there is no door. So, you have to create one.

There are two questions to worry about. Do you set your own agenda or what you are going to work on, or does your e-mail do it for you? And, do you block out time that e-mail cannot get you off task by just arriving? Do you establish a time when you are not checking it?

If you are going to spend your time doing what is important to you, you have to create agenda boundaries—or structure. It is like a school teacher saying, "OK class, it is now time for math," and spending the next hour on that lesson until it is done. It does not matter that a salesman showed up with a lot of cool history books and put them on her desk that morning. She has something called a "lesson plan," and she is going to teach it.

Certainly, checking your e-mail may—and probably should—indeed be a part of your plan for your daily work. You may look at what you have to do, and then begin to prioritize it, figuring out what has to be done first, what can wait, and what order of importance different tasks fall into. But the key is that your e-mail is just part of what is asking you for an appointment. So are all of the other things you have to do. Make sure you are the one deciding what is going to get your attention first, second, third, and so on. The problem comes when your lesson plan for the day is just your in-box, and your e-mail tells you what you are going to work on. This is not an agenda you are in control of. Much of this stuff can wait until you have first done what is important to you.

There are a lot of different methods for prioritizing what gets done when. You can pick one of the countless options available. The one that I like the best is a weekly and daily planning meeting with yourself to figure out what agenda you absolutely must move ahead in that time. (This does not mean ignoring the bigger picture, like the month, quarter, year, and longer periods of planning and objectives. You must do that to accomplish any big objective. But, here I am talking about the specific use of small chunks of time. I find that to plan at that level of detail is more realistically done on a weekly and daily basis.)

Early Monday morning, or late Friday, or whenever you find most helpful, have a meeting with yourself. Look at all that is on your plate—your important objectives—and plan the week with those in mind. Make sure you can answer the question, "If on Friday afternoon, I have gotten _____ done, it has been a good week." Then, figure out when those things are going to happen. Whatever else comes along will have to get in line, presumably in some extra space you have built in to the week to handle unexpected new issues, or maintenance work that comes up on existing ones, or when you purposely change your plan, not passively or reactively. But the key is that your agenda is set by you, certainly with awareness of what is in your in-box and including some of it, but it is not set by its very existence. Your in-box is not your boss.

Then, do the same thing for each day. Look at the time you have available and figure out what you have to get done that day for it to be spent well. "If by today I have gotten _____ done, it has been a good day." This does not mean that new things won't arrive and need your attention, but it does mean that they will get in line, or you will intentionally move them up in line. Sometimes, it means that they will not even be allowed in the door, sans emergencies. Remember, it is your day, and what you do with it is something you should be in charge of, not your e-mail.

By this, I am not trying to say not to return your boss's phone calls or respond to his or her mail. I am not saying that nothing exists in the world but you and what you care about. Certainly, we all have people and agendas we have to answer to that at times usurp what we would like to focus on. As singer-songwriter Bob Dylan said, all of us have to "serve somebody." However, many people have little or no plan for what they are going to deem worthy of focus, and they let their e-mail, i.e., other people's agendas, set that plan for them in a very passive way. Get in control of your agenda, purpose, and focus to the extent that you can.

There are times when you might like to work in a free-flowing way and see what arrives, and even respond in the moment. Great. But, if you do, make sure that you are doing that out of a choice that best serves your goals and agenda for what you want to have happen with your time.

CREATE TIME AND SPACE BY CLOSING THE DOOR

The first task is to set your own priorities and agenda, instead of allowing e-mail or other outside forces to do that for you. But now that you know what you are going to do, how are you going to make sure it gets done and not something else? Having an agenda is one thing. Sticking to it is another. Remember the analogy about people walking into the meeting and changing the focus? They had an agenda. But just because you have an agenda doesn't mean that the agenda really gets the time, unless you close the door.

Again, among successful people, you will find that there are many different ways of working. Some multitask, and some don't. Some do e-mail all day long, and some don't. Some do mail while watching Letterman at night in bed, and others do it at their desks at 5:00 AM with no distractions. There is certainly not just one way to work that is right for everyone, at least all the time.

But in this book, we are talking about having an integrated life by being in control, and control is the issue here. What I want you to ask yourself is this:

Am I the one deciding what I am going to be doing and when?

If you want to water ski and get an appendectomy at the same time, fine. Do whatever works for you. But, if you had planned to only have surgery, not water ski, and a Ski Nautique raced through the operating room and pulled you off the table, that is a different matter. You are no longer in control and your surgery may not go well, and not by choice.

The problem with e-mail is not so much when people tend to do it as when they don't not do it. The most effective people I know are people who have times when they give their entire focus to whatever they are working on—and there is no way they are going to stop what they are doing to see what just showed up in their in-box or on their BlackBerry. Certain blocks of time are guarded, and an e-mail or a phone call is not going to interrupt them or change the agenda.

So, what is important is that you are in control of your time and not e-mail or someone else. After seeing the way a lot of high achievers work, I would suggest that you think about protecting the important time in a way that an arriving e-mail or phone call or other intrusion cannot get you off track, or even distracted. Here are a few ways to do that.

Close Your E-Mail Program for a Specific, Blocked-Out Time Period

If you have decided that a certain task is important to you, like finishing a report or brainstorming a new project, assign and block out a time to do that. Then, close whatever e-mail program you use, so you will not be interrupted. Then, and only then, have you both set your agenda and protected it. Studies have shown that some people check their e-mail up to fifty times an hour. How much focus can they really have if they unplug and reengage every minute? Thought processes are not even allowed to make the associations needed to come up with the necessary ideas to solve or create something if attention is diverted to that degree.

Assign a Time for Checking E-Mail and Voice Mail and for Returning Calls

This is how a lot of high performers work. For example, they assign an hour in their schedule to read and respond to e-mail and to listen to voice mail and make calls. Or they meet with the people who handle their mail during that time, and give direction. Some might do this two times a day, others more or less. But the idea is that they are in control of when they answer mail, not the alert on their screen. Many people have a morning time that they look at mail, and an afternoon time. A high-level executive recently told me that when he decided not to check e-mail until lunch time, many of the items that had arrived early that morning were already addressed by the time he read the e-mail. All he missed out on was the drama.

If you have important calls to make, treat them like an appointment and assign them a time on your schedule. Do them on your timetable if possible. Send the person you're calling an e-mail, or have your assistant make contact to set up the time and tell them how long you'll need.

Turn Off the Ringer on Your Phone

In the old days in movies, an executive went into the office and right before closing the door told his or her assistant, "Hold all calls." That usually meant something big was going down in the plot. Certainly, people still do that, but many don't, and if they do, they still have a cell phone and someone can find them if they want to.

At times, there may be few things that are more annoying to a person you are meeting with than a cell phone ringing in and interrupting your time. If you have agreed to meet with someone, and have decided to give them your time, do you really need to take calls at the same time? One of the most effective leaders I have ever worked with has a habit. As soon as he sits down to meet with someone in his office, before saying a word, he reaches over and turns off the ringer on his phone. Everything goes to voice mail. He protects the meeting time and the people he meets with know they are there to get things done.

Certainly, there are times that are more free flowing and you can multitask and take calls or do e-mail. You are doing a lot of things at once and none of them are of a nature that cannot be interrupted. (Some jobs, like that of an executive assistant, require that e-mail is monitored on an ongoing, real-time basis.) But for most people, consider two things. First, there are times when that is not true, and whatever you are focusing on should not be interrupted unless the building is burning down or some other emergency arises. Second, there are a lot of times when interruptions keep you from doing what you really would like to see get done, even if those things are by nature interruptible. You think it is OK, but it is really not serving you well. So, be careful about your "freedom" to multitask.

Turn off the phone ringer at times you need to guard for important work. If you are not a doctor who gets life and death emergencies, then whoever is calling can probably leave you a message, and you can call them back at a time that does not keep you from doing what you have deemed important.

Create Folders

If your in-box is a place where everything just lives, then you are probably wasting a lot of time rehandling e-mails you have already looked at and decided to deal with later, either soon-later, or later-later. But, you have already looked at them, and now you are constantly shifting through your in-box figuring out what is what.

Try this. Create three separate folders: one for e-mails that require action immediately, one for those that require action soon (as you define it), and one for whenever—meaning that there is no pressing time requirement to them, but you want to keep them to either refer back to, read, or respond to at some point. The first time you read an e-mail in your in-box, move it to the appropriate folder. Then, you will save time in your in-box by not rereading and sifting through it for what you need to do. It will all be new. You can then go to your "action required" folder to actually work.

In addition, archive e-mails that require no action by creating folders for specific projects or people. Get them out of your in-box so you are not continually rereading them when you do not need to.

Close the Door

Spatial boundaries are important, especially if continuous interruptions keep you from focusing on important tasks. We talked earlier about power drains and the ways in which certain people have the ability to get you off track. You will need to be able to deal with them, certainly. But, you will have to deal with fewer of them if there are times at which you are not accessible and can create a space for yourself by closing the door, hanging up a sign, or going somewhere to get it done. Do what you need to do to make sure that you have the space you need.

Sort E-Mails by Sender

If you and someone have had many interactions about a specific issue, it may be much further along, or even resolved, than your in-box would lead you to think. Using the sort function in the From mode, collect all the e-mails from a particular sender. By reading through the most recent messages, you may find you can quickly delete many others in quick succession, because the issues have been resolved and you are current with that person or project. Or you can store them in a folder for future reference.

Ask Why

Recall what we discussed earlier about power drains. Are there certain people whose e-mails or calls take over your mind, focus, and time? If so, ask yourself why. Why do they have that kind of power over you and your sense of self-control? What do they represent to you? What issue about you is driving that? In reality, there might be nothing in the content of that e-mail that requires that kind of attention, response, anxiety, or priority from you. But there is something about the person that is able to hook you in that way. Find out why.

When I was just starting out in business, a high-performance mentor told me, "When they are really, really mad at you and upset about something, don't return their call for two days. It is good for your head." Although it may not be good advice for all situations, I understood what he meant. His point was that just because other people have decided you have to jump through a hoop for them does not mean that this particular hoop is one that really needs to be jumped through. Train yourself to be principled and self-directed by values and priorities, not by what others are imposing on you.

Set Your BlackBerry on Silent

While we have seen how e-mail programs can interrupt workflow, the BlackBerry or PDA is also a threat beyond sitting at one's desk. It extends the reach of intrusion to an entirely different level. A PDA can really help someone who is mobile to stay in touch, and for that, it has great value. I carry one myself, and as mobile as I am, I could hardly function without it. But at the same time, if we do not possess the ability either to change the setting to Silent or ignore it when an e-mail comes in or to turn it off, it can be a constant intruder to both business and personal life. The same thing holds true for cell phones. There are times to just turn off both of them. Protect that space. If you are not a doctor on call, again, can't it wait? At certain times, give complete focus to yourself and the person you are with or the activity you are engaged in.

It can be difficult to protect certain pockets of time without rules. Think about your PDA or cell phone. Has it become an open door to you that devalues everything you are doing to whatever it decides? Do you check it constantly in meetings? At dinner with friends or loved ones, does it take priority when it buzzes? Do you really want it to be your master like that? At times, decide that your life is more important than that next e-mail and turn it off. Get back in control. By turning it off for a little space, you are putting up a sign that says, "Do not interrupt. Life in progress."

ARE YOU ADDICTED?

Sometimes, when activities are meeting some need other than those they are intended to meet, you can become attached or addicted to that behavior. You develop a need for it to perform some function that regulates how you feel. For example, some people develop an inordinate need for food when they are feeling lonely or stressed, and they cannot stop eating when they are in an emotional need state. Others act out impulsively with sex to make themselves feel better. Some may overspend. Others drink too much. Still other people work to avoid other issues or feeling states in their lives. I have had many executives tell me that there are times when they know they escape into work because of how something is going at home or in the rest of life.

If you cannot be away from e-mail for some period of time to do something vital in life, like connect with your loved ones or take a walk or play golf, then something is wrong. If you cannot go to a social dinner without checking e-mail or responding to someone, something is wrong. If you can't go on vacation without constantly checking in, are you really on vacation? What about at home when you are supposed to be having downtime?

If you want to find out if someone is an alcoholic, tell them to go for a certain period without drinking and see if they can do it, and what happens when they do. Can they do it? Do they have withdrawals? You can learn a lot that way. So, test yourself. Are you capable of turning your e-mail off for a while to work? Or to enjoy some time with someone you care about? Or to have some leisure time or time of spiritual renewal? If you cannot do that, and do it without withdrawals, then you might not be checking e-mail after all. You may be running from—or avoiding—something else.

If you find that to be true, listen to that awareness and face the issue. Talk to someone you can open up to. See a coach or a good shrink.

TO THE PURE, ALL THINGS ARE PURE

Above all, remember our goal here. I am not trying to be a killjoy or a second grade teacher. As I've said, there are a lot of different ways to work, and if it is working for you, then it is working. But, and this is a big but, how do you define "working"?

While your multitasking may be enabling you to do a lot, it may not be enabling you to do what you have determined is important. One of the things I hear the most around this topic is "I am so busy, but it seems like there is just not enough time for what I think is important." While you may be very busy, or even very productive, is what you are producing with all of this activity what you really want to be producing?

The workaholic is someone who certainly produces a lot. But besides getting work done or making more money, he or she might not be producing a lot in the rest of life. I have had many people in their late thirties and forties tell me they wished they had focused on their relationships sooner, as they have climbed the career ladder only still not to have found a satisfactory relationship, even though they have been through a few. They may have experienced a high level of production and achieved their goals, but not in the whole of life, or in an integrated life as we are calling it here. Others have said that it has been too much "all about me." They have neglected their spiritual development or service to other people or causes.

Sometimes other people have seen that their work lives have kept them too much from their spouses, children, or hobbies they care about. When this happens, we have to ask why. When someone tries to fill the whole pie chart of life with work, what is driving that?

At times, they are running. They are running from pain or emptiness they would feel if they ever slowed down. Give them a vacation or some time off, and they don't know what to do with themselves. They get restless or even depressed. This is always a sign that work is not "pure." It is being used to serve some kind of defensive function in their life.

At other times, work is being used to keep them from some kind of fear or feeling of inadequacy in another part of life. They may be strong in work, but they are threatened or have been hurt in love. So, they ask work to fulfill all of them, a task for which it was not designed. Ultimately, it does not work.

Be careful when you say to yourself, "Oh, but my work is my life. I love it." It is good that you love your work, but if it is literally your "life," then you have either defined life in a very limited way and do not know what you are missing, or you have retreated from some part of life that is too scary or painful to dive into. Ultimately, your work cannot be your whole life. It will break down at some point or leave you empty and unfulfilled. Also, it's important to consider what happens when you retire. Gaining a well-rounded life now will prepare you better for retirement, when you will need a life after the work is gone. So, if you are the multitasker who truly has all the pie working so well that you and those who love you are happy, then I say, "Awesome." But, if you are the multitasker who might love the way you work but has either colleagues or loved ones desiring more focus, or even your own heart, then find a way to turn it off and find the results that are missing.

eleven

Getting Your Balance Sheet in Order

"What do you do when you realize a client is toxic and you can't stand to deal with them?" a woman asked in a leadership workshop.

"It is not good for you, or for your client, to allow them to be a nightmare to you," I said. "You might have to give a bit of a 'performance review' to your client about the way your relationship is going and what your expectations are from clients."

"I can't do that," she said. "The CEO of this company is not the kind of person you give feedback to like that. I would lose them. He would say, 'Deal with it or we will find someone who can.'"

"Then you have to ask yourself if you want to deal with it or not, and it sounds as if you don't," I said. "So, you might have to fire the client." (I talk more about this in chapter 12.)

"But, I have to deal with it," she replied. "I don't have a choice."

"You have contractual obligations that would not let you get out?" I asked.

"No, I could get out contractually," she said. "I just could not afford to get out financially."

"What do you mean?" I asked.

"Well, this client," at this point she hesitated and turned a bit red, "provides over half of my revenue. I can't afford it," she said.

"Oh," I said. "That is a very different problem. Then you don't have a client problem at all. You have a business problem. Let's talk about that first."

And that is what this chapter is about: what to do first.

Obviously she could not just tell her client to shape up or go away. She would be out of business. And, just as obvious, at least to me, she could not continue in that relationship long-term and thrive, at least in the way it was at present. So, if quitting today is not an option, and staying long-term is not an option, what is the right action today? The answer? End the dependency by getting her balance sheet in order.

She had gotten herself into a situation, for good reason or bad, that is untenable long-term. She was dependent on a client for survival. Of course, there are seasons, like in start-ups or in transitions or "launch strategies," when that makes sense. And sometimes it is even done on purpose as one business helps launch another one, even one they do not own but rather need to exist.

END THE DEPENDENCY

One of the first orders of business is survival, and if a business is dependent upon another entity for survival, then its fate truly is in someone else's hands. There are many nonstrategic situations where a business or a person gets into a relationship they need for survival in some way, and whenever that happens, they are at the mercy of however the other person or entity wants to treat them. It could be a business, a boss, a job, a friend or lover, or other relationship. But the key indicator is that there is a dependency—financially, emotionally, or relationally—that is not healthy and keeps someone in bondage, even if that bondage is benign (which ultimately it never is).

Remember, this book is about self-control. You can never have the freedom of self-control if you are totally dependent on another person. The reason is that sometimes you cannot survive the consequences of making the choices you need to make. If you need to confront someone, for example, and tell them you are not going to tolerate certain treatment or certain conditions, you can't do that if you cannot survive their being angry at you, firing you, rejecting you, not talking to you, suing you, not liking you, or whatever the consequence is. Freedom is not needing anything from any single person or entity for survival.

But that does not mean that we do not need people and entities. We do. We need each other. We survive by needing each other—relationally, emotionally, and financially. The difficulty arises from needing any one particular person or entity in order to survive. On the one hand, if a man or woman cannot psychologically survive if their spouse is upset with them, for example, then they are not free to be honest with him or her when needed. But on the other hand, if they have many supportive relationships that will stand with them through a difficult period of confrontation, for example, then they do not have to endure abuse. That is one of the keys to turning a difficult relationship around, i.e., to have the strength in your corner to be able to do what is necessary to get the other person to change.

The woman in the workshop certainly needs customers to survive. But her business problem was not about this client at all. Her business problem was about the clients she didn't have, not the one she had. If she had had many others, so that this person did not have the leverage and power with her that he did, she could deal with him in a way that could potentially solve the problem. She could have said to him something like, "I want to talk about the way that we work together and see if we can do better. I get more calls and requests for problem solving and crises with you and your company than is the norm. Let's work together to find out why this is the case and come up with a solution."

It is very possible that from a strong position she could have helped him see how he had some issues inside his organization that were not only creating problems for her, but were likely problematic for other relationships and within the company as well. She could have been a good partner, and helped him, as she solved her own problem with him. Usually when we confront a friend, for example, about an issue we are having with him or her, it helps that person in other relationships as well. As I said to the woman in the workshop, any time you are so dependent on a client that you cannot be honest with him, then you are no longer serving that client well. We need to be able to be honest with people in order to serve them, to help them. If we are afraid of the consequences of being honest, then we have lost our usefulness to them.

So, the first order of business for the woman in the workshop was not to deal with her problem client. Her first order of business was to get enough other business so she was not dependent on him, at which point she could deal with him in a helpful way. Or, she needed to find a way, through other sources of capital or cutting expenses, to be able to survive without his business. Then, and not until then, would she be free from him.

Similarly, you will not be able to have good boundaries and self-control in your own situation, business or personal, if you are in a state of financial, relational, emotional, or any other type of dependency. Just like we want children to grow into a state of adulthood in which they can survive without parents, we want adults to be able to survive on their own and not be held captive by any toxic situation—to be able to walk if necessary. Are you in that position?

POSITION YOURSELF FOR STRENGTH

If you are going to get in control of your life, you are going to have to do just that—get in control. You cannot control other people, but you can get in control of yourself. You have to be able to make the choices you need in order to make your life work, belong to you, and integrate around the things important to you. That may require you to set some boundaries and limits with some people.

In the upcoming chapter on communicating your boundaries, we will talk about having some difficult conversations. In the chapter on endings and pruning, we will talk about why some relationships need to go away. But, to do both of those, you will have to be in a position of strength, not a position of dependency. Consider the following scenarios:

- You need to confront a spouse who is in denial about a significant problem, such as substance abuse.

- You need to confront a difficult boss about mistreatment.

- You need to talk to an unreasonable or abusive client.

- You need to tell someone you are dating that something needs to change.

- You need to tell your boss or team that their strategy is not going to work and they should wake up and smell the coffee before it is too late.

- You need to tell a direct report that there is something about his or her performance that must change.

But what if the following things are also true?

- You cannot handle your spouse being upset with you and you know that he or she will be upset if you confront the issue.

- You need the job so much you are afraid your boss will fire you and you doubt your ability to get another job.

- You can't survive without the client.

- You can't stand the thought of being without a relationship.

- You are afraid your boss or the team will react badly, and you can't stand for them to be upset with you.

- You have grown to need your direct report's performance so much that if he or she walked you do not know what you would do.

If these things are true, you are not in a position to deal with what you need to deal with, and are not really in control of you. But what if the following were true?

- You have joined a codependency or support group that is going to stand with you when you confront your spouse's substance problem, and will be there for you if things go really badly. You won't be alone.

- You have taken classes, increased your skills, have heightened your "hire-ability," and have gone on interviews and already have other offers.

- You have built up your business to the point that this client represents only a fraction of your sales, and you are so well connected that you will be able to use that extra time to build even more.

- You have a strong foundation of friends, a support system, and self-confidence. And while breaking up would be sad, it would not be devastating. You would not be alone at all, but would have lots of friends to be with as you move to the next stage.

- You have so many people who believe in you and like you, that any one person's disapproval of your opinion, or a conflict with them, would not unnerve you. You would be strong through the battle of ideas. And like the second scenario, if you got booted, you would be fine.

- You know that you are in charge of your business and have not allowed it to be dependent on any one person's performance.

So, remember, you will not be able to be in control of your own life until you have strengthened your personal balance sheet. Your "equity" has got to be strong. You have to have a lot of assets in order to be able to do two things:

- Be who you need to be for yourself and have what you need to have happen, happen.

- Be the servant of others you need to be. You cannot serve someone you are toxically dependent on as you are not free to love them in the way that they might need at times, i.e., through tough love.

Be in the business of upping your equity, which means increasing your assets over your liabilities, building up your balance sheet of life. Here are some of the assets that you will need to be in a position of strength:

- Develop a strong support system of friends who will stand with you when you have to do something difficult or when you might lose someone's approval or even relationship. This may take some time, depending on your situation. But, in the beginning, you could join some existing support groups until your own support system is in place.

- Go beef up your skills so that you will have more job opportunities than you want, and more people who need you than you have time for.

- Get more credentials, education, or training not only to raise your marketability but your confidence as well.

- Focus on business growth so that the vulnerabilities you have to any particular market, customer, or other downturn will not be fatal.

- Get strongly grounded spiritually so that when difficulties occur, relational turmoil happens, or other times of upheaval come, you have a foundation to depend on. Many times people face issues of meaning, spirituality, and the things that matter deeply to them in a crisis. But to be strong in those issues before a crisis is real strength.

- Find a few people who are specifically dedicated to helping you in the moment of dealing with the crisis, i.e., available to talk to you right before the difficult confrontation, role play it with you, and be there for you right after and in subsequent weeks.

- Get the coaching or counseling that you need to deal with whatever or whomever you are dealing with in the bigger picture. Pay for it if necessary, but get it. A mentor is good, and sometimes a professional is better as it is more directly focused, structured, and protected.

- Join a support group, or put a peer group together. I remember one group of women I knew who all were going through job changes and had a 7:00 AM conference call each morning for fifteen minutes to support each other, and hold each other accountable for the steps they had to take that day.

- Get your financial house in order. If you do not have savings, or are in debt, that is a weak stone in your foundation that makes it difficult to take strong stances. Go get help if you have not been able to accomplish this. You need to be able to sustain substantial periods of no income to truly have choices.

- Develop a dedicated growth path for your relational and life issues. If you have never been in personal counseling, therapy, or some sort of growth path to work through whatever your own relational and life issues are, do it now. It could be formal or informal, but if you do not repair those dynamics and cracks in the foundation, they will diminish your strength.

- Grow in specific relationship and life skills. Take a workshop on communication, assertiveness, or conflict resolution so you can face difficult situations with more strength. Take a listening course, or a course on negotiation, or others. The idea here is that successful people are people who have taken the time to develop the life skills they need to negotiate tough situations.

- Find a "growth community" of some sort. Whether that be a spiritual community, a recovery group, a professional network, or a community college, be a part of a community of people who are getting better at life. Growth begets growth in people, and it is good to be in some sort of community that encourages it.

Remember, we are talking about a balance sheet here, not a short-term loan. These are real assets, and like all assets, the more valuable ones take time to build. These are not quick fixes. Put the time and effort into these and see them as goals that are going to take months—some of them years—to get to where you ultimately want them. But it is well worth the effort.

In the short-term, seek to grow your assets on your balance sheet by going to places where you can immediately find the things you need. Go see a professional for immediate help or join an already existing support structure. Then, from that foundation, you can build out. See it as venture capital.

A LAW OF THE UNIVERSE

This principle of human functioning is what I call a law of the universe:

Strength and security precede the ability to be free.

It begins at birth. You do not see a hungry baby walk away from her mother. She does that years later, only after she has had her needs met. You do not see a weak, dependent spouse walk away from an addict. He does that later, after he has joined an Al-Anon group to give him the strength. You do not see people who have no savings or little chance for another job tell an abusive boss to stick it. They do that later, after they have saved enough money or gotten a further degree or gotten another job. You do not see people walk away from a negotiation with poor terms if they have to make that deal. You see the ones who do not need the deal walk away from terms that are not favorable to them. You do not see people who are spiritually and/or relationally bankrupt walk through tough circumstances unscathed and do well right after. You see them transcend those circumstances as a result of having spiritual and/or relational equity in their lives.

So, this begs a question. If there is some situation in your life in which you are out of control in a way that is disintegrating your life, heart, soul, or mind, what deficit is allowing that to continue, and what assets do you need to gain first in order to deal effectively with that situation?

Get this about your dilemma. Your problem in some ways is not your fault, but it is a result of the law that strength and security precede the ability to be free. By saying it is not your fault I do not mean you are not responsible for it. You are responsible to deal with it, as it is your problem. However, you may have remained stuck because your balance sheet is not in order. The weakness, or lack of security, keeps the gravitational force pulling you downward, no matter what you wish you could do otherwise. You want to stand up, but are not strong enough in some way. So, here is what I am asking you to do:

Admit that you need to get stronger, and focus on that first.

Admit to yourself that you have been stuck because you have omitted some form of personal, spiritual, financial, relational, emotional, or vocational growth in your life that has kept you in a place where you do not want to be. Then, get to work. And that probably means getting the help and support you need to get there. The people who are able to do what you cannot do are usually not better people than you, only stronger. In reality, when you hear someone say of mistreatment, "Who needs *that*?" they mean it. And it's true. They are not in need. So they walk. They do not need that job or relationship or whatever. And they do not need it because they have the resources inside—and outside—themselves to survive without whatever that situation was providing for them. Only then will you be free to have the self-control—and self-direction—that we have been discussing.

You see this in people with strong faith. It gives them the ability to function in superhuman ways in the midst of horrible circumstances, if they have been building that faith over a long time so that their spiritual balance sheet is strong. They have invested in it. You see it among singles in the world of dating when people have strong community, good friends, and then begin dating someone who is not good for them. They walk away, knowing that their lives will still be full, and they have the relational skills to find someone better. You see it in marriage when someone is secure enough to be a force of growth in his or her spouse's life, standing up for love, honesty, faithfulness, or sobriety. And, you see it in people's business life when they have worked out their insecurities enough to deal with a difficult boss or tough work culture and not let it get the best of them, or they possess the ability to go somewhere where they are appreciated and valued. It is true. The rich get richer. So your job is to enrich the part of your life or skill set that is causing the need that keeps you stuck. When you do that, you will find that you will be able to execute the kinds of boundaries you need to have one, integrated, fulfilling life of love and work.

twelve

End Some Things Now

"So, how is it going with the company?" I asked Richard, one of the VPs. I had not seen him in about six months, since the end of a consulting project I did with his team, which was part of a large retail chain. It was one of the most relationally difficult situations I had seen in a long time. When we began, the CEO, the executive team, and the department heads had been strongly divided and stuck in place, with a lot of acrimony.

"You seriously would not believe it," he said. "We are having the best time in years. It is really a great place to be. I am so glad that I did not throw in the towel back in the midst of all the drama."

"So, what is different?" I asked.

"I don't know all the whys," he said. "I just know that people don't hate each other anymore. It was getting so divisive last year when all of that was going on, and now, the same people are getting along fine. I think the changes in David (the CEO) have been a big part of it, but other than that, I don't know. I just know it is good again."

"That is so great," I said. "You guys have a boatload of talent, and it would have been sad to see it blow up. I am glad it worked out."

What I did not say was that I knew exactly why it was better, and it was not all just because the CEO had improved. Certainly that was part of it. David had become more of a leader who could take charge. That provided a lot of clear direction and security for people who had been lacking in David's consensus-building style. But one particular result of his growth had made all the difference. He had fired Jason.

It had taken me a while to get David to the point where he could do what he needed to do with Jason. And that was what had made all the difference. Jason, apart from his performance issues, had the kind of personality some call "divisive." He had a knack for stirring up conflict between people, playing one against the other. When anyone would try to confront him or give him feedback, he would negate it, be defensive, and not receive it. But worse than that, Jason would then go talk to a third person and find a way to have them come to his side by convincing them how bad the first person was. Then, the little triangle of conflict was set. A confronts Jason. Then Jason talks to C, persuading C to hate A, despite the fact that C had no reason of his own to hate A before Jason convinced him of A's villainy. Multiply his defensiveness, denial, and divisiveness by multiple interactions with numerous people, add in a factor of a lot of time, and you get a real mess with a lot of conflict. There were lots of people hating each other, without really having much of a reason.

What was confusing to people in the midst of it was that they could not see that the conflict and the "two sides" were really coming from just one person. When they were in the middle of it, it seemed like a lot of conflict, not just one problem person. While there were other personality dynamics involved, Jason was the big issue. If, for example, David had been more mature and had better skills, he could have dealt with Jason and others much earlier and prevented a lot of the chaos. But he wasn't and he didn't. Given that, the instigator was free to do his charm, and then his harm.

Finally, though, when he was gone, I was able to get the other team members to see each other in a more realistic light and enjoy working with each other again, without Jason's poison in their relationships. So, although this was not all his fault, removing Jason was what changed the picture. And the bottom line David had to learn is the theme of this chapter. Sometimes, some things need to end:

> Although hard, sometimes endings are both necessary and good.

David had to learn that Jason's tenure had to come to an end. Once he was able to pull that trigger, everything changed. But to do that, David had to get comfortable with the idea that endings are sometimes a good thing.

NECESSARY ENDINGS

It is true in life and in work that things end. Relationships end, projects end, careers end, and different seasons of life end. Some of those are planned, and some of them are forced upon us. Some of them we would never want, but find ourselves needing to execute, like David with Jason. But one thing is true. If someone does not have the ability to end things that need to end, they will never have the one life we are talking about in this book. They will also always be hampered by problems that should no longer be problems.

In life, you will get what you tolerate. Period. There is a natural drift south, in all aspects of life. Problems—and problem people—seek out situations and people who will allow them to exist and to have a space. As I told a woman in a seminar who asked, "How do you deal with overly critical people?" the answer is "Just be honest with them. You will never hear from them again." In other words, tell them that you are not finding their input helpful, and if you want it, you will ask for it. If you do not tolerate it, they will go away and find someone else who will take that kind of treatment. And you will have that space for someone who is more helpful.

So, at times, to make it all work, you will have to end some things. And not all of the things you need to end are bad. Now and then you will have to end some good things that are taking up space in your life. Sometimes putting up with something that is OK keeps you from finding the option that is best.

Here is the truth:

You are probably involved in and attached to activities that are good, in and of themselves, but that are keeping you from having time and energy for activities that would be the best for you.

But because you don't like endings, you are loathe to let them go. It might be hard to say good-bye to them. In my book *9 Things You Simply Must Do*, I tell the story of a private company whose owner took it from 25 million dollars in sales to half a billion in a handful of years, directly as a result of this important principle, the ability to do necessary endings.

When he bought the company, he immediately instructed the management team to "get rid of about 80 percent" of what the company was involved in.

"Were those activities losing money?" I asked.

"No, they were all profitable," he told me.

I was a little surprised at the thought of owning a new company and getting rid of 80 percent of what it was doing while those things were making money.

But then he said something that illustrates the principle we are talking about. "The more I analyzed things, I could see that the life of the company was really in about 20 percent of its overall activity. Although the rest of it was OK, I thought it was a drain and a distraction from where the real life of the company was. The real life was in that 20 percent I decided to keep." The rest of it had to go away for the best part to have the time and resources it needed to grow.

Think about it. If he had been uncomfortable with ending things, he would still have a 25 million dollar company. I am sure that shutting down those operations involved some good-byes and some tears. But they were necessary.

So, to get to the one life we have been discussing, you are going to have to, for the rest of your life, be committed to two kinds of endings:

- Negative things that are not fixable

- Positive things that are keeping you from the things you care about the most

And, if you are uncomfortable with ending things, then you will either delay both of those, or not do them. Either way, you will have predictable results:

- Problems that continue

- Problems that grow into bigger problems

- Mediocrity that you become comfortable with

- Lost opportunity that could have come along only by ending something else

While endings are often painful, for good reason, they are also an inherent, necessary part of life. For us to be living, thriving, and not just surviving, we have to come to grips with that fact of life, and get good at executing endings when the time has come.

SO, GET COMFORTABLE WITH THE IDEA AND DO IT

We have looked at several concepts that prepare you for this one. First, you have worked to get your vision together and know what you want things to look like in various areas of life. Then, you have learned to examine your own limits and abilities to take the steps to create those realities. Next, we saw that you might have some power drains with certain kinds of people that keep you from enforcing those limits, and talked about the need to address those. We said that doing an audit would let you know where those kinds of drains are occurring.

After that, we said that there are certain laws or principles of boundaries that will make it very clear when and how these limits operate, and that you might find that your relationship with certain words keeps you from living out those principles well. The no-choice option sets the playing field in the right direction and then some personal rules will help you get there. Finally, we talked about where your time goes, and that you might need to strengthen your position first before you were ready to take some tough stands.

Now, this step is one of the most important. It is probably time for you to consider ending some things. Some will be getting rid of negative things, and some will be getting rid of good things. But, you still have to take the step. In a house, sometimes you throw out trash and other times you give away or sell possessions that have value, but not to your current or future life. Let them go.

I am not, in any way, saying to jettison important relationships, people, or other activities of value because they are difficult. That is immature and avoidant, like the person who has never faced anything in their marriage and one day decides "I am not taking this anymore" and gets divorced. That is running away. Difficult situations call for mature people to take the kinds of steps we are talking about in this entire book to make those situations better, and to resolve them. That is not what we are talking about.

What we are talking about are the situations that clearly need to end, not resolvable situations that you are avoiding dealing with and seeing ending as an easy way out.

But, to do that, you have to get comfortable with the idea that endings are good and a part of life. If you have some issues that keep you from doing that, deal with them. If you are afraid of hurting someone's feelings, deal with that power drain. Sometimes the truth hurts, but that doesn't mean you are inflicting harm. If you are overidentifying with their problems, they will never get better until you stop enabling them and instead release them to face those problems. If you are afraid that they will be upset with you, deal with that. If you have been through a lot of loss and saying good-bye to things is hard, face the grief. Whatever you have to do to get comfortable with endings, you must do in order to deal with real life, because in real life some things end.

So, take an inventory, and ask yourself which relationships and activities need to end.

Work Relationships

Does someone need to be fired? Do you need to fire a customer? That is an idea that many people never think about, but there are some customers or clients you should fire. They are taking up too much of you and too much of your people for the return you are getting. They might be too demanding, have too many crises, not pay well enough, negatively affect your culture or environment, or other issues. Sometimes, it simply isn't a good return on investment. Or, in some cases, they are abusive.

If you really want to inspire loyalty in one of your employees, step in to a situation in which they are taking abusive behavior from a customer and tell the customer that you do not wish for your people to be treated that way and you would like for them to take their business elsewhere. Your employee will then find out what really matters to you, and feel very valued. Sometimes it is the day for mama lion to growl and protect her cubs.

Activities and Practices

What activities are taking up time that should end to give space for others? Certainly, the toxic practices should go. If you are past college, partying may be keeping you from getting where you want to be. But past the toxic practices, what about others? Is that softball or bowling league just taking up time now, when at one time it may have had real value? Is it time to move on to something more in line with your vision?

Friendships and Relationships

What friendships or other relationships take up a lot of time, but in reality are not the kinds of friendships you desire? I am not saying that all of your relationships should be deep and meaningful. You need some dysfunctional friends. They can be some of your favorite people, although they might not be the ones you call in the dark night of the soul. We all need some wacky friends. We love them, and they provide most of the comedy. But two dynamics come into play in figuring out with whom you spend your time.

First, are you spending appropriate time for the level of relationship that exists? If you have so many surface friendships that you do not have time to give to the ones that you would consider close, that might be a problem. It would be like spending as much time with all the kids in the neighborhood as you do with your own. The ones most in your heart should get the most time, and sometimes we do not allocate time well to our circle of friends. If there are people you want to go deep with, then you have to focus on them more than some others, and to do that, some might have to go.

Second, sometimes people find themselves hanging out with people who are the relational equivalent of "filler." I am not being pejorative, or saying that some people have no value. But there are some people who are pursuing activities in life that are not your values, and also, may even be destructive. For example, when addicts gets clean, they often have to say good-bye to their old circle of friends who still do drugs or party too hard. Their sobriety depends on it.

In less extreme cases, some people are in relationships or friendships that are keeping them in denial or stuck. Those relationships are not really adding anything to them and they have become mutually stagnant. If you are married, what couples do you hang around? Are those couples good for your marriage as well? Are they adding to your relationship, values, or growth?

Look at it this way. If you are a parent, you monitor who your children hang out with because their friends either influence them toward growth and maturity, or in the other direction. As an adult, you have to be your own chaperone, and ask yourself if certain relationships are good for you or not.

If you are single, you may be dating in a way that is not getting you where you want to be either. But what happens is that people stay stuck in dating practices or with certain people because they are unwilling to make an ending. In reality, what they desire cannot happen until they make that ending to create room for an entirely different relationship reality.

Financial Practices

Financial stress is one of the most common causes of the disintegrated life. Sometimes it comes from unavoidable events, such as illness or other catastrophes. Most everyone has known a time in life of financial stress for one reason or another. But, most times, financial stress comes from other issues, and it can be both devastating and thoroughly preventable. Marriage conflict, personal trauma, addictions, depression, and many other maladies can often be traced to a person's financial struggles that did not come from tragedy but from a lack of boundaries.

To get into a good financial picture may require some endings for you. When you look at your picture, if it is not as strong as you need it to be, then to get there may mean that you end some spending practices that are causing that reality. If you do not have proper savings, or have accumulated debt, it is time to act.

What do you need to let go of? What are you spending money on that has to end? Do the audit, and figure out what you do not need to survive, and make cuts until you are in a strong position and truly have disposable income. Right now, if you do not have savings and/or have debt, you do not have money to spend on things that are not necessities. That money should be going to getting rid of the cracks in your foundation, lack of savings, and debt. End the other spending activities and spend it there first.

So, now you have many of the tools you need: awareness, a vision, direction, values, support, power, and so on. By now, you are getting a picture of the kinds of steps and practices that serve to bring the one life together in a meaningful, purposeful way. All that is left is for you to take the steps. Since that is probably going to involve talking to some people, and having some difficult conversations with some of them, you are going to need to know how to say it. That is the subject of our next chapter.

thirteen

Communicating Your Boundaries

There are two truths to think about in communicating your boundaries to other people:

- If it is difficult for you, you can develop the skills to make it easier.
- If it is naturally easy for you, you might have a problem.

IF YOU FIND CONFRONTATION DIFFICULT

To set limits with people or define yourself or say no to people or tell them what you want can all be tough things to do. Having those conversations can sometimes cause conflict, separation, guilt, anger, abandonment and rejection, retaliation, and a host of other bad outcomes. In many situations, there is a risk there for any of those to occur. We can probably all remember at least one time when we told someone something that was necessary and experienced an ugly result. The bottom line to almost all of these is that they bring up fears about the relationship. In other words, having these conversations means that you care about people and your relationships with them.

But at the same time, you also care about the issues. There are issues that must be faced and talked about if things are going to get better. There are limits that must be set to keep you or someone else from being hurt, or to make sure problems are not allowed to continue. You rightly care about your needs and agendas, and to get them met, you must assert them. Ergo, the conflict. To do what you need to do, you risk relational conflict, or worse.

The good news is that most of the fears you have about communicating your boundaries are not based in reality. They are in your own head. They come from your experiences in other formative relationships or from not knowing how to have those conversations well; i.e., you may just lack the conversational skills. But where the fears are justified, you are usually better off having the conversation anyway and dealing with the conflict head-on. That will enable you to find out if the other person is able and willing to work it out (i.e., do they care as much as you do about resolution), or you will find out that they either aren't able or don't care. Either way, you win because you find out what the reality of the situation is, what you are truly dealing with, and you can proceed from there. It is better to know who your true friends, and enemies, are. So, even if it is hard for you, it is worth it to get better at having those difficult conversations.

IF CONFRONTATION COMES NATURALLY

If it is naturally easy for you to confront people, then your first growth step may be to start to care a little more about how the message is delivered. It can be good for you to learn how to care more about other people and their reactions—and the relationships themselves—and not to be so cavalier about it. Often, those who find it too easy to assert themselves—not caring about what the other person feels or thinks—create a wake of broken relationships (personal and professional) that follows them through life. Caring more about others would be a good step to take, so it is not so easy to be heartless. They could learn to be more sensitive in their delivery, and it would benefit them as well as others.

In this chapter, we are going to talk about how to have those conversations in ways that accomplish both of the above. We are going to look at easier ways to have "boundary conversations" than you might have tried in the past. And we are going to do it in a way that shows care and concern for the other people as well.

HOW TO MAKE THE MOST OF A
HARD CONVERSATION

I was talking to the HR director of a transportation company about their upcoming round of performance appraisals. She was not happy that it was that time of the year again.

"So, what's the problem?" I asked. "You don't even have to do them. Their bosses do."

"I know, but I have to deal with the fallout afterward, especially with one employee. Last year it was awful. They got into a big conflict, and now I have talked to the employee and he doesn't want to meet with his boss for a review again, and the boss doesn't want to do it either. Both of them hated it."

"What went wrong?" I asked.

"I think it was just too aggressive, but the person had some real issues, and I think he is a little oversensitive," she said.

"So, which one do you think was the problem? Do you think the boss was too hard on him, or was he just not able to take negative feedback?" I asked.

"That's really hard to tell," she admitted. "It just did not go well."

And that is the problem.

In many boundary-setting conversations or confrontations or conflicts, the real issue gets lost, and it is difficult to figure out who actually has the problem because the way the conversation is handled becomes the issue—instead of the issue itself. People go into a conversation to talk about some problem and the conversation is hurtful, and it becomes a bigger problem than the problem was. When a person brings up an issue, the issue should remain the issue. But if they say it in a way that is demeaning, disrespectful, judgmental, or toxic, then two really bad outcomes follow. First, there is a new problem to be solved, i.e., the hurt that just occurred. Second, the old problem gets lost in the interaction and still remains.

When we feel hurt, our brains get flooded as a result of the emotions, and when that happens, judgment, the capacity for self-observation, insight, and connection can all be diminished. But to resolve problems, you need as much of those elements in the room as possible. So, you want to learn how to have these conversations in the best possible way, minimizing hurt and maximizing problem solving. Remember, you are there to aid in self-observation and problem observation in the other person, not to reduce it. In addition, you are there to strengthen your relationship with them as well.

For a successful outcome, you have to realize that there are two possible ways for the conversation to go badly. First, you can go about it in a way that will make the other person hurt or defensive. Second, you may be dealing with one of those people who gets hurt and defensive just because the sun comes up every day. The first one is the only one you can control, but you will be better off by being aware of the second possibility as well, and delivering the news in the best way possible.

The Tone

The first dynamic you need to be aware of is what I refer to as "tone." You often hear people say that "the tone of the conversation was ___." When they say that, we always know what they mean. The trick to establishing a good tone is to know why sometimes it goes well and sometimes it doesn't.

The field of psychology has been very helpful in demonstrating that communication and the experience of communication has a "valence" to it. Think about this definition of the word "valence" from *Merriam-Webster's*: "a: relative capacity to unite, react, or interact (as with antigens or a biological substrate), b: the degree of attractiveness an individual, activity, or thing possesses as a behavioral goal."

In other words, the way you say something to someone has a capacity to unite you, cause the other person to react, or to interact with you. And, it affects the degree of attractiveness that you and your issue have for the other person. The street wisdom has always been that you catch more flies with honey than with vinegar, and most communication experts would agree. And this all begins with the tone and its valence, whether positive or negative.

Remember, there is a difference between negative information and negative communication. Let me say that again for emphasis, as it expresses much of what you need to know in a difficult conversation, or one that may have difficult meanings for the other person:

There is a difference between negative information and negative communication.

Negative information, in simple terms, is information that someone doesn't like. It already has its own valence to it. If you tell me you don't like my performance in some way, I don't like to hear that as much as I like to hear that you think I did a terrific job. That is natural, my own self-image problems aside. But negative communication is what happens if you give me that information in a way that ends up with my being hurt, angry, or defensive. And we are probably no closer to a solution than when we began. So the first thing to remember is that negative information is a part of life, but negative communication doesn't have to be. The goal of problem solving is to deliver negative information through positive communication so that there is a good outcome, and not to avoid it because of the fear of negative communication. Remember, successful people, in life and work, communicate negative information as an ongoing practice. That is how they make success happen, by confronting and resolving problems.

Tone is the first step in avoiding negative communication. People respond to tone as much or more than they do to information. The sweetheart airline ticket counter agent who empathically tells you that your flight has been delayed will get a much better response and more cooperation from you in rescheduling than the jerk who says things like, "Look Buddy, I don't control the weather. This is all we have, so do you want it or not?" (Who hires those people anyway? I fly a lot, and it is very tempting to begin naming airlines.)

To help you keep the conversation positive, remember the big tone issues that trigger problematic responses:

- Anger in your voice

- Aggression in your stance

- Condescending expressions, words, or attitude

- Guilt-inducing words or expressions

- Shame-inducing words, phrases, or implications

- Cold, indifferent demeanor

In short, people know when you are for them, and when you are against them or down on them. I like the word "down" as it expresses a spatial metaphor of coming from above someone, looking down on them as if you are superior, a parent, or someone above them in some way. It is a surefire way of making someone react negatively. So rule number one is:

> Soften your tone and avoid wording that
> may leave someone feeling somehow bad.

To do this, there are times when you may need to wait to talk to someone. When you get the bad news or become aware of someone's screwup, if you are prone to becoming aggravated, your blood pressure is shooting up, and your irritation is showing—wait. This is not just me the psychologist telling you that you ought to be nicer to people. This is the leadership consultant telling you that you will get less of what you want and more of what you don't want (sabotage, secret job hunting, lost deals, hidden agendas) if you talk to others while you are angry. Take a time-out, even if as one leader told me, "I have a lot to be p.o.'d about!" He felt, and rightly so, that some of his team were not performing and were doing some pretty stupid things and that his anger was justified. Certainly, it was, but it was not going to solve the problem. A calmer approach that did not ignore the problem but got the communication done without turning people against him would solve the problem and get the results he wanted. So, take a time-out until you can do it right.

Affirm the Person, Relationship, and Desired Outcome

Remember, when you come into someone's space with a communication, their brain is scanning to determine whether you are friend or foe. That doesn't mean in the literal sense as the two of you may be good friends for a long time. What it means is that their brain is asking how to treat the interaction itself. The person's system is either going to be open to the information and to you, or if it perceives a threat, it will go into fight or flight, the natural option for dealing with adversaries. In addition, if you are talking to a male, it will be worse. Their brains will be more apt to react to negative information in a heightened way. So, often it is important to begin with an affirmation of either the person or the relationship, and where you want things to end up as a result of this conversation. If people know that you are talking about this issue so you can be better friends or make something easier, they know from the beginning that the outcome is not going to be that they are fired or rejected. That will calm down their brains and allow the information to come in. So rule number two is:

> Begin with affirming the person, the relationship,
> or the desired outcome.

Here's an example of how one might go about this. "Joe, I like working on projects with you, and I love how we work together, so I wanted to talk about a couple of things that could make it even better for me. When we have a deadline . . ."

If it is an issue that is more serious or problematic, a little more focus may be needed, but the same elements apply. "Sandy, I think you know how important you are to me and how much I am on your team. And I want us to be the best team possible and do great things together. To do that, there is something that happens that makes it hard for me sometimes, and I wanted to talk about it so we can do better."

Certainly you will have your own wording and style. But the important thing is that the person knows that you are for him and not against him, that your relationship is important, and that there is a positive future to this conversation. Knowing up front that your desire is for a better working relationship, or personal relationship if that is the case, helps the person to be at ease, and defensiveness goes down.

Be Specific about the Issue, Not the Person

When talking to a person about an issue, it is vital that you stay away from broad descriptions and labeling of the person's character. Consider this common attempt at getting someone to perform better. "You're so irresponsible. I want you to be more responsible in your work habits and act as if you care."

What am I supposed to do with that, if I am that person? First, the labeling makes me feel crummy. Second, there is nothing specific that I can work on. I just know I am supposed to be "more responsible."

Here is a better approach. "I need something from you. When you get the report to me past the deadline, it holds me up and I can't get my project in on time. The last two months, I did not get yours until a week after the deadline, and then we were pretty chaotic on our end trying to catch up. So, can we talk about how to get it done in the agreed-upon time?"

Here is another example. "You're abusive to me. You are always critical, no matter what I do. It is never enough for you."

This approach is more effective. "I don't like to be yelled at or called names. Yesterday in the meeting when you started screaming and then said what I did was 'moronic' was a good example, and that is not the first time something like that has happened. It is very hurtful to me, and it gets in the way of our work. I want to know that it won't happen again."

The second approach in both cases stays away from creating another problem by labeling the person. They are also specific to the issue and give the person an actionable item. They know what to do to make it better, other than to be more responsible, a term that has a different meaning to different people, or to be nicer. One person's irresponsible is another's laid back, and one person's abusive is another's banter. Tell them what the problem is, specifically.

Get Agreement

Often, especially in problematic interactions in which there is the possibility for defensiveness or denial, it is important to make sure that you get agreement after the conversation that both of you are on the same page. This is also important if someone is not defensive, but oversensitive. They can experience what you are saying as hurtful, even when you did not mean it.

So check it out at the end. "So, what are you hearing me say here?" or "Let's make sure we are understanding each other and what we are really saying. Tell me what you are hearing me say. I fear it may sound like I am saying something that I am not saying, that I don't like you or am down on you in some way. That is not the case at all. Does it feel that way to you?" or "What is your understanding of what we've discussed?"

Then, you can reconcile their understanding with what you were trying to communicate. If there is a miscue, then clarify it. Empathize with how it felt, and state it clearly. "I can see why it feels that way to you, and I am sorry about that. I am just trying to say that I want us to solve this issue so we can work better together. Nothing more."

In addition to agreement about what you have said, get agreement about what is going to happen in the future, and what you desire from the person. Make sure that you both understand what you are expecting and that there is agreement to fulfill that expectation. Also, ask the other person what he or she needs from you to make this happen. Many times, we can be a part of the solution as well as making someone aware of the problem. I was in a meeting with a team in which a conversation went down where a department head was upset that someone was not performing in a certain way, and told him. The other person was caught totally off guard, and had no idea that the first one had even needed certain things from him. So, part of the resolution was that the "nonperformer" asked the one who was upset to let him know much earlier in the future if there was something he needed and was not getting. That way, it could be addressed and the frustration circumvented.

When a team does this, it can be huge. I like to have teams come together and define the behaviors they need from each other to be an effective whole and to reach the goals they want to reach. "What will you need from me?" and "Here is what I will need from you" are all good conversations in which there is enough specificity to know two things: how to deliver on the desired request and how to hold someone accountable. Specificity in the agreed-upon outcome does both.

Make very actionable and specific requests for change. Tell the person what you want them to do.

Balance Care and the Whole Truth

We began this chapter by seeing that most of us, stylistically, fall on one side of the equation or the other. We are either too nice with a tendency to fudge on saying the hard things, or too brutal, forgetting to be very caring. The effective communicator does both. She shows care for the person, and does not skirt the issue at all. If you can do both of those together, then you will get the best results, even from the most difficult people.

My favorite mantra for doing this is to "go hard on the issue and soft on the person." Hard on the issue does not mean that you yell or push aggressively. It means simply that you are unyielding and do not minimize the issue with your choice of words. By suggesting that you be unyielding, I do not mean rigid and not open to input or compromise, but that you do not yield before you say what you need to say, or that you do not get pushed around. Some people are so flimsy that they are not clear. Remember, clarity adds structure. If you are not very direct and clear, the boundaries of what has to happen and what the issue itself is will get lost. Do not go soft on what should be firm.

Soft on the person means that you are preserving their feelings and personhood in the process. You can be unbending and nice at the same time. A "no" with a smile is just as firm as a scream. What makes it firm is that you are serious about it and are not going to change your mind, or skirt saying it. Firm and soft can go together, and should, in most situations. There are times when you need to growl or even yell, but those are few and far between and should always be for a good reason. A German shepherd can communicate a boundary without a growl or bark, and yet there are those times . . .

What you are doing is taking an integrated approach in which your structure is intact. You are staying connected to the relationship, and at the same time, connected to the truth and the need or the issue. That is an integrated approach that will also integrate the person as well. People who are difficult have often lost touch with caring about the other people, or have gotten too comfortable in getting away with things. When you are relational and firm, you are helping to restore balance in them by structuring them and getting them back in touch with the maturity they may have lost touch with.

I once gave a seasoned president of a manufacturing company with twenty-five thousand employees a month-long assignment to go have some direct conversations with some people that he had been indirect with, after which we would review it. Halfway through the month, he called me and said, "You know, this being direct thing really cuts down on a lot of anger." He did not even have to wait the entire month to get results. One of the complaints that came up when I had interviewed twenty people under him was that things were chaotic a lot of the time, and there was a lot of frustration. People were irritated and angry. When he began to get direct, the anger, chaos, and frustration reduced. The reason was that he was adding structure by being direct with people, like the difference in a classroom where the teacher is a pushover compared with one where the teacher is firm and clear about expectations. Communicating clearly, and nicely, adds that kind of integration to people who have gotten off balance in their own emotions and performance. It shapes them up without a scolding. Directness and firmness help people settle down.

Hold On to Your Perspective through Separateness

When you are going to communicate, remember to remain separate from the other person. This means that you make sure that his issue, perspective, defensiveness, feelings, or opinions do not become your own unless you choose to make them yours. What happens is because of the kinds of personal power drains we discussed earlier, you lose your sense of separateness and his agenda becomes yours because of other things going on inside of you. Your desire to please, or not knowing what to say, or your fear of his anger, can cause you to lose who you are and what you want, think, or feel. If it helps you, visualize a circle around each of you, with your own different perspectives, and stay inside your own circle. Realize over and over in your mind that "this is me, that is him."

In your communication, be aware to emphasize your separateness through clearly stating so, if needed. Some people need to be reminded, and it will help you keep your position. Make it clear for them. "I understand that you think A. But my perspective is different than that. I think B." Years ago, I had an employee whose responsibility was to make sure I had all of the information I needed for various events and activities and put them together in a usable form, so when I went to the meeting or event I would not be scrambling at the last minute for the documents, background information, etc. that I would be depending on. "I would like for you to make sure that you have all of those details written down before I need them," I told her.

As time went on, there were several occasions when I did not have the information I needed at the time I needed it, and I brought it up to her. I told her that I needed her to do better at making sure I had it all together and on time.

"But, we had already talked about that stuff before, so I knew you already had it," she said. "So, I figured you would just bring it with you."

"I understand," I said. "But what I asked for was that you gather it all together for me, and give it to me in a folder, ready to go."

"But I had sent it to you a week ago," she said. "So, you already had it."

"I get that. I understand you, that you feel as if since you had already gotten it to me, you didn't need to do it again. And I understand that you feel good about the job you did. I get it. You think you did it right. But here is what I need you to hear. I need it put all together for me, in one place, the day before I will need it. That is what I want. So, I need to know if you can do that, no matter what you might have given me before that time."

"Sure," she said, somewhat tersely. "I can do that."

If you look at this interaction, what was happening was something that was a pattern with her. She wanted me to accept her reality as "job well done." In her mind, she had done her part; i.e., she had gotten me my info. She was fine with what she had done. And, what happens sometimes is that when we understand and empathize with a person's feelings or intentions, we take the bait and allow those to become ours. In the process, the issue is lost. I still need my info all together. That is the real issue. No matter what her intentions were or are, that is not the issue. She was trying to change the issue to her view of the world, which was about her good intentions or that she had tried and done her job. Or worse, that I should not need it again in the form I wanted. She was fine with it, but I was not.

In another interaction with her, I had asked her to put a meeting together that an organization had requested, and after several weeks, it floated through my mind that I had not heard anything about it since then. So, I called her.

"What happened with the Wyatt meeting?" I asked.

"Oh, I haven't heard back from them," she said.

"Oh. Are we waiting to confirm a date?" I asked.

"Not yet. They haven't sent me any. I am waiting on them," she explained.

"But they have not even sent a date? When did you call them?" I inquired further.

"When you told me to," she said. "And they never called me back. I am waiting on them."

"You mean you called them only once? And they haven't responded, so you haven't called again?" I asked.

"Right," she said. "The ball's in their court. I called and they never got back to me."

"Did you think of calling them to follow up and see what was wrong?" I asked.

"No," she said. "Look, I did what you asked. The ball is in their court, and I am waiting on them. It is their responsibility now."

"OK, I understand," I said. "You think that because you called, you have done your part, and now it is up to them. Am I getting it?"

"Right," she said. "I don't know why you are bugged with me. They are the ones who are holding things up."

"OK, let me try to make something clear. When I ask you to do something, it is not done until it is done. Making a call, to get it off your list, is not getting it done. It is only done when it is done, when we have a meeting set. And if they are not doing their part, then that does not mean that you have done yours, just because you have made a call. Does that make sense to you? I need to know that when I ask for something that you understand it is not done because you tried, but it is done when it is done. That is what I want." She actually got it, put a sign up on her wall that said, "It is not done until it is done," and saved her job. If this communication had not worked, the ending could have been much different.

The issue here is that sometimes people will try to get you off of your issue or what you need to have happen by giving you all sorts of reasons about their side. Sometimes those are worthy, sometimes not. When they are legit, you can make a change and accommodate. But be wary of how easy it is to not remain separate from all of their reasons, excuses, and explanations. Hold on to yourself when you are getting maneuvered. Stay firm with your differentiated positions, and make sure you communicate them. Of course, there are times when you will rightly change your mind as someone's perspective has informed yours. But that should happen because you were convinced, not because you were weak. Be informed, not overpowered.

Stay Separate from the Difficult Person

We would not have problems with communicating our boundaries if people loved to be confronted or loved to have to adapt to what we want. If they just said, "Oh, thanks for confronting me. You have changed my life and I will be forever indebted to you," then we would probably all be communication experts. (Actually, that is what mature people do, by the way. Good feedback is seen as a gift, not an insult.) But that does not happen all the time, and probably you have had some difficult experiences in the past that make it hard for you to even try sometimes. But you have to if you don't want to end up living in the proverbial van down by the river. It is important to not give up because of the difficult ones, but instead, get your skills together so that when they show up, you are ready to deal with them.

The idea of staying separate when people are defensive or in denial is very important. Their strategy is to not have to take ownership of whatever it is that you are trying to get them to own. So, they will deflect, excuse, minimize, blame, or throw out a whole host of responses to keep from being responsible. When they do, staying separate from all of that noise is important. Staying separate from all of their attempts to avoid responsibility means that you will not get sidetracked and lose the focus of what you are trying to communicate.

First of all, remember the above. Stay in touch with what you want and what you think. Do not lose that and get talked out of it, unless you are truly being shown the light. And with a defensive blamer, that is unlikely. So, hold on to yourself.

Second, remember a little formula:

Empathize, and return to the issue.

People get lost when defensive people try to get them off track or whine or get angry or give a thousand reasons why A is really B. Remember, that is just noise. It is not germane to anything relevant. It is just so much static. You are responsible for delivering your message, and they are responsible for delivering theirs. Your job is to deliver yours until they are delivering one back that you are looking for. If not, then you have a different kind of discussion. Here are some examples of defensiveness, and the formula in action:

Sara: "What are you talking about? I do more than you ask all the time. I knock myself out for you. How can you say that I am not doing all that I am supposed to do?"

Regina: (with empathy) "I understand that it is frustrating to hear this, and that you feel like you do a lot. I can appreciate that. What I am saying is that when the things don't get done that I just told you about, that creates problems for me, and I want you to do them. That is what I want you to hear."

Robert: "Well, you do that very same thing to me, all the time. What about the other day when you totally ignored what I was talking about and went right on working on what you were working on? Or last week when I called you and you said that you didn't have time to even take a look at my report?"

Scott: "I understand that you are frustrated with me also, and we can talk about that at a different time. But right now I am talking about what just happened, and I want you to understand why that is a problem for me and that you won't do that to me again."

Diane: "You don't understand the pressure that I am under around here. Joe is all over me all the time to do his projects, and Ross has got his agenda, and the monthly reports are always hanging over me. I can't believe you are on my case about this."

Laurie: "I get it that you are under a lot of pressure. That's hard. But I still want you to hear that I am not happy with the way that you have been handling the things that we agreed upon that you would do."

In each of these scenarios, their quick bob is to deflect the issue with a victim cry, a move to shift the blame, or an excuse. While sometimes these are valid points, that is not the issue here. The issue here is that these are not real discussion points, but a bid to invalidate what you are bringing up. When that happens to you, stay on task, and do not take the bait. Remember that their deflections are only noise, or static.

Set Limits

Remember when we discussed the abilities a person with good boundaries possesses? One was to stay separate, as above. But another two of them had to do with dealing with destructive behavior in others. Those were to contain and limit destruction when it appears in other people. If you are in any kind of management role, these functions are required by your job, and even the law. If not, they are required by your personhood, to make sure that you are not being hurt, abused, or defrauded.

Limits are basically the boundary line that says how far you are going to go with a certain issue. It could be a behavior, an attitude, or even a time issue. It may be a financial limit, or how much you will agree to do for someone before you begin to feel as if you are being used. It may be to limit the degree of freedom that someone has with you to not live up to certain commitments. Whatever the context, a limit says how far you will allow something to go, and how far you won't.

It is important to remember a basic law of the universe when thinking about limits:

You get what you tolerate.

That law holds true whether you are raising a puppy, a child, a direct report, or a spouse. (Hopefully you are not raising a spouse, but it happens.) It holds true when you are negotiating a deal, working with an account, or supervising an employee. It will come into every context of life, in some form or another. Many times it is innocent, as in very good relationships. One person will have a habit or a practice that is not a problem for him or her, but is a problem for the other person. If the other person tolerates that behavior and does not talk about it, then it will remain in place until the other person finally says, "Excuse me, but you are stepping on my toe." And in good relationships, the ebb and flow of the relationship is to talk to each other about what you would wish to not have in the relationship, and then you will not have it. That is normal.

I once did a joint venture with another organization, and in the first year, it was a lot of getting used to the practices of each organization, its systems, expectations, and the like. As it turned out, there were practices we each had that were not foreseen on the other end, and needs that were not foreseen, that caused some heartburn. Both of us just behaved as a puppy does until someone says, "Don't chew on my shoes." Neither of us wanted to continue to have those things happen, so we addressed them on an ongoing basis for the first year. It was a little testy at times. But we got there.

After the first year, I remember being with the CEO of the other organization as we planned a strategy retreat, and he was talking excitedly about the future. He said, "I am really looking forward to this year and building on what we have done. Now that we have gotten the bumps and lumps out, it is going to be great."

Bumps and lumps. What a great way of expressing a natural occurrence, where two people or organizations basically said, "Hey, I do not want to put up with this forever. Let's change the way we do it." That is normal, and it is how the law operates in good relationships.

But sometimes one of the parties is not so innocent, and not so eager to adapt to the wishes of the other. The initial "Hey I do not like this, so let's please change this" message is not working. The person continues to do whatever he or she is doing, and it is destructive to the other person, family, team, or organization. At that time, remembering the law is vital. You get what you tolerate. It's especially important to remember this when dealing with the kind of person who does not observe his own behavior and correct it when he becomes aware of it. It's vital for you to set limits with these people. Their behavior must be limited in its ability to affect you or your organization. If not, you will only get more of it.

Once you come out of denial, or at least into the realization that if you do not limit this behavior it will continue, it requires some proactive behavior on your part, often a confrontation. (Sometimes it is advisable to not confront, but allow others to set the limit, like the police. But for now, let's talk about the people whom it is safe to talk to.)

The first step is to simply confront the behavior, using all of the appropriate principles we have already discussed. Affirm the relationship or the person, along with the outcome, and get your tone in order. Be specific, and talk about what you specifically want to focus on and what you want to see that is different:

Rachel: "Rolf, I want to talk to you about something because our working relationship is important to me, and I want us to be able to work well together. I would like to get an understanding around something so that we can do well from here on. The issue is that sometimes your anger is too much, and the way that you express it is hurtful to me and creates a lot of stress around here. I do not like the put-downs, like when you called me 'stupid' the other day in the meeting. Those reactions hurt and make it difficult for me to do my work, and I do not allow myself to be treated that way, by anyone. It is one of my values. So, I want you to stop yelling, or demeaning me, in private or in public. If you can do that, I think we can do well together."

That is a simple limit, a direct confrontation of the behavior that you do not want to tolerate. If Rolf listens, then all is well. The limit has contained the destructive behavior and not allowed it to spread. But if he does not listen and stop, further limits are needed, and that is when it is time for Rachel to go to the next step. It is time for the "don't think I won't do it" talk:

Rachel: "Rolf, I want to talk to you about your angry expressions. I asked you to not do that again, and you have continued to demean me, and get angry in a hurtful way toward me and others. As I explained to you, I do not allow myself to be talked to like that. So, I am going to let you know that if it happens again, I will file a formal complaint with HR, and I do not think that I will be lacking for witnesses. Please be assured that I will follow through on these consequences. You are free to do what you would like, as I cannot stop you. But I will follow through. I want a good outcome here, so I hope you can agree. Do we have an understanding?"

This time the limit went to the next level, which is to invoke consequences. While she has not done that yet, and would be naturally in her rights to go ahead at this point, this is an example of how to communicate a warning, or better yet, a promise. There are some issues that after having talked once—or sometimes not talked at all—consequences are the very first step. But here for illustration we see the warning talk.

The next level would be to follow through on the consequences and allow those to set the limits for you. These consequences, depending on the context, could be talking to HR, firing, demotion, resigning, not allowing yourself to be in the room with the person, legal action, separation or divorce, probation, etc. All of these involve more than words, as the person truly suffers some sort of pain as a result of his or her choices. Remember, a boundary without a consequence is only a suggestion. Real boundaries have real teeth to back them up, and consequences must cause some pain or loss for them to be helpful to the person.

But to help the other person is only one of the desirable outcomes. The other is that the behavior itself has been limited and the destruction contained. While we long for the other person to get it and turn around, and for the relationship to be restored, we cannot control that outcome. We can desire it and manage to it, but we cannot control it. But we always can limit the destruction either by limiting your own exposure to it (you could quit or walk away) or by using institutionalized powers, such as management, legal, and the police. You might not be able to get someone to change, but you can stay away from them or have them thrown in jail. Limits are good. Here are some more examples, adapted from my 2003 book with Dr. John Townsend, *How To Have That Difficult Conversation You've Been Avoiding*:

> "Joe, I won't allow myself to feel taken for granted, so if you call me at the last minute to go out, I won't be going anymore."
> "Debbie, if you leave things for me to do without asking, and just expect me to do them for you, I won't do them anymore. I want you to ask and not assume."
> "Brian, I do not want you to drink when I am with you anymore, because you can't control it. If you do, I will leave the party, or dinner, and will not see you again until you get some help."
> "Steve, I have told you that your suggestive remarks are not wanted. If you do another one, I will be gone and you will be hearing from legal."

While you may not like playing sheriff, sometimes it is necessary. There are people who will not stop their behavior when limits are set. And, if they won't, then the limits are there to protect you, other people, the organization, or the family. And here is the extra good news. Many times they can actually turn someone around and they change.

Strength in Numbers: Bring Others with You

One of the most important boundaries we can have is the help of other people. After having a one-on-one talk with a person and getting nowhere, it can be very helpful to bring someone else to the meeting. Several good things happen when you do not go alone.

First, it is tougher for a difficult person to split, deny, blame, dodge, or excuse with two people than with one. It is easier to get one person confused. Two can stay on the issue better.

Second, the mere presence of someone else has a commanding symbol to it; i.e., "This is serious enough to bring in two of us." People usually get that something is up when it is no longer just you that they are dealing with.

Third, you have a witness in case the next step needs to happen, and formal proceedings occur. People can (and often will) distort what you have said or lie outright. It is always good to have a witness. In addition, you can get feedback on how you did the confrontation. You might find that you were not as harsh, or as soft, as you thought. We all need that at times.

Plan the Conversation about the Conversation

Often, with a difficult person, you have talked with them about the problem before and nothing has happened. There has been no change. At that point, it is no longer appropriate to just do it again, expecting different results. It is time for what I call the conversation about the conversation.

> "Sue, I want to talk to you about something. As you recall, we have spoken several times about your summary reports to the team on your trips to our branches. I have told you that we need them, and we have not gotten them. That is still a problem, but that is not what I want to talk about.
>
> "What I want to talk about is a bigger problem, that being that when I talk to you about it, nothing happens. In other words, talking to you about it is not helping. I get a promise, but no response. So, I want to talk about why talking about this is not helping, and where we have to go from here."

Here, you are showing the person that there is a bigger problem than the summary reports, or whatever the issue is. The bigger problem, and one that can be a deal breaker, is that it does not do any good to address problems with them. So, where does that leave us? Often, that breaks through the denial and if not, consequences are next. But it lets them know that the pattern is being addressed and will not be allowed to go on.

This can be helpful in many different kinds of relationships, with subordinates, peers, friends, even bosses. After talking has not helped, to talk to them about that problem lets them know that you are not going to be OK with the problem continuing to go unaddressed.

Make a Plan

Related to that is to get a plan for what the two of you are going to do if this happens again. "So, if we go from here, and it happens again, what shall we do at that point? Let's agree on what will happen, so we both know what to expect."

I worked with a leader one time who had an anger problem, and the change came when the team and he agreed that if it happened again, they would all leave him there alone and not complete whatever they were doing. He knew beforehand. I have seen teams do the same thing with tardiness. "Let's agree that if you are late again, we will leave without you." To know ahead of time what our plan is gets ahead of the behavior.

Role Play

"You are kidding, right?" Shawn asked me. He was a seasoned manager, and could not believe that I was telling him that I wanted him to practice a conversation before he went in with his boss. "That seems so juvenile, to 'role play.'"

"Well, let me ask you something. How has it gone so far when you talk to him?"

"Terrible," he said. "He always gets me befuddled. I almost feel like I am going to pass out."

"OK, so, you want to do that again? What makes you think you are going to be able to pull it off this time?" I asked. "If Tiger goes to the practice range before a round, maybe you could learn to get it right before you go in there as well."

"It is so embarrassing," he said.

"Get over it. Now, I will be him, and you be you."

Sound juvenile to you? If so, remember that there is little that any of us can do well the first time without practice. Communication is no different, especially with difficult people. If they are defensive, you might have to practice knowing how to respond. You might have to even write it out, as a script. But do not expect yourself to do what you have never done before, especially under the heat. Practice, and then you will have done it before you go in there. Some of the best "aha" experiences I have seen with leaders are in role-play situations, from negotiations, to listening, to dealing with difficult people. When they practice, they learn, and they get courage. So, get with someone and get ready before you have the difficult conversation.

Related to that is to get support from someone right before you go in, go over what you are going to say, and then call them right after. I call this the "support sandwich." That way, you are encouraged beforehand and held accountable after, knowing that your friend is going to ask what you said. Also, they can help you lick your wounds, if needed.

PEOPLE ARE NOT THE SAME

In dealing with people, remember that one size does not fit all. There are wise people who listen to feedback, take it in, and respond to it. They correct themselves, and own their behavior. They learn, and they are a joy to work with. My suggestion with them is to resource them, give them more input, knowledge, training, teaching, and whatever you have because they tend to use it. It is a good investment.

With people like this, you do not have to do much except have a good tone, be clear, be specific, listen well, and you will get great results. Hire them when you can, work for them whenever possible, and stick with them as long as they perform. They are of good character.

The second group is not so much fun, but sometimes workable. They are the defensive ones, who sometimes blame and excuse and cause what I call "collateral damage" for others. They are not trying to hurt anyone, but because they won't take responsibility for themselves, they do cause other people problems. And, part and parcel of that problem is that when you give them feedback, they do not accept it.

With this group, remember, more feedback usually does not help. So, why are you continuing to do what does not help? You are wasting your breath trying to continually talk about a problem that the person is not owning. That is when you have to move to the other strategy above, making the lack of responsiveness and lack of change the problem of focus. Focus on that, and move away from talking, to consequences. Then, you sometimes will get a turnaround, and other times they will go away as they do not like to be held accountable. Either way, you are better off.

And then the third group are just destructive people—not by accident, but by intent. They like to bring you down. They enjoy it. These are the ones who like it when you fail or take glee at someone else's demise. They would rather be right or be seen as good than have good outcomes happen. They are not looking out for anyone, but are actually trying to bring others down.

With them, there is not only no talking, there is also usually no hope. Get serious about protecting yourself and others from their agenda, and take appropriate action. While group number one needs input, and group number two needs consequences, with the third group, you have to go into protective mode. I always say "lawyers, guns, and money," to quote Warren Zevon. They are out to harm, so make sure your strongest boundaries are intact.

DEFINE YOURSELF TO GOOD ENDS

Boundaries are about self-control in the service of your vision, mission, goals, and purposes, including good relationships with others. But, as the law of exposure says, they cannot be in secret. They have to be visible to others, through our communication. The best leaders and most successful people in fulfilling the call of one life are the ones who can communicate their boundaries well. If you can't, that is understandable. You might never have seen it done or never been taught. Just look back at your family of origin if you want to see your earliest schooling in communication. How did that go? Now you get it.

But, if you have had no training since then, then how can you expect to be better? You can't, but you need to. Go get some. Take a course, a workshop, get a book and practice, meet with a friend, or meet with your team. Any way you learn, getting better at it will pay for itself many, many times over. You will get what you tolerate, and what you communicate.

The Path Ahead

There is a saying you hear often in business circles after all the explanations, excuses, spin, and interpretations have played out, and only the stark reality of the numbers remain: "It is what it is." The performance—the profits or the losses—are what they are. No amount of editorializing can change them or the real-life implications. And in turn, these results reflect something very real about the people who generated them, more so than anything else. Our lives, in the long run, reflect more about us than the circumstances in which we lived them. As Heraclitus said more than two thousand years ago, "Character is destiny." Where we end up has a lot to do with who we are.

We have seen in this book how your own makeup, specifically, the character of your personal boundaries, has incredible impact on the outcomes in your personal and your professional life. In more than twenty years of leadership consulting, I have seen this reality lived out in many, many situations. No matter what "potential" someone has, or the talents, brains, or opportunities they possess, if they do not have the personal makeup to bring it all to fruition, success rarely happens. Dreams go unrealized and are sometimes destroyed. Who you are really, truly matters.

Our focus in this book has been on a particular set of abilities a strong identity provides. This consists of the ability to:

- experience oneself as separate and differentiated from others,

- contain destruction and keep it from spreading,

- define oneself and know who you are,

- set limits when needed,

- possess and live out values, and

- have self-control and thereby be free and autonomous.

Possess these traits and, over the long haul, personal and business fruitfulness will be yours to the degree that your talents and opportunities afford. Ignore them, and what matters to you most will suffer.

So, given that our success depends on having a strong sense of our own boundaries and freedom and that there is no getting around the reality that "it is what it is," where does that leave any of us today? In my experience, it leaves most of us in one of two places. The first is that you might be the kind of person who had the good fortune to grow up in a way that afforded you the sorts of experiences that built the abilities we are talking about, and, for the most part, you are clearly in control of yourself. This means that when you read the list of traits above, you find you possess them in large enough measure that living in a one-life kind of way comes naturally to you. If that is true, be thankful.

The second possibility is you find yourself, like the vast majority of us, possessing some of these traits, but also keenly aware that life could be a lot different if you could grow in these abilities. You know you experience power drains, and your personal and professional missions could benefit from regaining that power. In my experience, from CEOs all the way down the org chart, most honest humans identify more with group two than group one. We all can identify some areas where growth would benefit not only us but also the people we lead and care about.

If you follow the advice in this book, you will find that wherever you came from in your life, and whatever experiences left you with some holes in your boundaries, you will have gotten stronger and be on the path to experiencing an integrated life because you are a more integrated person. And, when you look at the fruit of your time and efforts, and "it is what it is," you will find more of what you desired.

As I have been privileged to walk this path with many people over many years, I can promise you two things: first, you might be amazed at how quickly you find yourself making great strides and getting great results. And second, you will also discover that this journey is not altogether instantaneous; it takes both time and work. It is a process. But the results are worth it, and the consequences of not walking the path are already evident in the realities currently haunting you. It is what it is, and will continue to be the same if you don't do the work you need to do.

There are a few things to consider as you begin the path.

First, realize it is our relational experiences that build our identities and boundaries. The "holes in your fences" came from formative relationships, and to repair them, you are going to need some new relational experiences. So, find them. Get a coach. Find a good therapist. Join a leadership network or group. Get together with a few trusted friends and go through this book together. Ask someone to mentor you. There are many forms and structures through which we find the kind of help we need to grow in these areas, and no particular one is right for every person. However, the one reality that will always be true, no matter what the form, is there is no such thing as the "self-made" man or woman. We develop in relationships with others who possess the wisdom and strength we do not possess. We get it from them, and then we live it out and pass it on to others. Life begets life, and there is no other way.

Second, do not be afraid to look at where your patterns came from. Recognize their roots and their history. This will enable you to overcome old patterns, as you recognize there are reasons you came to fear certain kinds of situations or people and that your history plays a part in who you are now. When you know your patterns of feelings and behaviors came from another context, probably when you were young, you can pick and choose which ones you want to no longer dominate you. In doing so, you have taken the first step in defining who you want to be instead of being defined by external forces that no longer have to have control of you. Find a wise guide, if needed, to help you make those connections. If there are deeper hurts and wounds that are holding you back, seek help for those, too.

Third—and I cannot overemphasize this—gain new skills. Growth is about learning to do things you have never done before. This means that you may have to take a communication workshop or a listening course. You may need to join a growth group to learn to communicate to others what you are feeling and thinking, and actually practice for a while before these skills carry over into real-life situations. Maybe you need to learn how to manage your time and gain some life-planning skills. That is OK. Like anything else, from riding a bicycle to performing brain surgery, it is going to take practice. Go wherever you need to go to grow in your skills. Be a learner, and one who practices.

Fourth, enlist the people with whom you live your life to join this path with you. In your personal life, invite your spouse, children, and close friends to process together what you want your relationships and your life to look like. Hold each other accountable to your shared vision and goals for your relationships. Do this as a team, with shared values and goals. Likewise, take this vision to your work teams at your company as well. Hire a team-building expert or coach to work with you. Make it a shared experience and covenant with each other to become the kind of team or company you want to become *together* and "on purpose."

Last, take the necessary time to define your life values. Invest the necessary time and energy figuring out what is important to you as well as the spiritual and transcendent values you would like to guide and define the outcomes of your life. Without a plan, life is something that just happens to us. Make sure you are the one who is deciding the texture, shape, and outcome of that vision and the values that will ensure it becomes a reality.

I strongly believe that you can. Humans were created and designed with the capacity for deciding which path, of the many available, they will take. I have seen people, from each and every rank, regain that capacity where it has been lost, and create the kind of life they once thought was not available to them. My hope and prayer for you is that you will find the path you were designed for, and rediscover the ability to make that a reality. God Bless,

Henry Cloud, PhD
Los Angeles, 2008

Helpful Hints

In writing this book, I discovered several tidbits of information that have proven to be very valuable to people I have worked with in my consulting and coaching practice. These thoughts don't really require separate chapters, so I am including them in this appendix. While all of these seven helpful hints might not apply to you and your team, some will probably help you build and maintain the kind of structure in *your* "one life," within which success and fruitfulness may grow.

DON'T HIRE SOMEONE YOU CAN'T FIRE

We have all experienced the trauma that inspired someone to invent this phrase. It goes something like this: If you work with, or are the boss of, someone who is also a friend or family member, then you have two relationships with that person: work and the friend/family relationship. You may love them deeply, and would never want to do anything to jeopardize your personal relationship with them. But, as a co-worker, partner, employee, or boss, you find there are issues with that person (usually, issues of performance).

If it were anyone else, you would be more clear about your expectations for them, review their performance, and if they did not live up to those requirements, either discipline them or fire them. Simple enough. And if you did all of that, the relational fallout would be limited to the workplace. It might be bumpy there, but it would be contained.

But this is someone you have another relationship with as well, and if you do the above, it will make that holiday dinner, vacation, golf game, or friendship weird, strained, or worse. It could even end it. You are just not "free" to discipline or fire them. By "free," I don't mean that you can't do it, but that when you do, it will not be without cost and consequences, from awkwardness to heartbreak.

That said, there are some people who have incredibly fulfilling dual work/personal relationships and love the fact that their business partner is also their best friend. And there are many people who say they will never work with family or friends again and will always keep them separate. If you choose to hire a friend or family member, here are some guidelines and practices that are helpful.

First, Ask Yourself "Why?"

If you have not already entered into this complicated scenario, stop and ask yourself why you are really doing it. You already have a good friendship or family tie, so why are you adding business to the equation? If it is because you have so much fun together that it would be fun to work together, then this is not enough. You can have fun without going bankrupt. You did not select that person to be your friend because he or she was good in their job. Likewise, you do not hire someone because they are a good friend. There must be a vital, real business reason as well as something they bring to the table that would make you choose them for that position. So, keep this the main thing.

Give Appropriate Position and Authority

One of the big mistakes is to give someone a position or authority that is not earned or warranted because he or she is family or friend. This happens in family businesses all too often. If you are going to hire your son or daughter, for example, then start them at the appropriate level and have them earn their way up, ideally reporting to other bosses than you. Make sure you empower those bosses to be real bosses as well, treating them like they would anyone else. The other employees will like this more, and it will be better later on if they have had to perform from day one. There is nothing worse than when workers in a company know that someone would not have a particular position or job if he or she did not have an inside track. It erodes the culture, as well as not being good for the person in question. I often tell business owners to have their kids work somewhere else after college for several years. Kids need to prove themselves, and they need to learn how to answer to reality and become adults before entering the family business.

Name the Elephant in the Room

This entire book has been about defining yourself and the boundaries of reality. When you have a friend you are managing, or vice versa, then define the boundary. Name the problem—not as a problem per se—but a real issue: "Sara, let's talk about this. We are good friends, and I am also your boss. This is not always comfortable for me. Friendship doesn't usually have a performance review as a part of it, or other similar, tricky issues. So, let's talk about how to do this. I need to know I can be your boss, and I need to know how to do this in a way that does not affect our friendship. You probably need to know the same. So, let's talk about it."

Ask your friend how he or she feels about the dynamic and about your correcting, training, or disciplining him or her—whatever you might have to do, or are already doing. Talk about how there are things that you have been afraid to mention because you didn't know how it would affect the friendship, which you would have already addressed if the friendship weren't there. Get it out in the open, and talk about how that affects your friendship.

I worked with one company that had a few of these relationships, and the staff decided to wear hats! They would literally wear hats to define who was talking in what role. If someone had to have a real clear "boss" talk and wanted to have real permission to do this, then that person would put on the boss hat and literally say, "OK, this is not your friend talking. This is the boss. I am putting on my boss hat." And they would go from there. A silly little symbol, but it defined things for each of them.

Set Clear Expectations

Nothing is better than clear expectations. Sit down together and talk about what each of you expects from the other, and write it down. What are your responsibilities and what are the other person's? How will you measure those? What will you do when they are not kept? What will be your method for addressing them? How will that feel? How will you keep that from becoming an issue?

Some of the biggest conflicts occur the same way that they do in marriage: stylistic differences that get moralized. One person is naturally more disciplined, structured, and linear than the other, who is more laid back, looser, and takes it all as it comes. In friendship, this can be fine, but in work the more disciplined one begins to feel taken advantage of. "Why do I come in at 8:00 AM and he doesn't get here until 9:00 AM? That's not fair!" he or she may feel.

The reality is these workers would come in earlier no matter what was required, because that is who they are. This has to be negotiated and decided upon. Usually the more responsible one tends to live with more "oughts" and places those expectations on others, and that is where conflict occurs. Make sure that the "oughts" are mutually defined and agreed upon. Remember also that "fair" is not the same as "alike." At the end of the day each person has to feel like they are mutually benefiting from the other. The other person's contribution may be different than yours, but of great value nevertheless. Just make the expectations of who is contributing what, and how, very clear. Then hold each other accountable to those expectations. Also, what will the consequences be?

Have a Plan for Conflict

When conflict occurs, what will you do? You need to talk in advance about handling potential disagreements. First, look at your history of resolving conflict. How has it worked? Do you avoid it together? Is it adversarial? Or does it go well? That pattern will continue in a work relationship, so plan for it. If this history isn't positive, name the pattern, talk about it, and think about how you will do it differently. You could start your discussion with, "At times when something has been wrong, we have avoided talking about things. In business, we are not going to be able to do that."

Another idea is to have a mutually agreed-upon mediating person: another manager, friend, or boss, whom you can take disputes to for resolution. If he or she is someone you both trust and who has your best interests in mind, it can work wonders. Sometimes just knowing there is a way out of a logjam creates the space to find resolution.

Determine the Exit Strategy

If this is not working, what will you do then? How will you unwind it without destroying the friendship? Each of you needs a defined way out of a bad relationship—unhappy endings can be pretty ugly if they are unplanned for. Make sure each of you can end the work relationship without damaging the other relationship. Define this ahead of time.

Sometimes the exit may be forced. Someone you cannot fire must be fired. Talk about that ahead of time. "OK, I am going to be your boss, and like any boss, theoretically, I might have to fire you one day. How are we going to do that and what will it be like between us if I have to tell you that this is not working out?"

If this has not been agreed upon ahead of time and it is that time now, go back to the communication chapter and practice those guidelines. Affirm the relationship, and talk about the desired result: that your friendship remains intact.

RESTRAIN YOUR NURTURING IMPULSE

Please do not send me angry e-mails about this sounding sexist. I include this section because so many women asked me to as I was researching this book. So, if you are a woman and this section isn't for you, that's terrific. But many women do feel this way, so this is for them. Conversely, there are many men out there who may find this section of use!

What women frequently tell me is that when they find themselves getting close to someone at work who is struggling in some way, their mothering, nurturing instincts kick in. Sometimes, they say, those instincts don't just kick in, they take over. In other words, they become more a caretaker of the person and his or her personal struggles than a boss or a colleague. They begin to feel bad for the person and talk more and more about personal struggles and less about work. And this boss finds it difficult to maintain performance expectations for a person going through something difficult.

First, you have to ask yourself if caring and nurturing may be getting in the way not only of your role as supervisor, boss, or even team member, but also in the way of the other person's getting better. There is a point where you are not helping the other person. Your lack of holding him or her to expectations is actually what is keeping them stuck. It is good for people to be held accountable, and this can help them get better. Even in psychiatric hospitals, patients have requirements as part of their treatment. They have meetings to go to on time, homework assignments, chores, and the like. Responsibility helps most emotional and relational problems to improve.

Second, why are you doing this? Are you empty in some way in another part of life? Is there a vacuum that over-helping is filling? Do you feel complete only if you have someone to take care of? Make sure that all of the helping that you are doing is coming from truly helpful motives. It may be more for your benefit than theirs, if you are the codependent type.

Third, structure your help so that work can continue. Talk to the person about your two roles with them: "I want to help you with some of this personal stuff, but I am still your boss and we have to have some expectations for performance. Let's talk about how to do that. How about we have a specific lunch on Fridays, when we can just focus on how you are doing and work on some of those things?"

I have worked with many companies where there is someone in a department who has a strong gift in helping people. So, they will meet with a person to do just that. They get together on break time and go through a self-help book, watch a DVD on personal growth, or work through a personal budget. But it is structured not to be a part of work; it's on personal time, like lunch. It is not job related; it's a friend helping a friend. This leaves work more clearly defined than the nurturing role.

WEIGH CAREFULLY A SPOUSE'S ADVICE

Another issue I have seen frequently is when a spouse begins to speak about the job of their husband or wife. While input can be very helpful from a spouse, it can also be problematic at times, especially if the one giving input or criticizing is not a part of the company and has no role other than critic.

Spouses can be good objective sounding boards and bring great wisdom and experience. The problem is when the one at the job does not take the advice, or does things in a way that the one at home would not do or does not like, and because the advice is not taken, it affects the relationship at home. The advice-giver gets bugged.

Over the years, I have come to believe in a twofold principle, which holds opposites in tension. First, if a spouse does not have to live with the consequences of implementing his or her advice, then the advice should be given freely as a take-it or leave-it offering. The spouse offering the advice should not let it affect how he or she feels toward or relates to his or her partner if the advice is not taken. It is the classic authority and responsibility issue: give the person who is held responsible for the consequences the authority to make their decisions, with your input, but with freedom. And then, do not punish them for it.

But the opposite is true as well. Sometimes the person on the job is doing or not doing something that is not really about a business decision but says more about character than business, and that *does* affect the marriage. If a spouse is tolerating things that are wrong or unethical, for example, instead of dealing with them, then this can affect the other spouse as well. A spouse loses respect for a partner who is not taking their advice, because not taking it shows a character deficit. At that point, work is coming home. I have heard so many spouses say, "I began to lose respect for him or her when . . ."

So, spouses should be free to do their jobs But, their decisions and practices should reflect being the kind of person that their spouse fell in love with, and can continue to feel good about being married to.

DON'T LET UNBALANCED TIMES BECOME A PATTERN

There are times when you will not be able to live the balanced life, period. Work and life have seasons or periods of time when unusual demands are placed upon you, for good reason. The birth of a child is one of those times, for example—odds are you won't be sleeping much during the baby's first few months, with a consequent impact on the rest of your life. But it would be wrong to think you could sustain that sleep deprivation for a long time. You would begin to break down and could not function well. It is not sustainable, and it should not be. It is only a season.

Accountants know this at tax time. They work like fiends. I am like that during "writing season." When I am in the process of writing a book, there is a deadline, and during those months, I find I am working much more than usual, because a book always seems to grow in its needs for attention over time. As I get into it, there is more to it than I had thought at first. In this season, I am usually overwhelmed. The first sign is my in-box, and my desk. Then my car. Next my mood, and sometimes the bathroom scale. When a ship's captain is navigating through a storm, the decks are going to take on a little water. I understand that the last few months of writing a book won't be a dry, clean trip. I have come to live with this, and even to somewhat expect it.

But, I *know* there is a deadline, just like April 15 for an accountant. It will end. And when it is over, I can go back to some sense of being normal. I know it will end.

But there are times when people get into those kinds of overstretched, fragmented, scattered, worn-down, depleted states . . . and these are not seasons. *These have become patterns without an end.* And this is not sustainable.

In the same way that a company or a person looks at cash flow, and asks whether or not the current expenditure in the red is sustainable for a longer period of time, a person has to look at workload and energy and ask the same questions. Is what you are doing sustainable over time? Is it a season? How long can you continue it?

Take a hard look at your expenditure of time and energy, and the way that you are having to feed a particular initiative, project, or even job. How long has that overload been going on? Is it truly a season that will end? Is there really an end in sight to this abuse? Why? Is that an objective or just wishful thinking?

What areas of life are suffering and not getting the attention they deserve? Family? Health? Spiritual life? Personal? Marriage? Hobbies? If what you are doing is not sustainable for any of these reasons, and you do not see an end in sight, then you have to come out of denial and see that you have an unhealthy pattern and do something about it. The answers are in the previous chapters; review them as you define your missions and purposes and then create the structures and boundaries necessary to sustain and protect those. A big part of change is going to come from dealing with your power drains. The question to ask yourself is this:

How long can you, your marriage, or your family
sustain what you are doing and not be diminished or
broken in the process?

If you have gotten used to numbing the pain, then the answer is probably a lot less time than you think. Before you even realize it, you might have lost some things that are very important to you, and you never even knew it.

MANAGE THE MANAGER

In chapter 6, I told the story of the first, part-time assistant I hired and how she calmly strode into my office to inform me that I had assigned her forty hours worth of work for that first week and had hired her for only twenty hours. I was stunned by her poise and also by the simple fact that she was right: I had not managed my workload very well, and it was my problem, not hers. I also know now that part of why I was stunned was the effect that a good boundary has, as we have talked about in this book. It defined where she ended and I began, and who was responsible for what. It was about well-formed structuring. So, my stunned feeling was a wake-up call, a splash of cold water on my face as a problem was revealed that I had not known was mine, and now here it was. Good boundaries bring clarity.

So, part of what you might find is that some of your being overwhelmed is because of a problem above you. You may be doing something that is unsustainable, or causes you to not be able to do the best that is needed because the level above you has overwhelmed your resources. And the people who work for you need to know that. Not just for your sake, but for the sake of the mission. The captain of the ship should know when there is a problem and should listen to those who report it. It is good feedback for leaders to have, especially if there is something they are really depending on you to deliver, and because of too many other things they have given you, they are not going to get the results they desire. If you communicate it that way, it *will* get their attention.

DEALING WITH A DIFFICULT BOSS

Few relationships in life can get to people like a difficult boss. There are many reasons for this, but two are big ones. The first is this person has real power over your life in some significant ways. He can fire you, and he can make demands on time and energy, our two greatest finite resources.

This is enough to really affect your well-being, if your boss is a crazy one.

Second, besides this real power, bosses have psychological power. They fit neatly into a parental slot in your head, simply by the fact that they are authority figures. Authority figures will pull feelings and reactions out of you that can go all the way back to your own parents or other early authority figures. If some of those relationships were hurtful or problematic for you, your boss may tap into some of how you used to feel when you were young. You may find yourself reacting to him or her in old ways, or feelings may surface that you have not felt in a long time. A boss may have the power to make you feel bad, insignificant, or afraid like no one else does, simply because of his or her position.

In dealing with the real power, remember the concept of getting your balance sheet together. You will not be able to address negotiating points in your relationship, especially in your needs for decisions about time and energy, if you are in a weak position. You will feel such a need to do whatever is necessary that you can be pushed into a position that is not sustainable for the rest of the areas of your life. The demands of the job may be destroying your home, but if you have to have it for survival, you are not in a good negotiating position. I have seen many times when because of a person's strengths, great concessions were made in job structures to accommodate the talent. But you have to be one of the real talents to get those deals. So, get your balance sheet up, and be so good at what you do that they need you more than you need them. This is when you will see those conversations go better.

With the second issue, the psychological one, the concept of power drains applies. Who does this boss remind you of? Is he a critical father? A domineering mother? (By the way, do not believe that you only have father feelings with men, or mother issues with women. If you had a harsh father, for example, a harsh woman will be able to trigger that same issue with you.) Maybe a boss brings up feelings about early teachers or church figures.

Figure out why your boss is able to get to you the way he or she does. What is getting triggered? Then, *use this as a growth step for your own good.* He or she is not your problem, remember this. The way he or she is able to get to you is your problem, and you will either resolve that or take it with you long after this person is out of your life. So, develop some psychological separateness from the boss, so he or she cannot get to you. Let the boss's stuff be the boss's stuff, as they say. Stay clear, and separate.

Then, respond in the ways we have talked about. Here are some quick tips. First, figure out the issue. Does your boss make you feel stupid? Afraid? Powerless? Then, figure out where the feelings come from and get some help, perhaps some counseling. Before you go getting bugged that your boss has the power to send you to therapy, think about what I said above. This is for *you* to grow. The boss has played a role in your life, and you have discovered you have an issue. Your issue may be learning how to deal with a complete jerk, but this is still a growth step that is good to take. We all need to know how to do this.

Finally, develop a plan to deal with your boss. When you go into planning mode, you are taking back the power. You get active and are no longer a victim. The plan could be:

- Role play before going to talk to the boss, and get support.

- Talk to your boss directly, speaking to the issues, as I mentioned in the communication chapter.

- Approach your boss with a buddy—talk to him or her with someone else who has the same issue. This can be very powerful. When two or three of you go to the boss and say, "We would like to discuss something with you," it is more difficult for him or her to retaliate against several people and more difficult for the boss to be in denial.

- Go to HR and enlist their help. They are trained to handle personnel situations, and they will know what to do.

- If your boss is abusive, you may have to follow through on the consequences. Go through the proper channels and file a grievance, work with HR, or in extreme cases where the law and your legal rights have been violated, talk to an attorney.

Some key things to remember: Make sure you go in on the solid ground of doing your job well (so they can't throw poor performance back at you). Be prepared to have that difficult conversation with your boss: "I have talked to you about the way that you demean me. In yesterday's meeting you called me and idiot in front of my team. This is an example of what I have asked you to not do. Promise me that this will not happen again; or document my file for poor performance, if you think I am doing a bad job; or let's talk about my leaving and severance. It is up to you, but I am not going to continue to be treated this way."

It can also help to see it as a team and strategic issue for the company. Many times a VP will call me in as a consultant to facilitate a leadership-development project—the ultimate goal is to help people deal with the CEO, and to perhaps affect change with him or her as well. If you have the power to suggest or drive a leadership-development project, do it. Once you bring new information and process into an organization, people begin to grow and change and that can filter all the way up. I have seen it many times over the years. A good consultant can do wonders to influence an entire system, working upward through other levels.

Finally, if you do not want to do any of the above, which a lot of people don't for good reasons, then manage around the boss. Find a way to firewall yourself and then work around him or her. People have done that for centuries, and there are times when you should do the same. This is not an expression of powerlessness or of being a victim. It is a calculated decision. Remaining where you are is good for you, and you are not going to allow one person to ruin it for you, so you will manage him or her like any other obstacle.

Do a gut check. Look yourself in the mirror and ask, "Do you really want to be the kind of person that anyone can have that much power over? Will you commit to doing something about this and no longer be a psychological victim?" Then, do it. Do what is necessary, but no person, no one, should have the power to ruin your psychological well-being. See this as an invitation to get to an entire new level of maturity and strength.

DO THE HARD THING FIRST

"Easy Hard versus Hard Easy." I don't remember the first time that I heard this saying, but it rings true in most every area of life, especially in the creation of boundaries. What it means is that there are two ways of doing most anything. The first one is to do what is easy first. It takes less effort, is not scary, and you probably will enjoy it. But if you do that, then it is going to be a lot harder later to do whatever you did not do earlier. Here's a familiar example: Going to the dentist is hard for you. It takes a little effort and maybe a little discomfort. So, you do the easy thing, and you skip the appointment. But, later, the hard thing—going to the dentist—is going to be a lot harder than if you had gone earlier: It is root canal time.

So, doing the hard thing first usually means that it will be a lot easier later. Do the tough thing and finish school first, and then making a living is easier later. Do the easy thing first, like dropping out, and making a living later is going to get a lot harder. Exercise a little now, even if you find it kind of hard to get out of bed early a few times a week, and then the easy part is later when you are enjoying good health. Take it easy now, and the hard part of open-heart surgery comes later after the heart attack.

The reality is that there is no option where hard does not exist. That is denial. The question is not whether or not we want hard. The question is when do we want it, and therefore deciding how hard do we want it to be. If we do the hard part first, then it is over and even the hard part will be easier than if we wait. Later is always harder.

With boundaries, this law applies in so many ways it would be difficult to think of most of them. It is true across the board. Take confrontation, for example. Hard to do, but put it off and it is guaranteed to get a lot harder and the messes and consequences will be much bigger. Setting limits early on is uncomfortable, but it will keep a lot of bad things from happening down the road.

So, think about this law in the areas where you need to add structure to your life. Chances are there is going to be a little discomfort. I will almost guarantee that it will be easier and the losses will be smaller than if you wait. Pick up the phone and start the hard part; the easier parts will eventually follow.

BOOKS BY DR. HENRY CLOUD

INTEGRITY
The Courage to Meet the Demands of Reality

ISBN 978-0-06-084969-6 (paperback)

In this groundbreaking book, Dr. Cloud shows what integrity is, how it is lived in everyday experience, and how to determine whether you are perceived as someone with character and integrity.

THE ONE-LIFE SOLUTION
Reclaim Your Personal Life While Achieving Greater Professional Success

ISBN 978-0-06-146643-4 (paperback)

Dr. Cloud extends his bestselling formula to the workplace and convincingly demonstrates that setting physical, mental, emotional, and spiritual boundaries at work is not only helpful, but essential to establishing a successful, happy, and rewarding career.

Made in the USA
Middletown, DE
15 March 2019